COMMUNICATION AND SOCIAL INFLUENCE PROCESSES

Gerald R. Miller, 1931-1993

COMMUNICATION AND
SOCIAL INFLUENCE PROCESSES

Edited by Charles R. Berger
and Michael Burgoon

Michigan State University Press
East Lansing
1995

Copyright © 1995 Michigan State University Press

All Michigan State University Press books are produced on paper which meets the requirements of American National Standard of Information Sciences—Permanence of paper for printed materials ANSI Z39.48-1984.

Michigan State University Press
East Lansing, Michigan 48823-5202

03 02 01 00 99 98 97 96 95 1 2 3 4 5 6 7 8 9

Library of Congress Cataloging-in-Publication Data

Communication and social influence processes / edited by Charles R. Berger and Michael Burgoon.
       p.   cm.
   Includes bibliographical references (p.) and index.
   ISBN 0-87013-380-2 (hard : alk. paper)
  1. Interpersonal communication. 2. Persuasion (Psychology)
  3. Social Interaction. 4. Attitude change. 5. Social influence.
  I. Berger, Charles R. II. Burgoon, Michael.
BF637.C45C644   1995
302.2—dc20   95-2096
                                             CIP

Dedication

May 20, 1995

This volume has been prepared in honor of the late Gerald R. Miller, who was a professor in the Department of Communication at Michigan State University. All of the authors of this volume were both his students and friends. Gerry's intense and enduring interest in communication and social influence processes sparked similar interests in his students, as the chapters of this volume clearly demonstrate. A more subtle but perhaps even more profound gift Gerry gave to his students was his consistent encouragement to take intellectual risks and to advance and develop new ideas. His influence is reflected in the diversity of topics included in this book's chapters and the innovative approaches used to investigate them. Although Gerry is no longer with us physically, in so many ways he is present in each of these chapters. We all miss him very much, but his ideas will always be part of our thinking, writing, and continuing conversations about communication and social influence processes.

Contents

Preface

S tudents of social influence, from Aristotle to contemporary scholars, have viewed communication processes as fundamental to the induction of attitude and behavioral change in people. When the experimental study of persuasion became popular at the midpoint of the 20th century, researchers sought to isolate the causal variables responsible for producing attitude change (Hovland, Janis, & Kelley, 1953). While research reported during that era examined the role of personality variables in the persuasion process (Janis & Field, 1959), such message factors as fear appeals and message sidedness, as well as the order of presentation of persuasive communications, were deemed central to the induction of social influence (Hovland, 1957). With the introduction of television, increased concern was expressed over the persuasive effects of mass media, especially with respect to such issues as violent media portrayals and their influence on children (Schramm, Lyle, & Parker, 1961). However, almost identical alarms were sounded more than two decades earlier by the Payne Fund researchers with respect to the potential deleterious effects of movie attendance on children (Charters, 1933; Wartella & Reeves, 1985).

Whether studied within the confines of the laboratory or in the context of survey research, it was generally assumed during this period, as it is today, that persuasive messages disseminated in either face-to-face communication situations or mass mediated contexts are the currency with which influence agents ply their trade. Under this conceptual umbrella, the induction of social influence is viewed as a linear process in which sources or influence agents devise messages that they send through channels to influence receivers. Not only did these early, linear models of the communication process employ such terms, but the source, message, channel, receiver model of communication was used explicitly as a framework for organizing landmark reviews of the persuasion literature (McGuire, 1969, 1985).

The source, message, channel, receiver model of communication and social influence was especially compatible with the research design preferences and the statistical tools employed by experimental researchers. Source, message, and channel variables were usually manipulated under controlled conditions, and their independent and conjoint effects on receivers' attitude changes were observed. Attitude change data were then evaluated using some form of analysis of variance (ANOVA) techniques. This linear conception of the persuasion process and the simpatico ANOVA designs held out to eager scholars of that time the promise of developing a reliable set of causal laws or law-like generalizations linking persuasive outcomes to antecedent communication variables. However, by the early 1970s it became apparent that such robust, causal statements would not be forthcoming. Instead, highly complex and somewhat ephemeral interaction effects were more the rule than the exception. Attempts to accommodate this welter of conflicting and sometimes paradoxical findings under a single theoretical rubric became exercises in futility. By the late 1960s, Ostrom (1968) counted some 34 different persuasion theories, none of which could provide a plausible explanation for the broad range of observed communication-persuasion relationships.

In retrospect, this somewhat disappointing result should have been anticipated. Although it is true that the linear model linking source-created messages with changes in audience members' attitudes is highly compatible with ANOVA techniques for assessing causal relationships between independent and dependent variables, a wide variety of communication episodes, within which social influence takes place, do not comport well with this linear conception of the communication process. In face-to-face interactions where social influence is exercised, the distinction between influence agents and influence targets is virtually impossible to maintain. In these contexts, not only do feedback loops abound, but the mutual thrust and parry of verbal and nonverbal messages are not easily accommodated within the standard ANOVA experimental paradigm. Unlike relatively straightforward agricultural experiments examining relationships between fertilizer constituents and crop yields, the dynamic relationships between people during social influence episodes simply cannot be captured by the garden variety split-plot design. When people engage in social interaction, they mutually influence each other's actions; consequently, the observations interactants provide researchers are not independent of each other. These correlated observations do violence to a fundamental assumption underlying the use of many experimental designs and a host of analytic techniques (Kraemer & Jacklin, 1979). What is needed is a new and more inclusive conceptualization of the role played by communication in exercise of social influence using methodologies that reflect this more sophisticated perspective.

The chapters of this volume represent a significant move toward redefining the relationships between communication and social influence processes. Instead of conceiving of the typical social influence venue as one in which a single source disseminates messages to an audience, as an individual presenting a public speech might do, social influence is viewed from a broad array of perspectives. These perspectives include such individual-level processes as cognition (Berger), language (Burgoon) and personality (Steinfatt) through interpersonal processes such as deception (Stiff), compliance-gaining (Boster), and social exchange (Roloff and Sunnafrank) to more macro social network interactions (Parks). Regardless of their general views concerning the nature of communication, the authors explicitly acknowledge the reciprocal nature of social influence processes in interpersonal communication contexts, and incorporate this perspective into their theoretical thinking about communication and social influence relationships. An important implication of these conceptual moves is that the "law of the instrument" (Kaplan, 1964), as represented by the standard ANOVA experimental paradigm, has been repealed by these authors. This law stipulates that like the small child who indiscriminately pounds everything in sight when given a hammer, researchers wedded to a particular methodological orthodoxy may uncritically apply their approach to any and all research questions. Strong methodological commitments constrain conceptual developments, thus ensuring that the only research questions asked are those that can be answered by using the preferred set of research techniques. As these chapters reveal, the narrow constraints of the standard experimental paradigm have been abandoned in the authors' thinking about the relationships between communication and social influence processes, resulting in a more catholic view of these linkages.

The view shared by this volume's authors—that interpersonal influence processes are inherently reciprocal—is testament to their common intellectual heritage.

Charles R. Berger   Michael Burgoon
University of California University of Arizona
Davis   Tucson

REFERENCES

Charters, W. W. (1933). *Motion pictures and youth: A summary*. New York: Macmillan.

Hovland, C. I. et al. (1957). *The order of presentation in persuasion*. New Haven, CT: Yale University Press.

Hovland, C. I., Janis, I. L., & Kelley, H. H. (1953). *Communication and persuasion*. New Haven, CT: Yale University Press.

Janis, I. L., & Field, P. B. (1959). *Personality and persuasibility*. New Haven, CT: Yale University Press.

Kaplan, A. (1964). *The conduct of inquiry: Methodology for behavioral science*. San Francisco: Chandler.

Kramer, H. C., & Jacklin, C. N. (1979). Statistical analysis of dyadic social behavior. *Psychological Bulletin, 86*, 217-224.

McGuire, W. J. (1969). Attitudes and attitude change. In G. Lindzey & E. Aronson (Eds.), *The handbook of social psychology* (2nd ed.) (Vol. 3, pp. 136-314). Reading, MA: Addison-Wesley.

McGuire, W. J. (1985). Attitudes and attitude change. In G. Lindzey & E. Aronson (Eds.), *The handbook of social psychology* (3rd ed.) (Vol. 2, pp. 233-346). New York: Random House.

Ostrom, T.M. (1968). The emergence of attitude theory: 1930-1950. In A. G. Greenwald, T. C. Brock, & T. M. Ostrom (Eds.), *Psychological foundations of attitudes* (pp. 1-32). New York: Academic Press.

Schramm, W., Lyle, J., & Parker, E. B. (1961). *Television in the lives of our children*. Stanford, CA, Stanford University Press.

Wartella, E., & Reeves, B. (1985). Historical trends in research on children and media: 1900 to 1960. *Journal of Communication, 35*, 118-133.

Inscrutable Goals, Uncertain Plans, and the Production of Communicative Action

Charles R. Berger

Any communicative act, be it verbal or nonverbal, which is apprehended by another, will alter that individual's perceptions, attitudes, beliefs, and motivations, even if ever so slightly; therefore, it is axiomatic that communication and social influence processes are inextricably linked. Accepting this postulate, however, does not obviate the necessity of specifying the processes responsible for the production of the communicative actions that induce social influence. Traditional approaches to the study of communication and social influence have focused on the source, message, channel and receiver variables responsible for producing attitude and behavioral changes in audiences (Burgoon & Miller, 1985; McGuire, 1969, 1985), and numerous social psychological theories have been advanced to explain why individuals alter their attitudes and actions in response to persuasive messages (Eagly & Chaiken, 1993; Petty & Cacioppo, 1981).

In addition to theories and models of persuasion advanced by social psychologists, communication researchers have studied aggressively the strategies individuals say they employ to gain compliance from others and the conditions under which these compliance-gaining strategies are used (Miller, Boster, Roloff, & Seibold, 1977, 1987; see Chapter 5). While all of these efforts have yielded insights into the processes by which individuals are influenced, the social psychological theories have focused almost exclusively on explaining why audience members are influenced and avoided the issue of how persuasive messages are produced in the first place. Moreover, even though compliance-gaining researchers have been concerned with identifying strategies and the conditions under which they are likely to be deployed, little attention has been given to the details of how such strategies are devised and the problems that strategic communicators confront when they construct such strategies and instantiate them in their verbal and nonverbal actions.

In his review of the persuasion literature, Miller (1987) noted these problems with the compliance-gaining research paradigm and suggested that those interested in understanding interpersonal influence should devote more attention to the study of social influence in ongoing interactions. Specifically, he asserted:

> If persuasion researchers want to understand how compliance-gaining message strategies function in interpersonal settings—or, for that matter, how any symbolic inducement functions in any communicative setting—they must come to grips with the necessity of observing actual message exchanges (Miller, 1987, p. 474).

In order to fill these theoretical gaps, the present chapter will focus on the message construction problems faced by social influence agents and the strategies they use to overcome them. As will become clear, these problems and strategies are not only relevant to communication situations manifestly concerned with social influence, they are germane to all communication situations in which individuals attempt to realize their intentions through communicative acts.

SOURCES OF UNCERTAINTY

From the point of view of the producer of communicative action, even the most innocuous communicative acts are fraught with potential uncertainty (see Chapter 8). In the present context, uncertainty is related to the ability of individuals to predict the responses of their conversational partners to their utterances and nonverbal actions. Uncertainty also is related to the ability of message producers to explain others' responses to their actions (Berger, 1979, 1987, 1988; Berger & Bradac, 1982; Berger & Calabrese, 1975; Berger & Gudykunst, 1991; Miller & Steinberg, 1975; Ritchie, 1991; Shannon & Weaver, 1949). It is true that ritualistic and routine communication situations, where response alternatives are relatively few, are inherently less uncertain than less mundane communication episodes. However, there is always the possibility that one's conversational partner will respond unconventionally to even the most routine message, as the following exchange illustrates:

> Manny: How are you today, Moe?
> Moe: Why do you want to know, Manny?

Setting aside the possibility that Manny and Moe engaged in some kind of disagreement or altercation recently, Moe's response to Manny's message would very likely create considerable uncertainty in Manny's mind because Moe enacted an extremely unlikely message alternative in response to Manny's innocuous greeting. For the most part, however, ritualistic communication situations are routine precisely because the levels of predictability in them are extremely high. The number of alternative messages generally enacted in such situations is usually highly constrained.

However, many communication situations in which individuals find themselves, including situations in which they wish to exert social influence over others, cannot be dealt with by enacting highly practiced rituals. In some social influence situations, for example, persons attempting to wield influence find that the targets of their attempts accept, resist, or actively attempt to counter their persuasive efforts. Consequently, the problem facing influence agents is how to anticipate these alternative responses from their targets and to deal with them in their own communicative action. Repeated attempts to influence the same targets on different occasions may help reduce the amount of uncertainty experienced by influence agents. Even after numerous encounters with the same targets, uncertainty cannot be completely reduced since targets' moods and emotional states can show short-term fluctuations, of which influence agents are unaware, that may significantly affect targets' receptivity to agents' influence attempts.

In addition to communication situations in which social influence is a primary goal there are other uncertainty-saturated communication episodes. Individuals may be called upon to generate messages to deal with exigencies that they have never before had to face. Consider, for example, the case of people who receive telephone calls meant for others in which the caller is seeking to inform the intended recipient of the call that a close relative of theirs has been killed in an automobile accident. It then falls upon the third party, who just happened to be present when the telephone call arrived, to inform the intended recipient of the death. For most individuals, except those who have to deliver such news to others on a regular basis, the construction of messages designed both to provide the necessary information to the intended recipient and to do so in such a way that the amount of emotional distress experienced by the recipient is minimized involves careful choice among numerous communicative alternatives and is, thus, an exercise in decision-making under uncertainty.

Having established that a class of high-uncertainty communication episodes exists and that even ritualistic and routine communication episodes can become fraught with uncertainty, it is important to identify specific sources of uncertainty in such episodes. From both theoretical and practical perspectives, it is of little utility simply to assert that uncertainty presents difficulties to communicators in certain situations. Until various sources of uncertainty are identified, strategies for dealing with such uncertainty cannot be considered with any specificity. Consequently, attention now turns to various sources of uncertainty in communication episodes.

PRECONDITION UNCERTAINTY

Before initiating face-to-face interaction with another, individuals must determine whether the people with whom they intend to interact have the sensory and linguistic capabilities necessary for accomplishing social interaction. There are obvious situations in which these preconditions for carrying out face-to-face encounters may not be met. Individuals who are hearing impaired may find it difficult to understand incoming streams of spoken language and those who are visually impaired may not be able to process the gestures, facial expressions, and body postures that act to modulate the meaning of the verbal stream. In addition, even if the relevant sensory systems responsible for the supporting social interaction are intact, other preconditions for carrying out interaction may not be met. If, for example, individuals must rely primarily on verbal communication channels to reach their communication goals, they may find that their fellow interlocutors do not speak their language, thus making the accomplishment of their goals difficult, if not impossible.

When individuals encounter others, they are likely to assume that their co-interactants have the necessary sensory capabilities with which to carry out interaction. Unless there is visual evidence to the contrary, they further assume that their interaction partners share their language. It may not be until the interaction commences that it becomes evident that there are difficulties in one or more of these domains. Nevertheless, in a theoretical sense, when individuals encounter others about whom they know nothing, other than the fact that those they have encountered are humans who appear to be alive, there is some measure of uncertainty concerning the capabilities of the others to carry out interaction. Simply because it is generally assumed that those with whom we interact possess these capabilities does not mean that uncertainty is not present. It is frequently only after interactions have begun that we learn these capabilities may be at issue; this is testament to the existence of this source of uncertainty.

GOAL UNCERTAINTY

Students of interpersonal communication in general and compliance-gaining in particular have found it useful to conceive of social interaction as a goal-directed activity. Goals are generally viewed as desired end-states for which interactants strive (Berger, 1995). Strategies have been isolated for attaining a large array of instrumental goals, including affinity-seeking (Bell & Daly, 1984), comforting (Burleson, 1984), compliance-gaining (Dillard & Burgoon, 1985; Hunter & Boster, 1987; Miller, et al. 1977, 1987; Seibold, Cantrill, & Meyers, 1985; see Chapter 5), embarrassing others (Petronio, Snyder, & Bradford, 1992), and gathering social information (Baxter & Wilmot, 1984; Berger & Kellermann, 1983, 1989, 1994; Kellermann & Berger, 1984). In addition to these empirical efforts, attempts have been made to provide theoretical underpinnings for this research (Berger, 1995; Dillard, 1990a, 1990b, Greene, 1990; Kellermann, 1988; Read & Miller, 1989). Both the theoretical and empirical work done in this tradition is predicated on the twin assumptions that individuals pursue clearly defined goals in their interactions with others, and they frequently seek to achieve multiple goals simultaneously. Although these multiple goals may conflict at times (Kellermann, 1988), the widely accepted postulate is that both social actors and researchers can identify such goals. Consistent with the notion that the pursuit of multiple goals simultaneously should engender greater uncertainty in social actors than the pursuit of singular goals, Greene and Lindsey (1989) reported that individuals who were given the task of pursuing two interaction goals at the same time were less verbally fluent than their counterparts who were given the task of pursuing only one goal. Verbal fluency as indexed by non-vocalized pauses and speech onset latencies have frequently been used as empirical indicators of the uncertainty associated with linguistic decision-making (Berger, 1993; Berger & Abrahams, 1993; Berger & Jordan, 1992; Berger, Karol, & Jordan, 1989; Butterworth & Goldman-Eisler, 1979; Goldman-Eisler, 1968; Greene, 1984; Greene & Lindsey, 1989; Siegman, 1987).

Though individuals may sometimes have a well thought out set of goals they intend to pursue in particular interactions with others, the goals of many communication episodes are not well defined. Moreover, even in cases where goals have been well defined a priori, for a variety of reasons the clarity of these goals may decrease or the goals themselves may change radically as the interaction progresses. For instance, individuals may enter social influence situations with the clearly defined goal of persuading others to change their actions or beliefs only to find that at the conclusion of the episode it is their partners who have persuaded them to alter their course of action or their beliefs. Or, persons who enter a particular interaction with the intention of establishing only a friendship later may find themselves involved in a love affair.

Individuals' goals may be unclear as they begin interactions or goals may transmute in the course of interactions, which raises goal uncertainty levels. Also, in social interaction situations it is not only one's own goals that count, it is the goals of one's interaction partners that are critical. From the perspective of the individual interactant, partners' goals generally must be inferred. Consequently, there is always room for uncertainty with regard to the intentions of one's interaction partner, which makes the generation of optimal messages for achieving one's goals more difficult. In general, the theoretical and empirical work on goal-directed social interaction has been mute with respect to this source of uncertainty in strategic communication episodes. This is a curious oversight since it is routinely assumed by those interested in the study of discourse comprehension that inferences about the goals and plans of co-interactants are vital for understanding discourse (Carberry, 1990; Cohen, Morgan, & Pollack, 1990; Green, 1989).

As observed previously, individuals may find that their goals change during the course of their interactions. One potential explanation for these goal shifts concerns the opportunistic nature of social interaction. As they conduct their interactions with others, individuals may realize the time may be right for broaching particular issues with their interaction partner. Comments made during the interaction may trigger memories of intentions that were thought of at another time but which were not available in working memory when the interaction began. Such instances are frequently introduced by the phrase "That reminds me..." where the "that" generally remains unspecified. Of course, instances of such reminding may be triggered by visual cues and individuals who are reminded may not necessarily verbalize their recollection. Instead, they may seek to change the direction of the interaction toward the new goal or goals by using more subtle strategies. In the crucible of social interaction, goals are hardly static entities that typically are pursued from the beginning to the end of particular communication episodes. One's own goals, as well as the goals of one's interaction partner, exist in a continuing state of flux. It is this dynamic property of social goals, then, that contributes to overall uncertainty in social interaction episodes and makes social interaction a rich matrix for opportunistic behavior.

PLAN UNCERTAINTY

Not only may there be considerable uncertainty surrounding one's own goals and the goals of one's co-interlocutors in many social interaction episodes, there may also be uncertainties connected with the plans that interactants use to pursue their goals. Plans may be viewed as cognitive representations of action sequences that are oriented toward achieving goals, and it is generally assumed that plans are hierarchically organized with more abstract actions at the top of the hierarchy and progressively more concrete actions toward the bottom (Berger, 1995; Levelt, 1989; Lichtenstein & Brewer, 1979; Schank & Abelson, 1977; Wilensky, 1983; Srull & Wyer, 1986). Even when individuals have clearly defined interaction objectives, there may be high levels of uncertainty with respect to the actions that might be taken to attain these goals.

Given the hierarchical organization of action plans, uncertainty may occur on single or multiple levels of the plan. For example, planners may have a clear idea of the abstract actions that need to be taken to achieve their goals but be quite uncertain concerning the specific actions that must be deployed to realize these abstract plan features in social interaction. Or, planners may have a clear idea of the particular actions that might be used to achieve a specific goal but be unable to link them together into a coherent action sequence at more abstract levels. While the discussion so far has viewed the relationship between plans and uncertainty from the perspective of the individual pursuing a goal or a set of goals, social actors can also experience uncertainty with respect to the inferences they make about the plans their co-interactants are following during interaction episodes. Again, in such instances, people may have relatively low uncertainty levels regarding the goals their fellow interactants are pursuing in a given situation but be very unsure of the plans they are using to guide their actions while pursuing their goals.

Plan uncertainty may arise from a number of sources. Planners may have multiple sub-plans for reaching a specific goal. As these sub-plans proliferate, the decision-making task faced by planners becomes more uncertain. This phenomenon was demonstrated in a series of experiments in which individuals were asked to devise plans for persuading another person to accept their opinion on a specific issue (Berger, et al., 1989). In one experiment, some individuals were asked to construct a persuasion plan before engaging in the influence task. A second group also devised a plan before starting the task; however, just after they completed their plan but prior to engaging in the persuasive interaction, they were asked what they would do if four randomly selected actions, proposed in their plan, failed. A third group was given no time to plan, and proceeded immediately to engage in the persuasion task. In the persuasion task, all participants were asked to try to persuade an experimental confederate who, unbeknown to the participant, was instructed to disagree with the opinion expressed by the subject.

Results of this experiment showed that the group whose plans were questioned demonstrated lower levels of verbal fluency than their counterparts who planned but were not questioned, or those who did not generate plans before the interaction. Furthermore, among those who planned before engaging in the persuasion task, individuals who included more specific arguments for their position in their plans were less fluent than those who included fewer arguments in their pre-interaction plans. Another experiment in this series showed that the process of questioning individuals about their persuasion plans had the effect of increasing the number of specific arguments in subsequent plans. Apparently, then, individuals with more specific arguments in their plans also were more uncertain of which specific arguments they should deploy as they failed to persuade their partners. Because of the increased complexity of their decision-making task, occasioned by the large numbers of arguments from which they had to choose, planners with more specific arguments were less fluent than those who had relatively few specific arguments in their plans.

Not only are these findings somewhat counterintuitive (after all those whose plans were questioned should be better able to deal with failure during their interactions than those whose planned actions were not questioned or those who did not plan at all), the data raise some questions about the utility of complex planning before initiating goal-directed social action. Since it is well established that such speech disfluencies as vocalized and non-vocalized pauses undermine perceivers' judgments of individuals' credibility (Berger, 1985, 1994; Newton & Burgoon, 1990; Miller & Hewgill, 1964), complex interaction plans may have the effect of lowering planners' credibility because of the reduced levels of fluency with which complex plans are carried out at the level of social action. Although it is possible that the debilitating effects of plan complexity on verbal fluency observed by Berger et al. (1989) could have been ameliorated to some degree by greater opportunity for pre-interaction rehearsal of planned actions, there remains the seeming paradox that complex planning in advance of action may disrupt performance.

Not only may the complexity of plans themselves increase the amount of uncertainty interactants experience while enacting the plan, but there are other sources of plan uncertainty during social interactions. As suggested previously, goals can and do change during the course of particular interaction episodes; consequently, plans must be abandoned completely or modified on-line as goal metamorphoses play out during interactions. Or, goals may remain relatively constant, but the plans instantiated to reach goals may prove to be ineffective, thus necessitating abandonment or modification of plans. In either case, social interactants may be forced to rethink their plans while in the process of interacting with the target of their planned actions. Simultaneously rethinking plans while performing the actions necessary for maintaining the flow of conversation is cognitively demanding. Consequently, when these parallel demands are made during interactions, they should be marked by significant disruptions in verbal fluency or other potential indicators of uncertainty and cognitive load (Greene & Lindsey, 1989).

AFFECTIVE STATE UNCERTAINTY

While those concerned with the relationships between cognitive processes and social interaction have recognized that emotions may significantly influence the relationships between cognition and social action (Berscheid, 1983; Isen, 1984; Sternberg, 1986), relatively little research has been done to explore these effects. Nonetheless, the affective state of their message targets is a critically important datum for some semblance of rational decision-making by social actors concerning the content and style of messages transmitted for the purpose of achieving instrumental goals in social interactions. Within the realm of social influence episodes, message planners may conclude that the targets of their planned influence attempts are very likely to be unreceptive to their requests because they are "not in the mood." Such attributions might lead social actors to abandon, at least temporarily, any attempts to influence their targets, or these attributions may lead to significant modifications of extant message plans. By contrast, positive assessment of targets' affective states may encourage influence agents to actualize their plans.

In many circumstances, however, the current affective states of message targets may be unclear to those attempting to reach various goals. Given that potential message targets may engage in impression management activities, it might be difficult for those seeking to realize their goals to obtain confident readings of targets' emotional states (Schlenker, 1980). In addition to this source of uncertainty, message planners may be unsure of the kinds of emotional impacts anticipated messages might have on the affective states of their receivers, regardless of their present states. Adult language users have well articulated expectations that link various message types with the effects they are likely to have on emotional states of others. For example, informing an individual that they just have won $100,000,000 in a lottery versus telling someone that they will die within a few months of a painful terminal illness will produce considerable variance in the affective responses of message targets. However, even at the extremes, perverse emotional responses are possible. Individuals may be considerably less than euphoric about winning a lottery when they recognize the potential negative impacts the public notoriety they receive may have on their lives, and individuals whose lives are hopeless in a social-psychological sense may welcome the news of a quick and natural end to their living hells. Thus, even when messages appear likely to induce clear-cut affective responses in their recipients, some measure of uncertainty inevitably surrounds individual responses to them.

Although as social actors we assume that we have "privileged access" to knowledge of our own emotional states, a variety of theoretical perspectives and lines of empirical research from the James-Lange theory of emotion (James, 1950) and social comparison theory (Festinger, 1954) to Schachter's (1959, 1964) work on the social determinants of subjective emotional states, Bem's (1972) self-perception theory, and recent work on the facial feedback hypothesis (Cacioppo, Martzke, Petty, & Tassinary, 1988), suggest that individuals may harbor considerable uncertainty concerning their own affective states. When such conditions obtain, observations of one's own actions (Bem, 1972) and the actions of others (Schachter, 1959, 1964) may exert considerable influence on the subjective emotional state reported. Not only may social actors be uncertain of their current emotional states, they may also be uncertain of the potential affective consequences for themselves of sending various message types to potential targets; that is, individuals may not only be uncertain of the potential emotional impacts of their messages on others, they may be equally uncertain of how delivering these messages to a target will affect their own emotional state, and these effects may be considerable. Delivering bad news may be just as difficult emotionally for the messenger as it is for the recipient.

BELIEF UNCERTAINTY

A final source of uncertainty considered here concerns the beliefs that parties involved in social interactions hold about the world. In the context of social influence episodes, certain of these beliefs may be crucial in determining message choices, and uncertainty about these critical beliefs may make the task of constructing and disseminating persuasive messages very difficult. It is axiomatic that in attempting to change attitudes and behaviors, beliefs not directly at issue but those implicated by the target beliefs may be critical for the successful induction of change. For instance, in attempting to persuade a roommate to go to the movies instead of studying, a given influence agent might appeal to the belief that if one has spent considerable time studying in the past, one is entitled to take some time to relax. Obviously, the success of this line of argument depends upon the degree to which the roommate endorses this belief concerning the relationship between work and play.

Since individuals have a large number of beliefs about themselves and the world (Rokeach, 1968), it is virtually impossible for influence agents to know the status of the totality of targets' relevant beliefs. Moreover, even if the status of relevant subsets of these beliefs is known at a given point in time, beliefs, like goals, are subject to change without notice. Consequently, knowledge of others' beliefs may become outdated and provide a less than optimal guide for making decisions about the structure and content of social influence messages. Message appeals based on previous knowledge of targets' beliefs that worked perfectly well in the past may fail to work in the present situation, thus creating a potentially chaotic and bemusing situation for message producers.

COPING STRATEGIES

We now turn our attention to strategies used to cope with these potentially chronic uncertainty sources. Although at first blush it might be reasoned that reducing these uncertainties is the straightforward way to alleviate their disruptive effects, uncertainty cannot be reduced completely. Consequently, in addition to deploying strategies to reduce these uncertainties, message producers must employ strategies for dealing with uncertainties that inevitably remain even after extensive uncertainty reduction efforts. At the very least, message producers must protect themselves from the downside risks of constructing and disseminating specific messages.

Given that message producers can never be absolutely certain of their targets' communicative competence levels, goals, plans, affective states, and beliefs, they must somehow protect themselves against the most negative consequences of guessing wrong; thus, potential strategies for hedging against such risks will also be considered.

INFORMATION SEEKING

A general strategy for reducing any of the uncertainty types delineated above is to acquire information. It has been suggested that within this general strategy individuals can employ passive, active, or interactive strategies for attaining desired information (Berger, 1979; Berger & Bradac, 1982). Using *passive strategies* individuals garner information about targets by observing them unobtrusively. Evidence suggests that unobtrusive observers prefer to gather their information in informal social situations where the target persons are actively engaged in social interaction with others (Berger & Douglas, 1981; Berger & Perkins, 1978, 1979). In the case of *active strategies*, information seekers ask third parties for their assessments of targets. Although these third-party assessments may be biased, individuals feel that they are able to compensate for these biases by employing "second guessing" techniques (Doelger, Hewes, & Graham, 1986; Hewes & Graham, 1989; Hewes, Graham, Doelger, & Pavitt, 1985; Hewes, Graham, Monsour, & Doelger, 1989). Active strategies also involve the acquisition of information by subjecting targets to tests in which targets' responses are observed unobtrusively. These tests do not involve direct interaction between observers and targets. Finally, *interactive strategies* require face-to-face interaction between observers and targets. Within this strategy domain, information seekers can attain uncertainty-reducing information by asking their targets questions (Berger & Kellermann, 1983). In addition, those seeking information can reveal information about themselves with the hope that their targets will reciprocate, and information seekers can simply relax targets to induce them to be more talkative and potentially revealing (Kellermann & Berger, 1984). Of course, information gathering strategies of any kind may be thwarted by a number of counterstrategies (Berger & Kellermann, 1989) and information seekers may be forced to alter their strategies in response to these countermeasures (Berger & Kellermann, 1986, 1994).

Although information acquisition is an obvious route to uncertainty reduction, it has limitations. First, individuals have limited capacities to process information. The flood of information available to observers through verbal and nonverbal communication channels cannot all be heeded and evaluated. Furthermore, when individuals attempt to acquire information while involved in face-to-face interaction with their targets, a considerable amount of their information processing capacity must be diverted to monitoring their own actions in the encounter thus reducing their ability to process incoming information. Second, even if information is heeded, it may not be germane to the type of uncertainty that must be reduced. As discussed previously, uncertainty may stem from a number of different sources; hence, it is vital that information being acquired "match" the relevant uncertainty source. Finally, concerns for social appropriateness may severely limit certain kinds of information gathering activities (Berger & Kellermann, 1983; Kellermann & Berger, 1984; Kellermann, 1988). Asking sensitive questions, for example, may be inappropriate in a wide variety of communication contexts. Consequently, individuals cannot rely solely upon information acquisition strategies to reduce their uncertainties about various features of social interaction contexts and the individuals acting in them.

GOAL FOCUS

As indicated earlier, the instrumental and communication goals being pursued by interactants may be either unclear at the beginning of interaction episodes or they may become less clear as goals transmute in the course of interactions. Frequently, conflict episodes between those involved in close relationships manifest both of these processes. Individuals may initiate a discussion about an issue with no particular goal in mind other than to "pass the time." As the interaction progresses, however, they begin to disagree over the issue. They then find themselves arguing about issues unrelated to the original issue they began discussing. This "kitchen sink" variety of conflict, in which a laundry list of sources of dissatisfaction is dragged into the discussion, moves from a discussion focused on a singular issue to one in which the individual's goal is to demonstrate to the partner how the partner exploits them and how long-suffering they are. These patterns of escalating conflict between intimates may occur even when the parties involved do not wish to enact them (Cronen, Pearce, & Snavely, 1979). Toward the end of such episodes, a particular goal may become clear; however, the goal states in which parties found themselves on the way to the final goal state may be extremely obscure in retrospect.

From the point of view of individuals initiating social influence episodes in which their objectives involve the alteration of others' beliefs, attitudes, or actions, it is critical that goal focus be maintained; however, some detours from the path to the influence goal during the episode may be

advantageous strategically. As exemplified by conflict episodes between intimates, however, allowing primary goals to go out of focus invites the instan-
tiation of other goals that may be counterproductive to the achievement of
desired goals. Maintaining goal focus is crucial for at least two reasons.
First, if individuals have done at least some planning prior to the interaction
episode, allowing goals to go out of focus during the influence episode may
obviate the strategic insights gained during the planning process. It may be
difficult for social actors to remember the details of their plans for long time
periods; thus, if the focal goal or goals of the interaction are lost for some
period of time, it may be difficult for social actors to retrieve their sophisticated and potentially effective pre-interaction plans from memory. Second,
since individuals understand others' actions and discourse by inferring the
goals they are pursuing and the plans they are using to attain their goals, by
maintaining goal focus influence agents enable their targets to understand
better their actions and messages thus rendering the social influence process
potentially more efficient. Of course, under a limited set of conditions,
social influence might be accomplished more expeditiously by obfuscating
intent, for example, confidence or "con" games (see Chapter 4); nevertheless, under a wide variety of conditions, maintaining goal focus is more
likely to produce potentially efficient outcomes.

CONTINGENCY PLANNING

One way to hedge against unexpected interaction states created by either
the individuals involved or the interaction context is to build contingent
actions into interaction plans. Potential blocks to goal-directed actions can be
anticipated and alternative action sequences for attaining goals can be constructed and enacted if necessary. There is evidence that children who
believe in the efficacy of planning generally include more contingent actions
in their plans when asked to plan for specific goals than do their counterparts
who believe that goals should be pursued with greater spontaneity (Kreitler
& Kreitler, 1987). Some findings suggest that college students planning to
reach such social goals as ingratiating themselves to a new roommate or asking a person out for a date generally include relatively few contingent
actions in their plans to reach these goals (Berger & Bell, 1988; Berger &
diBattista, 1992a). Some analysts have concluded that planning disasters in
the public policy domain frequently stem from the inability of planners to
anticipate relatively obvious limitations in their plans (Hall, 1982). There is a
tendency, for example, for transportation planners to assume that new transportation technologies will work flawlessly when first implemented. In fact,

new technologies are almost certain to demonstrate a significant number of problems that require both time and money to remedy. Thus, contingent planning is a good idea in the abstract, but one that people do not seem to take too seriously, even when the stakes are relatively high.

While the research and analysis suggest that contingent planning is a relatively rare activity, there are some variables that seem to moderate the amount of contingent planning in which individuals engage. First, as noted previously, individuals who hold the general belief that planning before initiating goal-directed action is a desirable procedure to follow include more contingent actions in their plans for reaching specific goals (Kreitler & Kreitler, 1987). While this finding suggests that there may be stable individual differences in the propensity to plan in advance of initiating goal-directed action and to include contingent actions in plans, other evidence indicates that goals themselves may affect the extent to which contingent actions are integrated into plans. Although Berger and Bell (1988) found that spontaneous contingent planning was not evidenced in most plans, their study revealed that plans developed for pursuing the goal of requesting a date contained significantly more contingent actions than plans devised to reach the alternate goal of inducing a new roommate to like one. One interpretation of this difference is that because the potential loss of face involved in a failed attempt to obtain a date might be considerably greater than the threat accruing from failure to ingratiate one's self to a roommate, when individuals constructed their date-request plans, they were more motivated to hedge against this contingency by devising alternative action sequences. This finding suggests the broader proposition that as the magnitude of potential negative consequences of goal-failure increases, the likelihood that planners will include more contingent actions in their plans also increases.

This theoretical proposition notwithstanding, Hall (1982) has suggested that when individuals plan large-scale public projects, they focus on those actions that are likely to bring about the desired goal state. While this bias is understandable, it may lead to the unrealistic view that goal failure is impossible if the plan, as conceived, is followed. Moreover, planning carried out in the context of "group think"—the tendency for group members to be of one mind on an issue—may reinforce the view that a particular plan is certain to succeed, as members of the Kennedy administration apparently concluded about their plans for the ill-fated Bay of Pigs invasion (Janis & Mann, 1977). Given this potential "success bias" in both individual and group planning, it is little wonder that contingent actions are relatively rare events in plans. It is only when potential sources of failure are taken seriously that contingent planning processes are activated. Unfortunately, even mentioning the possibility of plan failure in group planning contexts may invite ostracism of the dissenter by other group members, especially if the plan under consideration is one developed or endorsed by group members who have considerable power. Pressures for conformity in groups or the anticipated disapproval of others, then, may inhibit contingent planning.

As the number of contingencies included in a plan increases, the complexity of the plan also increases by default. We have already seen that increases in plan complexity are associated with increases in cognitive load, as manifested in increases in the frequency and duration of non-vocalized pauses (Berger et al., 1989). Consequently, while contingent planning may be used to hedge against uncertain events that may arise during the execution of a particular goal-directed action sequence, this advantage may come at the cost of large increases in cognitive load. Moreover, one may pursue goals that clearly do not demand much in the way of contingent planning. Under most circumstances, a plan to walk to the corner store to purchase a pack of chewing gum should be considerably less complex than a plan to persuade a prospective employer that one is the right person for the job. Of course, if the corner store were located in an area with a high crime rate, one might be forced to devise a complex plan, including numerous contingencies, to go to the corner store and at the same time preserve one's life. Nonetheless, it is possible, in theory at least, to invest too many scarce cognitive resources into devising complex plans with numerous contingencies. This possibility suggests the desirability of careful goal analysis and reasonable estimates of the difficulty in reaching goals before engaging in specific planning activities.

ALTERING FAILED PLANS: THE HIERARCHY HYPOTHESIS

In spite of their attempts to anticipate various sources of goal failure through contingent planning, planners may encounter unanticipated contingencies that may undermine the effectiveness of their plans. The inevitability of such unanticipated contingencies was captured by Robert Burns (1785/1819) in his poem To a mouse, in which he observed:

> But Mousie, thou art no thy lane,
> In proving foresight may be in vain:
> The best-laid schemes o' mice an' men
> Gang aft a-gley,
> An' lea'e us nought but grief and pain,
> For promis'd joy!

When unanticipated contingencies appear, plans must be modified on-line as they are being enacted—assuming, of course, that those carrying out the plan wish to continue to pursue their goals (Waldron, 1990). Given these conditions, how do individuals go about altering plans when their plans fail to bring about desired end-states?

A line of research designed specifically to shed light on this issue has explored how individuals alter their message plans in response to not being understood by their conversational partners (Berger, 1993; Berger & Abrahams, 1993; Berger & diBattista, 1992b, 1993). The theoretical grounding for these experiments is encapsulated by the *hierarchy hypothesis*. This hypothesis asserts that when individuals are thwarted in their attempts to achieve goals in communication situations, their first tendency is to alter concrete, lower-level elements of their message plans rather than higher-level message plan units. Low-level, more concrete elements of message plans include the vocal intensity and speech rate at which the message is delivered, while higher-level message units are concerned with the structure and the sequencing of message content. The propensity to alter lower level units first is predicated on the twin assumptions that: (1) higher-level message plan alterations require more cognitive resources for their implementation, and (2) individuals are "cognitive misers" who are wont to expend large amounts cognitive effort to perform cognitive operations (Fiske & Taylor, 1984).

Experiments performed to assess the veracity of the hierarchy hypothesis generally have supported the line of argument underlying it. First, two studies have shown that geographic direction-givers, who were requested to provide their directions a second time but to use an alternative walk route—a high-level message plan alteration—required significantly more time to begin the second rendition of their directions than did individuals who were asked to provide their directions a second time but at a slower speech rate, which is a lower-level alteration (Berger, 1993; Berger & Abrahams, 1993). Moreover, those who were asked to provide more landmarks in the second rendition of their directions demonstrated average response latencies that were between these two extremes (Berger, 1993). In both of these studies, response latency was used to index the amount of cognitive load experienced by the research participants. Second, Berger and diBattista (1992b, 1993) found that regardless of the locus of communication failure, individuals showed higher levels of vocal intensity—a low-level alteration—while providing the second rendition of their directions than they did when they gave the first rendition of their directions. Moreover, in both of these studies only 4% to 5% of direction-givers spontaneously changed the walk route of their directions—a high-level alteration—when those receiving the directions indicated that they were having difficulty following the directions but did not specify the walk route itself as the locus of the communication failure. These findings support the view that when given the choice, individuals prefer low-level to high-level message plan alterations in response to goal failure because low-level alterations require fewer cognitive resources for their implementation. The hierarchy hypothesis and its postulates also provide an explanation for the often-observed tendency of individuals interacting with others who do not understand their language, including English as a second language (ESL) teachers, to repeat what they have said previously but to say it in a louder voice— clearly a dysfunctional strategy for overcoming non-acoustic-based communication failures!

Just as planners may be insensitive to the necessity for anticipating potential roadblocks to their planned actions through contingent planning, the research germane to the hierarchy hypothesis teaches us that when goal failures occur, communicators may not necessarily make optimal adaptations for surmounting the barriers that may be placed in the path of their goal-directed actions. In the context of social influence episodes, this latter tendency is no more apparent than in the behavior of parents toward their non-compliant children. In such cases it is commonplace to observe parents who, having failed to secure compliance from their children in an initial influence attempt, simply repeat the content of their first compliance-gaining message but do so in a louder voice during the second rendition, as if increasing vocal intensity is likely to be the most efficient or effective way to secure the child's compliance. As we have seen, this strategy may require considerably less effort than one requiring the reformulation of arguments and appeals used in the message; however, this savings in effort may not match the potential loss of efficiency and effectiveness. Besides, the act of speaking, let alone shouting, tends to increase blood pressure, suggesting the long-term health benefits of higher-level message plan alterations. These health issues aside, increased vocal intensity not only may be ineffective in securing compliance per se, it may promote angry and hostile responses from those subjected to the intense voice, thus further lowering the likelihood of compliance and raising the probability of long-term relationship deterioration between the influence agent and the target (see Chapter 2).

Although we have done no research on this issue to date, an important theoretical and practical question is how to encourage those who experience goal failure to: (1) take the time to diagnose the source of the failure, (2) take time to alter their plans, and (3) alter their plans at the appropriate levels of the message plan hierarchy. Clearly, some failures may require only low-level alterations—for example, speaking louder to someone who is hearing impaired or speaking more slowly to a non-native speaker of one's language. However, I suspect that many, if not most, goal failures require higher-level, more cognitively demanding modifications for their successful repair. Finding ways to encourage communicators to acquire the skills and the levels of motivation necessary for making these high level alterations to message plan hierarchies is an important theoretical and research challenge.

ACCRETIVE PLANNING PROCESSES

The logic of the hierarchy hypothesis suggests that it is neither necessary nor desirable to abandon completely a particular message plan when it fails to bring about desired end-states. Even high-level alterations to message plan hierarchies may require only minor modifications to render the plan successful. The addition of a few facts, statistics, or a new argument may transform an ineffective plan into one that is quite successful. Consequently, major investments of scarce cognitive resources may be wasted if an entire message plan is abandoned when it fails; although, as has been noted, planners need to be prepared to make such investments when necessary.

There is some evidence that individuals may make relatively conservative adaptations to goal failures. For instance, Berger and Kellermann (1986) reported that individuals (High Seekers), whose goal was to find out as much as possible about conversational partners they had just met, asked no more or fewer questions of partners who were instructed to provide as little information about themselves as possible (Low Revealers) as partners instructed to reveal as much information about themselves as possible (High Revealers). That is, the High Seekers did not vary the number of questions they asked of their partners in response to goal failure. Rather, the High Seekers who were thwarted by the Low Revealers tended to ask more questions about their partners' goals and plans than their non-thwarted counterparts. In addition, the thwarted High Seekers provided more verbal backchannel responses like "Oh, really?" or "Is that so?" to encourage their low-revealing partners to disclose more information about themselves.

Apparently, then, the High Seekers whose information acquisition goal was blocked did some of the same things they would do under normal conditions; that is, they asked the same number of questions, but varied other aspects of their message plans such as backchannel responses and types of questions. These patterns of message plan alterations suggest an accretive planning strategy in which the planner continues to do what normally works at some message plan levels but adds variations at other levels. Presumably, if the High Seekers found evidence that their increased backchanneling brought about more personal revelations from their formerly reticent partners, they would continue to elevate their backchanneling levels, although this possibility was not assessed directly in this study. The findings of this study also suggest the possibility that incremental, trail-and-error approaches to message plan alterations are used when goal failures occur. Whether such strategies themselves would be modified under conditions of a priori contingency planning is an issue worth research attention.

FRAMING STRATEGIES

Messages designed to reach such focal goals as persuasion and behavioral compliance may not only fail to bring about the desired goal state, they also may cause the influence agent to lose face (Brown & Levinson, 1978, 1987; Goffman, 1959, 1969). Consider the potential threats present when, for example, an individual asks another out for a date—a situation in which a refusal may be read as personal rejection. When such requests are made, it is rare for requesters to be perfectly certain that targets will accede to their requests; as a consequence, people may frame their requests in such a way that any refusal's threat to their face is nullified. Humor is clearly one such framing device. If a date request, for example, is delivered in a humorous context and is turned down, the individual making the request can claim that it was just a "joke" and direct the conversation to more innocuous topics. A similar "just kidding" or "lighten up" frame is used frequently to defuse potentially angry responses to comments, when those making the comments sense that their conversational partners are becoming miffed at what they have said to them. Although in these latter cases no attempt is made to build a humorous context before the comment is delivered. The "just kidding" or "lighten up" frame is clearly an ex post facto attempt to undo unanticipated negative side effects produced by one's messages.

Both of these cases illustrate attempts to cope with the inevitable uncertainties that accompany the dissemination of messages in face-to-face encounters. Message producers can seek information about their targets, have their goals in sharp focus, devise plans that contain numerous contingencies, and alter plans that fail at various levels of abstraction. In spite of these planning and plan alteration efforts, however, messages may still fail to bring about desired goals; and, what is worse, they may precipitate such unanticipated negative consequences as loss of face. Consequently, given the vagaries inherent in all communication situations, it behooves message planners to activate these framing strategies to hedge against potential worst-case scenarios, which in the present case would involve both failure to reach substantive goals like compliance-gaining and simultaneous loss of face. To fail to gain compliance from a given target is one thing, to loose face in the process probably makes future attempts to gain compliance from the same target that much less likely to succeed, since one's credibility is that much more compromised. Thus, a fundamental planning objective should involve face preservation, at least if one anticipates a long-term relationship with the target of one's influence attempts.

CONCLUSION

When individuals construct and disseminate messages in both face-to-face and mediated communication contexts, there is always some measure of uncertainty about the effects that the messages will produce. Uncertainties concerning communication competence, goals, plans, affective states, and beliefs may conspire to produce either pleasant or unpleasant surprises. For the most part, message producers are not conscious of the manifold outcomes—both desirable and undesirable—that their messages may effect in those who receive them. Nevertheless, such strategies as seeking information, focusing on primary goals, contingency planning, plan adaptation, accretive planning, and framing can be used either to hedge against unanticipated effects, a priori, or to nullify them as they arise during ongoing communication episodes. The framework articulated here does not require that these coping strategies be deployed consciously, although each one of them can be used intentionally.

Constructing and disseminating verbal and nonverbal messages is always a risky undertaking, as attested to by the frequency with which people wish they could "take back" things they have said to others. The perspective advanced in this chapter suggests that if human communicators were to utilize more often their unique capacities for forethought and planning and their ability to monitor carefully ongoing communication episodes, they might find themselves regretting what they have said a lot less often.

REFERENCES

Baxter, L.A., & Wilmot, W.W. (1984). Secret tests: Social strategies for acquiring information about the state of the relationship. *Human Communication Research, 11*, 171-201.

Bell, R.A., & Daly, J.A. (1984). The affinity-seeking function of communication. *Communication Monographs, 51*, 91-115.

Bem, D.J. (1972). Self-perception theory. In L. Berkowitz (Ed.), *Advances in experimental social psychology* (Vol. 6, pp. 1-62). New York: Academic Press.

Berger, C.R. (1979). Beyond initial interaction: Uncertainty, understanding, and the development of interpersonal relationships. In H. Giles, & R. St. Clair (Eds.), *Language and social psychology* (pp. 122-144). Oxford: Basil Blackwell.

Berger, C.R. (1985). Social power and interpersonal communication. In M.L. Knapp, & G.R. Miller (Eds.), *Handbook of interpersonal communication* (pp. 439-499). Newbury Park, CA: Sage Publications.

Berger, C.R. (1987). Communicating under uncertainty. In M. E. Roloff & G.R. Miller (Eds.), *Interpersonal processes: New directions in communication research* (pp. 39-62). Newbury Park, CA: Sage Publications.

Berger, C.R. (1988). Uncertainty and information exchange in developing relationships. In S.W. Duck (Ed.), *Handbook of personal relationships* (pp. 239-255). Chichester, England: John Wiley & Sons.

Berger, C.R. (1993, November). *Planning, plan adaptation and cognitive load: An assessment of the hierarchy hypothesis.* Paper presented at the annual convention of the Speech Communication Association, Miami, FL.

Berger, C.R. (1994). Power, dominance, and social interaction. In M.L. Knapp & G.R. Miller (eds.), *Handbook of interpersonal communication* (2nd ed., pp. 450-507). Newbury Park, CA: Sage Publications.

Berger, C.R. (1995). A plan-based approach to strategic communication. In D.E. Hewes (Ed.), *The cognitive bases of interpersonal communication*, (pp. 141-179). Hillsdale, NJ: Lawrence Erlbaum Associates.

Berger, C.R., & Abrahams, M. F. (1993, May). *Altering communication plans in response to goal failure.* Paper presented at the annual convention of the International Communication Association, Washington, D.C.

Berger, C.R., & Bell, R.A. (1988). Plans and the initiation of social relationships. *Human Communication Research, 15*, 217-235.

Berger, C.R., & Bradac, J.J. (1982). *Language and social knowledge: Uncertainty in interpersonal relations.* London: Edward Arnold.

Berger, C.R., & Calabrese, R.J. (1975). Some explorations in initial interaction and beyond: Toward a developmental theory of interpersonal communication. *Human Communication Research, 1*, 99-112.

Berger, C.R., & diBattista, P. (1992a) Information seeking and plan elaboration: What do you need to know to know what to do? *Communication Monographs, 59,* 368-387.

Berger, C.R., & diBattista, P. (1992b, October). *Adapting plans to failed communication goals.* Paper presented at the annual convention of the Speech Communication Association, Chicago, IL.

Berger, C.R., & diBattista, P. (1993). Communication failure and plan adaptation: If at first you don't succeed, say it louder and slower. *Communication Monographs, 60,* 220-238.

Berger, C.R., & Douglas, W. (1981). Studies in interpersonal epistemology III: Anticipated interaction, self-monitoring, and observational context selection. *Communication Monographs, 48,* 183-196.

Berger, C.R., & Gudykunst, W.B. (1991). Uncertainty and communication. In B. Dervin (ed.), *Progress in communication sciences* (Vol. 10, pp. 21-66). Norwood, NJ: Ablex.

Berger, C.R., & Jordan, J.M. (1992). Planning sources, planning difficulty, and verbal fluency. *Communication Monographs, 59,* 130-149.

Berger, C.R., Karol, S.H., & Jordan, J.M. (1989). When a lot of knowledge is a dangerous thing: The debilitating effects of plan complexity on verbal fluency. *Human Communication Research, 16,* 91-119.

Berger, C.R., & Kellermann, K.A. (1983). To ask or not to ask: Is that a question? In R. N. Bostrom (Ed.), *Communication yearbook 7* (pp. 342-368). Newbury Park, CA: Sage Publications.

Berger, C.R., & Kellermann, K. (1986, May). *Goal incompatibility and social action: The best laid plans of mice and men often go astray.* Paper presented at the annual convention of the International Communication Association, Chicago, IL.

Berger, C.R., & Kellermann, K. (1989). Personal opacity and social information gathering: Explorations in strategic communication. *Communication Research, 16,* 314-351.

Berger, C.R., & Kellermann, K. (1994). Acquiring social information. In J.A. Daly & J.M. Wiemann (Eds.), *Communicating strategically* (pp. 1-31). Hillsdale, NJ: Lawrence Erlbaum.

Berger, C.R., & Perkins, J.W. (1978). Studies in interpersonal epistemology I: Situational attributes in observational context selection. In B.D. Ruben (Ed.), *Communication yearbook 2* (pp. 171-184). New Brunswick, NJ: Transaction Press.

Berger, C.R., & Perkins, J.W. (1979, November). *Studies in interpersonal epistemology II: Self-monitoring, involvement, facial affect, similarity and observational context selection.* Paper presented at the annual convention of the Speech Communication Association, San Antonio, TX.

Berscheid, E. (1983). Emotion. In H.H. Kelley, E. Berscheid, A. Christensen, J.H. Harvey, T.L. Huston, G. Levinger, E. McClintock, L.A. Peplau and D.R. Peterson (Eds.), *Close relationships* (pp. 110-168). San Francisco: Freeman.

Brown, P., & Levinson, S.C. (1978). Universals in language usage: Politeness phenomena. In E.N. Goody (Ed.), *Questions and politeness* (pp. 56-289). Cambridge: Cambridge University Press.

Brown, P., & Levinson, S.C. (1987). *Politeness: Some universals in language usage.* New York: Cambridge University Press.

Burgoon, M., & Miller, G.R. (1985). An expectancy interpretation of language and persuasion. In H. Giles & R. St. Clair (Eds.), *The social and psychological contexts of language* (pp. 199-229). London: Lawrence Erlbaum Associates.

Burleson, B.R. (1984). Age, social-cognitive development, and the use of comforting strategies. *Communication Monographs, 51,* 140-153.

Burns, R. (1785/1819). To a mouse: On turning up her nest with a plough. In J. Currie (Ed.), *The works of Robert Burns* (Vol. 3, pp. 132-134). London: William Allason & J. Maynard.

Butterworth, B. (1980). Evidence from pauses in speech. In B. Butterworth (Ed.), *Language production Volume 1: Speech and talk* (pp. 155-176). New York: Academic Press.

Butterworth, B., & Goldman-Eisler, F. (1979). Recent studies in cognitive rhythm. In A.W. Siegman & S. Feldstein (Eds.), *Of speech and time: Temporal speech patterns in interpersonal contexts* (pp. 211-224). Hillsdale, NJ: Lawrence Erlbaum Associates.

Cacioppo, J.T., Martzke, J.S., Petty, R.E., & Tassinary, L. G. (1988). Specific forms of facial EMG response index emotions during an interview: From Darwin to the continuous flow hypothesis of affect-laden information processing. *Journal of Personality and Social Psychology, 54,* 592-604.

Carberry, S. (1990). *Plan recognition in natural language dialogue.* Cambridge, MA: MIT Press.

Cohen, P.R., Morgan, J., & Pollack, M.E. (1990). *Intentions in communication.* Cambridge, MA: MIT Press.

Cronen, V.E., Pearce, W.B., & Snavely, L.M. (1979). A theory of rule-structure and types of episodes and a study of perceived enmeshment in undesired repetitive patterns ('URPs'). In D. Nimmo (Ed.), *Communication yearbook 3* (pp. 225-240). New Brunswick, NJ: Transaction Books.

Dillard, J.P. (Ed.). (1990a). *Seeking compliance: The production of interpersonal influence messages.* Scottsdale, AZ: Gorsuch Scarisbrick.

Dillard, J.P. (1990b). The nature and substance of goals in tactical communication. In M.J. Cody & M.L. McLaughlin (Eds.), *The psychology of tactical communication* (pp. 70-90). Clevedon, England: Multilingual Matters.

Dillard, J.P., & Burgoon, M. (1985). Situational influences on the selection of compliance-gaining messages: Two tests of the predictive utility of the Cody-McLaughlin typology. *Communication Monographs, 52*, 289-304.

Doelger, J.A., Hewes, D.E., & Graham, M.L. (1986). Knowing when to "second guess": The mindful analysis of messages. *Human Communication Research, 12*, 301-338.

Eagly, A.H., & Chaiken, S. (1993). *The psychology of attitudes*. Fort Worth, TX: Harcourt Brace Jovanovich.

Festinger, L. (1954). A theory of social comparison processes. *Human Relations, 7*, 117-140.

Fiske, S.T., & Taylor, S.E. (1984). *Social cognition*. New York: Random House.

Goffman, E. (1959). *The presentation of self in everyday life*. Garden City, NY: Doubleday Anchor.

Goffman, E. (1969). *Strategic interaction*. Philadelphia, PA: University of Pennsylvania Press.

Goldman-Eisler, (1968). *Psycholinguistics: Experiments in spontaneous speech*. New York: Academic Press.

Green, G. M. (1989). *Pragmatics and natural language understanding*. Hillsdale, NJ: Lawrence Erlbaum.

Greene, J.O. (1984). Speech preparation processes and verbal fluency. *Human Communication Research, 11*, 61-84.

Greene, J.O. (1990). Tactical social actions: Towards some strategies for theory. In M.J. Cody & M.L. McLaughlin (Eds.), *The psychology of tactical communication* (pp. 31-47). Clevedon, England: Multilingual Matters.

Greene, J.O., & Lindsey, A.E. (1989). Encoding processes in the production of multiple-goal messages. *Human Communication Research, 16*, 120-140.

Hall, P. (1982). *Great planning disasters*. Berkeley, CA: University of California Press.

Hewes, D.E., & Graham, M.L. (1989). Second-guessing theory: Review and extension. In J.A. Anderson (Ed.), *Communication yearbook 12* (pp. 213-248). Newbury Park, CA: Sage Publications.

Hewes, D.E., Graham, M.L., Doelger, J., & Pavitt, C. (1985). "Second guessing": Message interpretation in social networks. *Human Communication Research, 11*, 299-334.

Hewes, D.E., Graham, M.L., Monsour, M., & Doelger, J. A. (1989). Cognition and social information gathering strategies: Reinterpretation assessment in second-guessing. *Human Communication Research, 16*, 297-320.

Hunter, J. E., & Boster, F.J. (1987). A model of compliance-gaining message selection. *Communication Monographs, 54,* 63-84.

Isen, A. M. (1984). Toward understanding the role of affect in cognition. In R.S. Wyer & T.K. Srull (Eds.), *Handbook of social cognition* (Vol. 3, pp. 179-236). Hillsdale, NJ: Lawrence Erlbaum Associates.

James, W. (1950). *The principles of psychology.* New York: Holt.

Janis, I.L., & Mann, L. (1977). *Decision making: A psychological analysis of conflict, choice, and commitment.* New York: Free Press.

Kellermann, K. (1988, March). *Understanding tactical choice: Metagoals in conversation.* Paper presented at the Temple University conference on goals in discourse, Philadelphia, PA.

Kellermann, K., & Berger, C.R. (1984). Affect and the acquisition of social information: Sit back, relax, and tell me about yourself. In R. Bostrom (Ed.), *Communication yearbook 8* (pp. 412-445). Newbury Park, CA: Sage Publications.

Kreitler, S., & Kreitler, H. (1987). Plans and planning: Their motivational and cognitive antecedents. In S.L. Friedman, E.K. Skolnick, & R.R. Cocking (Eds.), *Blueprints for thinking: The role of planning in cognitive development* (pp. 110-178). New York: Cambridge University Press.

Levelt, W.J.M. (1989). *Speaking: From intention to articulation.* Cambridge, MA: MIT Press.

Lichtenstein, E.H., & Brewer, W.F. (1980). Memory for goal directed events. *Cognitive Psychology, 12,* 412-445.

McGuire, W.J. (1969). Attitudes and attitude change. In G. Lindzey & E. Aronson (Eds.), *The handbook of social psychology* (2nd ed.) (Vol. 3, pp. 136-314). Reading, MA: Addison-Wesley.

McGuire, W.J. (1985). Attitudes and attitude change. In G. Lindzey & E. Aronson (Eds.), *The handbook of social psychology* (3rd ed.) (Vol. 2. , pp. 233-346). New York: Random House.

Miller, G.R. (1987). Persuasion. In C.R. Berger & S.H. Chaffee (Eds.), *Handbook of communication science* (pp. 446-483). Newbury Park, CA: Sage Publications.

Miller, G.R., Boster, F.J., Roloff, M.E., & Seibold, D.R. (1977). Compliance-gaining message strategies: A topology and some findings concerning effects of situational differences. *Communication Monographs, 44,* 37-51.

Miller, G.R., Boster, F.J., Roloff, M.E., & Seibold, D.R. (1987). MBRS rekindled: Some thoughts on compliance gaining in interpersonal settings. In M.E. Roloff & G.R. Miller (Eds.), *Interpersonal processes: New directions in communication research* (pp. 89-116). Newbury Park, CA: Sage Publications.

Miller, G.R., & Hewgill, M. A. (1964). The effect of variations in nonfluency on audience ratings of source credibility. *Quarterly Journal of Speech, 50,* 36-44.

Miller, G.R., & Steinberg, M. (1975). *Between people: A new analysis of interpersonal communication.* Chicago: Science Research Associates.

Newton, D.A., & Burgoon, J.K. (1990). The use and consequences of verbal influence strategies during interpersonal disagreements. *Human Communication Research, 16*, 477-518.

Petronio, S., Snyder, E., & Bradford, L. (1992, October). *Planning strategy for the embarrassment of friends: An application and test of Berger's planning theory.* Paper presented at the annual convention of the Speech Communication Association, Chicago, IL.

Petty, R.E., & Cacioppo, J.T. (1981). *Attitudes and persuasion: Classic and contemporary approaches.* Dubuque, IA: Wm. C. Brown.

Read, S.J., & Miller, L.C. (1989). Inter-personalism: Toward a goal-based theory of persons in relationships. In L. A. Pervin (Ed.), *Goal concepts in personality and social psychology* (pp. 413-472). Hillsdale, NJ: Lawrence Erlbaum Associates.

Ritchie, L.D. (1991). *Information.* Newbury Park, CA: Sage Publications.

Rokeach, M. (1968). *Beliefs, attitudes, and values: A theory of organization and change.* San Francisco, CA: Jossey-Bass.

Schachter, S. (1959). *The psychology of affiliation: Experiments in the sources of gregariousness.* Stanford, CA: Stanford University Press.

Schachter, S. (1964). The interaction of cognitive and physiological determinants of emotional state. In L. Berkowitz (Ed.), *Advances in experimental social psychology* (Vol. 1, pp. 49-80). New York: Academic Press.

Schank, R.C., & Abelson, R.P. (1977). *Scripts, plans, goals and understanding.* Hillsdale, NJ: Lawrence Erlbaum Associates.

Schlenker, B. (1980). *Impression management: The self-concept, social identity, and interpersonal relations.* Monterey, CA: Brooks-Cole.

Seibold, D.R., Cantrill, J.G., & Meyers, R.A. (1985). Communication and interpersonal influence. In M.L. Knapp & G.R. Miller (Eds.), *Handbook of Interpersonal Communication* (pp. 551-611). Newbury Park, CA: Sage Publications.

Shannon, C., & Weaver, W. (1949). *The mathematical theory of communication.* Urbana, IL: University of Illinois Press.

Siegman, A.W. (1987). The telltale voice: Nonverbal messages of verbal communication. In A.W. Siegman & S. Feldstein (Eds.), *Nonverbal behavior and communication* (pp. 351-434). Hillsdale, NJ: Lawrence Erlbaum Associates.

Srull, T.K., & Wyer, R.S. (1986). The role of chronic and temporary goals in social information processing. In R. Sorrentino & E.T. Higgins (Eds.), *Handbook of motivation and cognition* (pp. 503-549). New York: Guilford Press.

Sternberg, R. J. (1986). A triangular theory of love. *Psychological Review, 93*, 119-135.

Waldron, V.R. (1990). Constrained rationality: Situational influences on information acquisition plans and tactics. *Communication Monographs, 57*, 184-201.

Wilensky, R. (1983). *Planning and understanding: A computational approach to human reasoning*. Reading, MA: Addison-Wesley.

Language Expectancy Theory: Elaboration, Explication, and Extension

Michael Burgoon

S o, let me tell you a story. There could be no more appropriate way to begin a chapter in a volume in honor of Gerald R. Miller than to use one of his favorite communication activities as the vehicle for discussion of a theory of social influence that has been developed over the last 25 years. The story is not so much about me, as a communication researcher, but rather a case study of sorts about the sociology of science, at least as it refers to the development of a theoretical perspective that has (1) evolved into a set of relatively formal, logical propositions with some nomothetic force, (2) generated a number of derived hypotheses with considerable explanatory and predictive power, and (3) been supported with a wealth of empirical data attesting to its generalizability cross-contextually.

LANGUAGE EXPECTANCY THEORY: ELABORATION

THE BASIC ASSUMPTIONS OF THE ORIGINAL THEORETICAL FORMULATION

The general expectancy model. Before telling the tale of how this theory developed over the past quarter of a century, perhaps a brief summary of the basic tenets of the theory is in order. M. Burgoon and G.R. Miller (1985) provided a rather complete exposition of their theoretical position on the relationship between language and persuasion with the following introduction:

> Our language affects our lives powerfully. Others make attributions about social and professional status, background and education, and even the intent of communication by evaluating our language choices. Those intrigued with social influence whether classical scholars or media image-makers, have long pondered the influence of such language choices on the success or failure of persuasive attempts. The decision to appeal to people's logic or emotional side is manifest in the language used in persuasive messages: persuaders try to mollify, justify, terrify or crucify by altering the language in their appeals.

The original logic underlying Language Expectancy Theory (M. Burgoon, 1989; M. Burgoon, Jones, & Stewart, 1975; M. Burgoon & G.R. Miller, 1985;), which is obviously a language-based theory of persuasion, begins with the assumption that language is a rule-governed system and people develop macro-sociological expectations[1] and preferences concerning the language or message strategies employed by others in persuasive attempts. These expectations are primarily a function of cultural and sociological norms. Preferences are usually a function of cultural values and societal standards or ideals for what is competent communication performance.

M. Burgoon and G.R. Miller (1985) also provide a detailed propositional logic outlining the formative explanatory calculus of Language Expectancy Theory, which will be explicated in some detail later in this chapter. M. Burgoon (1989, 1990) later presented a major refinement of the model and discussed the effects of both positive and negative violations of expectations in persuasive attempts. For the purposes of a brief summary, Figure 1 graphically presents the basic tenets of Language Expectancy Theory.

Briefly, change in the direction desired by an actor occurs when positive violations of expectations occur. Positive violations obtain in two ways (1) when the *enacted* behavior is better or more preferred than that which was *expected* in the situation, or (2) when negatively evaluated sources conform more closely than expected to cultural values, societal norms, or situational exigencies. Change occurs in the first case because enacted behavior is outside the normative bandwidth in a positive direction and such behavior prompts attitude and or behavioral changes. In the second condition, a person who is expected to behave incompetently or inappropriately conforms to cultural norms and/or expected social roles. This results in an overly positive evaluation of the source and, subsequently, the change advocated by that actor. Negative violations of expectations result from language choices or the selection of message strategies that lie outside the bandwidth of socially acceptable behavior in a negative direction. The result is no attitude and/or

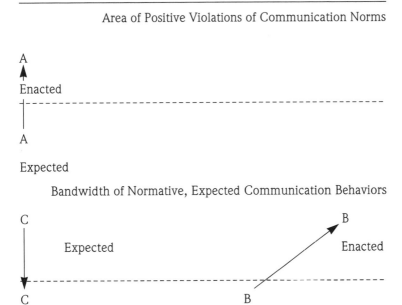

Area of Positive Violations of Communication Norms

A

Enacted

A

Expected

Bandwidth of Normative, Expected Communication Behaviors

C   B

Expected   Enacted

C   B

Enacted   Expected

Area of Negative Violations of Communication Norms

Case A: Positive violation of expectations by performing unexpected, positively valued behaviors. Enacted behavior outside the expected, normative bandwidth in positive direction. Attitude/behavior change in the direction advocated by the source.

Case B: Positive violation of expectations by negatively evaluated source conforming more closely to norms of communication behavior. Enacted behavior within the expected normative bandwidth. Attitude/behavior change predicted in direction advocated by the source because of overly positive evaluation of source behavior.

Case C: Negative violation of expectations by performing unexpected, negatively valued behaviors. Enacted behavior outside the expected, normative bandwidth in negative direction. No attitude/behavior change or actual changes in opposite direction advocated by the source.

Figure 1. Summary of Expectancy Theory Predictions about Message Strategies and Attitude/Behavior Change

behavioral changes, or changes in the opposite direction intended by the actor.

The etiology of the formulation of Language Expectancy Theory. The promised story is really about the rather serendipitous beginning of this line of research. In the last part of the decade of the 1960s, what would become the first in a series of studies (M. Burgoon, 1970a) was conducted. The predominant paradigm, or what might be termed normal science in communication was social psychological in nature. Fascination with the empirical study of attitude change was then (cf. Festinger, 1957; McGuire, 1969) distinctly cognitive in nature and primarily concerned with intrapsychic processes that facilitated or inhibited the reception and subsequent acceptance of variously structured suasory messages. Less, albeit some, research was focused on processual variables that moderated the impact of specific persuasive messages.

One line of inquiry was concerned with situations in which attitudes induced by one event influenced attitudes toward another event. Specifically, much earlier work concerned with source credibility and prestige suggestion (Hovland & Weiss, 1952) demonstrated that simply linking a message with different names could alter people's responses to that message. While this would not now qualify as any kind of novel finding, it did lead to a plethora of studies by psychologists and communication scientists concerned only with those instances in which the message and source are somehow directly linked.

In a wholly separate line of research being conducted by mass media scholars (Pool & Shulman, 1959), there was an attempt to examine situations in which effects, other than directly linked source-message combinations, were operative. They recognized that events preceding the reception of a given message by some receiver greatly influence the communication process. Pool and Shulman (1959) posited that such events created attitudinal response sets which altered the performance of professional encoders. Reporters thinking about liked people or pleasant events prior to receiving a writing assignment were better able to write a "good" news story than one containing "bad" news; conversely the reporter thinking about disliked people or events excelled at writing about bad news.

M. Burgoon (1970a) hypothesized that the same phenomenon exists in the reception of messages.[2] Support was found for the position that so-called differential attitudinal response sets dramatically affected interpretation and acceptance of messages of social import at the time, specifically message content discussing race relations on campus. All of this research was variable-analytic in nature, guided by little more than devising clever manipulations of response sets that might bias subsequent persuasive attempts. When the M. Burgoon (1970a) piece was accepted for publication in *Speech Monographs,* then-editor, Sam Becker,[3] forwarded to me an accepted but not-yet-published article by Robert Brooks (1970) that proved to be foundational for much of my own research.

This brief, four-page special report by Brooks was concerned with the early reversal of previously held affective responses to sources of public speeches which occurred immediately upon delivery of the text. While the content of Brooks's discovery was of some passing interest, his discussion of the early source reversal data—which I happened on fortuitously (Brooks, 1970, p. 155)—ends my story about what promoted the thinking and provided the spark that ignited my interest in developing Language Expectancy Theory. Brooks wrote in his concluding paragraph:

> ...the possibility of contrast effects should be considered. This principle assumes that we carry stereotypes into such social situations as the public speech. There, the speaker's behavior may be discrepant with stereotyped expectations. If the discrepant stimuli cannot be assimilated or ignored, they are likely to be exaggerated in a listener's perception. So viewed, mere civil behavior on the part of Malcolm X may be perceived as extraordinarily genteel by an auditor who expects barbaric actions from a black [sic] nationalist. One explanation...is this: unfavorable (or favorable) speakers may be perceived more (or less) favorably not because their behavior is intrinsically persuasive (or dissuasive) but because it contrasts with stereotyped expectations which audiences hold for notorious(or popular) public figures.

These comments prompted questions about the nature of what Brooks called stereotypes, and what determines what would later be called expectations. First, to what degree could the individual as a unit of analysis be jettisoned in favor of a more aggregate look at shared expectations of groups and even societies? Second, would it not be fruitful to pursue research to determine if there are indeed cultural and sociological forces that shape our patterns of ordinary language and determine normative and non-normative usage? There was ample evidence to assume that as communicators mature, they not only learn the mechanics of language, but what to say and when to say it. Finally, the question of whether such normative expectations were limited to notorious (or popular) public figures or applied to all communicators of a given type, group, class, or even all societal members was intriguing.

EARLY EMPIRICAL SUPPORT FOR AN EXPECTANCY INTERPRETATION OF PERSUASIVE EFFECTS

The studies of communicator expectancies. Turning specifically to the persuasion literature, the results of the previously discussed research (Brooks, 1970; M. Burgoon, 1970a) demonstrated that receivers do have shared expectations about the behaviors a communicator *should* exhibit. When these expectations are violated, receivers overreact to the behaviors actually exhibited. If a persuasive actor is initially perceived negatively, and then demonstrates more positive behavior than anticipated, receivers overestimate the positiveness of the unanticipated behaviors (McPeek & Edwards, 1975). The reverse also holds: when an initially positively valenced communicator exhibits unexpectedly negative communication behaviors, receivers exaggerate their negative evaluation of the communicator and/or the message.[4]

Expected message structure/style research. While much of the research on expectancy violations involved situations where persuasive actors took unexpected positions or advanced unexpected arguments, another line of research, co-occurring in time (M. Burgoon, 1970b, M. Burgoon & G.R. Miller, 1971) but not resident in any coordinated intellectual plan, was investigating the persuasive impacts of linguistic variations in advocacy attempts. Again, this research, which later proved quite valuable in developing Language Expectancy Theory, was originally little more than a garden variety variable-analytic program focusing on the effects of persuasive messages varying in language intensity (i.e., the degree to which some statement deviates from neutrality).

Theory construction often resists developing in the coordinated, orderly way imagined by philosophers and qualitative sorts short on experience in the messy world of empirical data. Burgoon and Chase (1973), working in the resistance to persuasion (inoculation) paradigm, found that refutational pretreatment messages, varying in the use of intense language, created linguistic expectations in subsequent attack messages. When those expectations were met, maximal resistance to persuasion obtained; when linguistic expectations were violated in attack messages, resistance to persuasion was not induced. Later, M.D. Miller and M. Burgoon (1979) further extended knowledge about the relationship between linguistic violations of expectations and the induction of resistance to persuasion by employing a simple expectancy theory model not requiring inoculation strategies (refutational pretreatment messages).

Toward a message-centered theory of persuasion. In a series of empirical studies, Burgoon and his research associates (M. Burgoon & Stewart, 1975; Jones & M. Burgoon, 1975; M. Burgoon, 1975),[5] provided experimental tests of the combined effects of the previously separate work on communicator-focused and structural linguistic expectations. They identified types of individual (females and low credible communicators) who were presumed to be expected to use less aggressive language choices in their persuasive messages. Such people, using more instrumental verbal aggression (a term coined much, much later), were seen as negatively violating expectations and, thus, attitude change was inhibited. Further it was revealed that males and high credible sources could use *either* aggressive or unaggressive verbal strategies and be persuasive. However, it seemed that more aggressive behavior was the expected and/or preferred mode of argument only for highly credible male advocates.

The results of this series of empirical tests of expectancy-based predictions was accompanied by a discussion of what was then called a message-centered theory of persuasion. What was actually presented was a kernel—perhaps more aptly called a skeletal—formulation of what would later be developed as Language Expectancy Theory. Arguments advanced in this discussion were markedly different from prevailing theories of social influence of the day.

First, the focus was distinctly sociological. It was argued that entire social categories (e.g., females, members of different ethnic groups, etc.) were bound by relatively rigid normative expectations of what was "appropriate" or expected communication behavior. Such expectations were not unique to specific communicators, but to aggregates of like individuals in this society. Second, the concept of normative bandwidths (refer again to Figure 1) of differential size, of expected language behaviors, was empirically demonstrated. People of high credibility, and male speakers in general, appeared to have a great deal of linguistic freedom (wide bandwidths) and could select from a number of persuasive strategies without violating pre-set expectations. On the other hand, large numbers of the population had constricted bandwidths of expected communication behaviors, and concomitantly constrained choices in how they could argue if they wished to be successful at persuasion. Finally, this elementary theoretical formulation provided a plausible explanation for "boomerang" effects, change opposite to the position advocated by the communicator, that had proven enigmatic to persuasion researchers at the time. People negatively violating expectations produce such a contrast effect that people move to opposing attitudinal positions in order to distance themselves from advocacy of such communicators.

LANGUAGE EXPECTANCY THEORY: EXPLICATION

THE ORIGINAL FORMALIZATION OF THE MODEL

M. Burgoon and G.R. Miller (1985) first attempted to explicate Language Expectancy Theory as an umbrella for understanding a wealth of diverse, often confusing, and contradictory empirical findings in three different persuasive paradigms. Several studies examined the traditional *passive message reception paradigm* (G.R. Miller & M. Burgoon, 1973), which had garnered most of the attention of social psychologists and communication scientists. Simply stated, these studies investigated situations in which communicators create messages designed to change the behaviors of message receivers. A second set of studies investigated a radically different persuasive context labeled the *active participation paradigm*. Most of these studies required the target persuadee to engage in counterattitudinal advocacy, taking positions that they themselves did not believe. The third situation was the *resistance to persuasion paradigm*, where inhibition of persuasive attempts was the paramount concern. Because of space limitations, only theorizing about the passive message reception paradigm will be presented here.

This attempt at theory construction was distinctly not variable-analytic in nature, nor guided by some brand of inductive inference making. Rather, the purpose was to develop as "grand" a nomothetic-deductive framework, composed of deductively embedded propositions, as possible to explain extant empirical regularities (and seeming irregularities) in the general body of published social influence research. Burgoon and Miller (1985) carefully articulated the nature of the body of knowledge that their resultant propositional framework would incorporate. They claimed that although their research (and that of many others) could be grouped under the above three broad headings, numerous other questions were also addressed in their examination of the research evidence. They listed the major issues dealt with at various stages as they formulated their propositional framework:

1. The research selected language variables commonly used in persuasive appeals.

2. Considerable attention was devoted to determining the relationship between specific communicator attributes (e.g. credibility and gender) and language choices as a determinant of persuasive success or failure.

3. Some attention was given to investigating selected receiver attributes as predictors of receptivity to varying persuasive strategies.

Though these receiver variables did not receive a great deal of attention, some knowledge was gained about the effects of sex of the receiver and relative open- and closed-mindedness on receptivity to specific messages.

The fundamental propositions (modified). The first proposition in the formal articulation of the theory merely laid out the fundamental assumptions of the theoretical model. This higher-order proposition, from which all else follows, approaches being axiomatic in content and structure:

> **Proposition 1:** People develop cultural and sociological expectations about language behaviors which subsequently affect their acceptance or rejection of persuasive messages.

Two corollary propositions, of obvious origin given the previous discussion, are required as a beginning point for developing a more complete theoretical synthesis of the relationship between language effects and persuasion:

> **Proposition 2:** Use of language that negatively violates societal expectations about appropriate persuasive communication behavior inhibits persuasive behavior and either results in no attitude change, or changes in position opposite to that advocated by the communicator.
> **Proposition 3:** Use of language that positively violates societal expectations about appropriate persuasive communication behavior facilitates persuasive effectiveness.

A complete review of the voluminous research literature encompassed under the umbrella of the following propositions is clearly beyond the scope and imposed page limits of the present chapter. However, detailed reviews of the fear-appeal literature, research on opinionatedness, and language intensity are readily available in the M. Burgoon and G.R. Miller (1985) initial review. M. Burgoon (1989) has extended that review to include a number of micro-level message variables as special cases of what has been called a type of instrumental verbal aggression. In a piece published shortly after that review and extension of Language Expectancy Theory, M. Burgoon (1990) also explained the results of more macro-level persuasion strategies—(e.g. sequential message strategies such as foot-in-the-door (Dillard, Hunter, & Burgoon, 1984) and door-in-the face (Cann, Sherman, & Elkes, 1975) techniques as well as the compliance-gaining message strategy research (cf Marwell & Schmitt, 1967a, 1967b; Miller, Boster, Roloff, & Seibold, 1977, 1987) from an Expectancy Theory perspective.

The propositions, with considerable nomothetic force and a wealth of empirical support, are as follows:

> **Proposition 4:** People in this society have normative expectations about the level of fear-arousing appeals, opinionated language, language intensity, sequential message techniques, and compliance-gaining attempts varying in instrumental verbal aggression appropriate to persuasive discourse.

> **Proposition 5:** Highly credible communicators have the freedom (wide bandwidth) to select varied language strategies and compliance-gaining techniques in developing persuasive messages, while low credible communicators must conform to more limited language options and compliance-gaining messages if they wish to be effective.

> **Proposition 6:** Because of normative impacts of source credibility, high credible sources can use low intensity appeals and more aggressive compliance-gaining messages than low credible communicators using either strong or mild language or more pro-social compliance-gaining strategies.

> **Proposition 7:** Communicators perceived as low credible or those unsure of their perceived credibility will usually be more persuasive if they employ appeals low in instrumental verbal aggression or elect to use more pro-social compliance-gaining message strategies.

> **Proposition 8:** People in this society have normative expectations about appropriate persuasive communication behavior which are gender specific such that (a) males are usually more persuasive using highly intense persuasive appeals and compliance-gaining message attempts, while (b) females are usually more persuasive using low intensity appeals and unaggressive compliance-gaining messages.

> **Proposition 9:** Fear arousal that is irrelevant to the content of the message of the harmful consequences of failure to comply with the advocated position mediates receptivity to different levels of language intensity and compliance-gaining strategies varying in instrumental verbal aggression. Receivers aroused by the induction of irrelevant fear or suffering from specific anxiety are most receptive to persuasive messages using low intensity and verbally unaggressive compliance-gaining attempts but unreceptive to intense appeals or verbally aggressive suasory strategies.

CRITICISMS OF LANGUAGE EXPECTANCY THEORY

Unfortunately, some of the research emanating from Language Expectancy Theory has been criticized for being teleological in nature. Since normative sociological or expected communication behaviors have not been specified on an a priori basis it is difficult, if not impossible in many situations, to determine when a positive or negative violation of expectations has obtained. Some investigators have concluded that when attitude/behavior change occurs, a positive violation of expectations must have occurred. Similarly, when no attitude/behavior change occurs or there is a boomerang effect, the conclusions drawn are that a negative violation must have occurred. Such interpretations of the empirical data make the theoretical model unfalsifiable. While such a criticism should be directed more at the way science is sometimes conducted than at the theoretical model per se, a priori specification of expectations in experimental situations would make for much stronger scientific claims.

It has also been suggested that the theoretical model ought to be less global or "grand" in its predictive and explanatory goals, less dependent on non-context dependent experimental research of the social psychological-type, and present evidence of generalizability beyond laboratory situations primarily relying on convenience samples of undergraduate students. While such criticisms might well apply to much, or even most, empirical work in communication, field tests of the theory in an applied context, using samples more representative of the population at large, would provide a more robust and useful test of the utility of the theoretical formulations. Language Expectancy Theory is not well supported with data illuminating how expectations develop between the same persuader and persuadee over time, or how they impact sequential message acceptance and/or eventual compliance with positions advocated. Moreover, little research has examined how *individual* expectations of specific communicators affect the persuasive impact of different types of advocacy messages.

LANGUAGE EXPECTANCY THEORY: EXTENSION

EMPIRICAL GENERALIZATIONS ABOUT THE HEALTH CARE CONTEXT

M. Burgoon and J. Burgoon (1990) collaborated to incorporate their separate expectancy models as an explanatory model in an applied communication context—namely, physician-patient communication. While all of the earlier expectancy models (M. Burgoon & Miller, 1985; M. Burgoon, 1989, 1990) made predictions on ideal (preferred communication) notions of expectations, M. Burgoon and J. Burgoon (1990) reasoned that an examination of the actual practice of medical communication (enacted communication) should be a potent predictor of what patients actually expect. Reviewing a large volume of research in health communication, they offered the following generalizations about how physicians actually communicate with patients in the clinical context:

> **Empirical Generalization 1:** Physicians report that they use expertise (moderately aggressive) strategies to gain patient compliance more than other types of available verbal compliance-gaining strategies.
> **Empirical Generalization 2:** As patients' medical problems increase in severity, primary care physicians report that they become more verbally aggressive in attempts to gain patients' compliance.
> **Empirical Generalization 3:** Physicians use more verbally aggressive communication strategies in situations where patients have not complied with previous recommendations or treatment regimens.
> **Empirical Generalization 4:** Severity of illness and past noncompliance interact such that physicians use the most verbally aggressive strategies in clinical situations in which the patient has a severe medical problem and a past history of noncompliance.
> **Empirical Generalization 5:** Physicians are more verbally aggressive with patients they have known for less time and less verbally aggressive with patients they have known for longer periods of time.

The empirical generalizations listed above incorporate much of the research and theorizing discussed in the extant research literature. The first empirical generalization is based upon self-reports, actual analysis of clinical encounters, and a number of other methodological techniques suggesting that differential expert power between physician/actor and patient/target prompts the use of expert power in the form of simple direction giving and appeals to the authority, knowledge, and expertise of the attending physician. Physicians tend to eschew threatening and/or antisocial strategies and more prosocial reinforcing strategies, while opting for expertise strategies to gain compliance.

The second empirical generalization is based upon the notion of personal benefits associated with compliance or noncompliance (Boster & Stiff, 1984; Cody & McLaughlin, 1980; Dillard & M. Burgoon, 1985). Simply stated, the greater the perception that compliance will be in the patient's own best interest, greater will be the number of verbal strategies—including highly aggressive communication acts—physicians use to gain compliance.

Empirical Generalization 3 is based upon the argument advanced by Dillard and M. Burgoon (1985) that, other things being equal, greater antic-ipated resistance should produce greater effort and selection of more ver-bally aggressive strategies. Thus, a history of past noncompliance should increase the probability of physicians using more aggressive language in the clinical context.

Obviously, the interaction effect posited in the fourth empirical general-ization is based upon the reasoning leading to the two previously discussed generalizations. In general, strong empirical support was found for the pre-dictions made above.

The fifth empirical generalization is based on a logic less intuitively obvi-ous than those advanced above. It was reasoned that as physicians gained more interpersonal information on patients they would respond by tailoring their messages to that individual, be able to avoid the more verbally aggres-sive strategies, and use more positive strategies in their compliance-gaining attempts with long-term patients. Physicians did use more positive (unag-gressive strategies) as the length of the relationship with a patient increased. However, regardless of the length of relationship with the patient, expertise strategies were still the predominant form of compliance-gaining attempts .

The most surprising finding in this research effort was how seldom physi-cians report using positive or reinforcing strategies in the medical context. As medicine evolves from a traditional focus on curative regimens to disease prevention and control, providers may need to expand their repertoire to be more attentive to a patient's performance of desired behaviors. Although beyond the scope of this chapter, an abundance of research on learning the-ory points to the importance of contingent reinforcement to obtain and maintain socially important behaviors. Given the relative dearth of such compliance-gaining strategies in the practice of medicine, low compliance rates are more easily understandable.

PATIENTS' PERCEPTIONS OF COMPLIANCE-GAINING STRATEGY USE BY PHYSICIANS

In a follow-up survey research project, M. Burgoon, Parrott, J. Burgoon, Coker, Pfau, and Birk (1989) explored physicians' verbal compliance-gain-ing strategy selections as reported by their patients. There was a great deal of veridicality between patients' reports of compliance-gaining strategies used by physicians and the research findings reported above. Patients also reported that health care providers rely on expertise strategies as the primary means of gaining compliance. Consistent with other investigations, it appears that patients perceive that physicians exert minimal effort to motivate or persuade them to comply with prescribed treatment regimens or suggested alterations in lifestyles. Moreover, patients do not perceive that physicians become more aggressive when they have been noncompliant, even when the medical condition being treated is potentially severe. This is one departure from the self-report data provided by physicians.

A number of other issues addressed in this field research allowed the following conclusions to be formulated:

> **Empirical Generalization 6:** No significant relationships exist between patient characteristics, structural variables in the health care delivery system, and perceived physician compliance-gaining message strategy selection.
> **Empirical Generalization 7:** Patients report that physicians are actually less verbally aggressive in clinical encounters in which patients have been noncompliant.
> **Empirical Generalization 8:** Severity of illness is unrelated to increased use of verbally aggressive communication strategies by physicians.
> **Empirical Generalization 9:** Altruism and negative esteem appear to be effective in increasing compliance even though neither strategy is often used by physicians.
> **Empirical Generalization 10:** In general, it appears that in most clinical encounters, physicians can obtain more compliance by relying less on simple direction-giving and expertise strategies, and more on use of aggressive verbal strategies.
> **Empirical Generalization 11:** Use of a greater number of unaggressive compliance-gaining strategies by physicians enhances patient satisfaction; however, use of aggressive communication does not reduce satisfaction with the quality of health care received.

Generalizations 10 and 11 run counter to many prevailing beliefs and many of the prescriptive injunctions offered by those interested in health communication. The empirical findings of M. Burgoon et al. (1989b) have not been well received by those who firmly believe that physicians must make every attempt to be warm and friendly in all aspects of the clinical encounter. Other research (Burgoon and Burgoon, 1990) has suggested that physicians can combine such relational management strategies designed to show more immediacy, involvement, and interpersonal affect with more aggressive verbal communication strategies that will (1) increase the likelihood of subsequent compliance, and (2) not significantly decrease levels of patient satisfaction. Finding the optimal combination of all available compliance-gaining strategies, direct/indirect and verbal/nonverbal, is the challenge facing those people interested in the medical context.

EXTENDING LANGUAGE EXPECTANCY THEORY TO THE HEALTH CONTEXT

Research was undertaken to build on the expectancy propositional framework by (1) providing more precision in specifying what communication behaviors patients expect of their physicians, (2) incorporating additional variables to provide a direct test of the effects of verbal aggression on satisfaction and compliance, and (3) determining if Language Expectancy Theory could be used to generate hypotheses and provide results that would be parsimonious explanations and potent predictors of the outcome variables of concern in the medical context. This research effort eliminates the possibility of a teleological interpretation of results in that differences in enacted and expected behaviors are clearly specified in advance. Moreover, given such precision in specifying expected behaviors in advance and measuring the valence of such communication styles, clear distinctions can be made between the expected, enacted and preferred communication behaviors of physicians. Such a procedure allows an unequivocal specification of what sets of behaviors should be considered as positive or negative violations of expectations, and what range of behaviors merely conform to societal norms about communication in the medical context.

M. Burgoon, Birk, and Hall (1991) claim that while the work by Burgoon and Burgoon (1990) provides a skeletal framework for applying the general expectancy model to the medical context, the above collection of statements does not incorporate some of the most important tenets of Language Expectancy Theory and are thus incomplete in their possible application of the theory to the practice of medicine. As previously indicated, early research (M. Burgoon, Jones, and Stewart 1975; M. Burgoon and G.R. Miller, 1985) that provided the foundations for Expectancy Theory clearly demonstrated that the bandwidth of normatively expected behaviors is invariant for neither individuals nor groups of people. For example, it has been clearly demonstrated that females have a much narrower bandwidth of socially acceptable behavior than do males in this society. In other words, females are limited in their choice of strategies if they wish to avoid negatively violating expectations and being ineffective in compliance-gaining attempts. It is very difficult for a female to positively violate expectations. Yet it is quite likely that any deviations, even relatively trivial changes, from the expected roles of females will result in negative violations of expectations and increase the probability of noncompliance. A significant problem in studying physicians' enacted and expected behavior is that any conclusions drawn may generalize only to male physicians. Little research has addressed the influence of gender on the physician-patient interaction and subsequent outcomes. The lack of research in this area is due, in part, to the fact that few women have until recently entered those medical specialties most responsible for adult health care, namely family practice and internal medicine. Thus, the generalizations advanced by Burgoon and Burgoon (1990) may be applicable only to male physicians.

While there has been little research on the effects of gender differences in the medical context, there is a wealth of research to suggest that females are more nurturant, less verbally aggressive, more likely to express caring and concern, and more empathic in their enacted communication behaviors (M. Burgoon, Dillard, & Doran, 1984; Eakins & Eakins, 1978; Infante & Wigley, 1986). To the extent that such behaviors are products of early sex role socialization, they are most resistant to change (Scanzoni, 1975). It is therefore unlikely that professional socialization would completely counteract sex-role differences among physicians. This is supported by the finding that female medical students tend to recognize more psychosocial issues for patients while males tend to see themselves in control of communication with patients (Rosenberg, 1979). If female physicians have been socialized to the traditional female sex-role, they should be more nurturant, expressive and have stronger interpersonal orientations than male physicians.

Another line of reasoning, based upon notions of credibility, would suggest that female physicians have a high probability of negatively violating expectations if they do not use verbally unaggressive message strategies in compliance-gaining attempts. The research by M. Burgoon, Jones, & Stewart (1975) is only one example of many studies that have shown that women, in general, are considered as less credible communicators than males by both males and females in this culture. According to Expectancy Theory, less credible communicators have a restricted bandwidth and the use of aggressive message strategies is non-normative and clearly a negative violation of expectations.

While physicians, male and female, have relatively high normative status in this society, there are differences in the perceptions of credibility of males and females in the health care professions. For example, Engleman (1974) found that a majority of both men (84%) and women (75%) preferred a male doctor as their regular physician. A limited amount of research attests to the fact that while female physicians are held in somewhat high esteem by most people in this society, they are still seen as less credible than their male counterparts and, therefore, should have less freedom to use aggressive strategies. This credibility differential, coupled with socialization processes, results in the enactment of unaggressive strategies because part of the female role suggests that any deviation from such verbally unaggressive compliance-gaining strategies will increase noncompliance.

It is clear that male physicians have a great deal of freedom to select compliance-gaining strategies. First, they have high normative status and the socialization process provides them with an extremely wide bandwidth of acceptable behaviors. Second, much research demonstrates that socialization makes aggressive behavior not only acceptable but preferred for highly credible male communicators in this society. However, the expected enacted behaviors for male physicians, as evidenced by the generalizations put forth by Burgoon and Burgoon (1990), are: to be affectively neutral, to give directions, and to use negative expertise. All of these strategies fall near the middle of the instrumental verbal aggression continuum. However, there is considerable evidence to suggest that high levels of verbal aggression on the part of male physicians are often perceived by patients as an expression of personal concern and considered a positive violation of expectations, increasing levels of compliance.

Moreover, since male physicians are expected to be affectively neutral in both treatment and prevention situations, affiliative strategies such as the expression of caring and concern can also be a positive violation of expectations for male physicians. Such personalization of the clinical visit is preferred by most people, but rarely experienced in a visit to a male physician. Thus, the only strategies which seem to be ineffective for male physicians are the ones presently most often used: a combination of simple direction-giving and expertise.

All of this taken together allowed M. Burgoon, Birk, and Hall (1991) to offer the formal statement of the following hypotheses:

>**Hypothesis 1:** There are perceived differences in expected communication behaviors such that male physicians are expected to use more aggressive verbal strategies while females doctors are expected to utilize less aggressive verbal strategies.
>
>**Hypothesis 2:** There will be an interaction between the source of a persuasive message and message strategy such that: (a) among male

physicians, a deviation from moderately aggressive language either in the direction of more instrumentally verbally aggressive or less aggressive strategies will result in increased levels of reported compliance; and (b) among female physicians, there will be an inverse linear relationship between level of verbal aggression and reported compliance.

In this study, manipulation checks were completed to establish on a priori grounds that there were significant differences in expected communication behaviors between male and female physicians. Using adult patients as subjects, compelling support for the above hypotheses derived directly from Language Expectancy Theory obtained. Moreover, there was no decrease in satisfaction when male physicians used either unexpectedly aggressive or unaggressive strategies.

WORK IN PROGRESS USING LANGUAGE EXPECTANCY THEORY

Two recent dissertation projects at the University of Arizona are directly dealing with issues designed to assuage some of the previously stated criticisms of Language Expectancy Theory. John Hall (1992) designed a study that measured *specific individual* communication expectations of receivers about two known sources. Given the individual-level expectation data, he used CD-Rom technology to present one of several broadcast-quality public service messages, varying in verbal immediacy, on a health-related issue. These messages either conformed to expectations, or positively or negatively violated previously held expectations by that individual for that communicator. He also chose communicators who were both liked and disliked by individuals in the subject population. Thus, he crossed source liking with individual expectations, and positive or negative violations to predict subsequent attitude change. Results provided support for the fundamental assumptions of Language Expectancy Theory.

Renee Klingle (1994) is currently completing a project in which a physician is shown interacting with the same patient in six sequential clinical visits. She is manipulating expectations for the final scenario by varying the amount of verbal aggression (positive or negative kinds of reinforcing messages) over time. Some subjects view only patients receiving negative feedback and aggressive communication; others see patients receiving positive regard and feedback for all six sessions. Still other subjects are evaluating different combinations of aggressive and non-aggressive physician communication behavior over time. She is also examining the gender of the physician as a predictor of how expectations will develop and to what extent a

violation of those expectations in the final physician-patient interaction scenario will affect attitudes toward the position, probability of complying
with the physician in question, and satisfaction with the communication in
this clinical context.

CONCLUSION

The paths taken to develop Language Expectancy Theory—from its
inception as little more than questions raised from interesting but relatively
unconnected empirical observations, to having some standing as a propositional framework with some explanatory and predictive power—did not follow some orderly textbook approach to theory construction. Rather, forks in
the intellectual road often led to misdirection and for every step taken for-
ward, often several steps were taken backward. But, it can be argued that
the clarion calls for more original theory construction in this discipline have
been partially satisfied by this communication-based theory, albeit incomplete at the moment. There is some logical interconnectedness in the set of
propositions that have guided research efforts for nearly a quarter of a century. A wealth of empirical data, often seen as confounded, confusing, and
even contradictory, are difficult to explain without invoking the tenets of
Language Expectancy Theory. The heuristic values of the theory are obvious when one examines this previously unconnected data bank.

New directions to answer critics of the theory, along with its application
in applied domains, attests to the relative health of this sociological view of
the role of expectations in shaping responses to persuasive messages.
Finally, perhaps this treatise will convince my collaborator on this volume,
Chuck Berger, to include this effort in his short list of extant theories, or
curios as he calls them, in the discipline of communication (see Berger,
1991).

NOTES

1. Some clarification of the nature of the theoretical formulation is in order. First, Language Expectancy Theory does *not* qualify, as mistakenly claimed by others, as having the assumptions or the form of a meta-theoretical "rules" approach, like Donald Cushman and Barnett Pearce attempted to formulate in their published work. Gerald Miller and I never exactly embraced those meta-theoretical leanings. While we proclaimed that language is indeed a rule-governed system, the propositional calculus is clearly nomothetic, with the end-goal being a law-covering framework. Moreover, the theory is primarily concerned with the sociological basis of expectation development and the impacts of deviations of groups, types, or classes from sociological or cultural expectations about appropriate communication behavior. Obviously, concerns with social-cognition processes are invoked to explain how people process messages that either positively or negatively violate such macro-level expectations, but no attempt was made to specify the *exact* nature of those psychological processes within the context of the full articulation of the theory.

2. No claim is made that the concept of cognitive response sets was invented as part of this research program. That construct had been around for a long period of time prior to this experimental effort, and remains a part of the psychology and communication literature.

3. This particular event attests to the "small world phenomenon" in this discipline. Professor Becker was the mentor of Gerald Miller when Miller was at Iowa; I was completing my Ph.D. at the time under the direction of Professor Miller, and Dr. Becker was kind enough to assist me in my initial effort at publication in a refereed journal.

4. Later work demonstrating the "negativity effect" (Kanouse & Hanson, 1972; Kellermann, 1984) demonstrates that negative information has more of a "biasing" effect than does positive information. This does not alter the basic assumptions of Language Expectancy Theory. No assumption of symmetrical effects of positive and negative violations is posited. In fact, the usually very dramatic reactions to negative violations of expectations is entirely consistent with the "negativity effects" findings. Thus, the *magnitude* of effects of positive and negative violations may differ without challenging the foundational assumptions of how such violations of expectations impact the persuasive process.

5. It should be noted for the record that a parallel but distinctly separate research effort, developing what is now called Expectancy Violations Theory, primarily concerned with nonverbal communication behaviors, had just been started by Judee K. Burgoon. Recent reviews (J.K. Burgoon, 1992, 1993) of this work describe the impressive amount of empirical support that has been offered for this theoretical formulation. Over the years, I have benefited greatly from advice and counsel from Judee Burgoon as I struggled to develop Language Expectancy Theory.

REFERENCES

Berger, C. R. (1991). Communication theories and other curios. *Communication Monographs, 58,* 101-113.

Boster, F., & Stiff, J. B. (1984). Compliance-gaining message selection behavior. *Human Communication Research, 10,* 539-556.

Brooks, R. D. (1970). The generalizability of early reversals of attitudes toward communication sources. *Speech Monographs, 37,* 152-155.

Burgoon, J.K. (1992). Applying a comparative approach to nonverbal expectancy violations theory. In J. Blumler, K.E. Rosengren, & J.M. McLeod (Eds.), *Comparatively speaking: Communication and culture across space and time* (pp. 53-69), Newbury Park, CA: Sage.

Burgoon, J.K. (1993). Interpersonal expectations, expectancy violations, and emotional communication. *Journal of Language and Social Psychology, 12,* 13-21.

Burgoon, M. (1970a). The effects of response set and race on message interpretation. *Speech Monographs, 37,* 264-268.

Burgoon, M. (1970b). Prior attitude and language intensity as predictors of message style and attitude change following counterattitudinal communication behavior. Unpublished doctoral dissertation, Michigan State University, East Lansing.

Burgoon, M. (1975). Toward a message-centered theory of persuasion: Empirical investigations of language intensity III. The effects of source credibility and language intensity on attitude change and person perception. *Human Communication Research, 1,* 251-256.

Burgoon, M. (1989). The effects of message variables on opinion and attitude change. In J. Bradac (Ed.), *Messages in communication sciences: Contemporary approaches to the study of effects* (pp. 129-164). Newbury Park, CA: Sage.

Burgoon, M. (1990). Social psychological concepts and language: Social influence. In H. Giles & P. Robinson (Eds.), *Handbook of social psychology and language* (pp. 51-72). London: John Wiley and Sons.

Burgoon, M., Birk, T, & Hall, J. (1991). Compliance and satisfaction with physician-patient communication: An expectancy theory interpretation of gender differences. *Human Communication Research, 18,* 177-208.

Burgoon, M., & Burgoon, J. (1990). Compliance-gaining and health care. In J. P. Dillard (Ed.), *Seeking compliance: The production of interpersonal influence messages* (pp. 161-188). Scottsdale: Gorsuch-Scarisbrick.

Burgoon, M., & Chase, L. C. (1973). The effects of differential linguistic patterns in messages attempting to induce resistance to persuasion. *Speech Monographs, 40,* 1-7.

Burgoon, M., Dillard, J. P., & Doran, N. (1984). Friendly or unfriendly persuasion: The effects of violations of expectations by males and females. *Human Communication Research, 10,* 283-294.

Burgoon, M., Jones, S. B., Stewart, D. (1975). Toward a message-centered theory of persuasion: Three empirical investigations of language intensity. *Human Communication Research, 1,* 240-256.

Burgoon, M., & Miller, G. R. (1971). Prior attitude and language intensity as predictors of message style and attitude change following counter-attitudinal advocacy. *Journal of Personality and Social Psychology, 20,* 240-253.

Burgoon, M., & Miller, G. R. (1985). An expectancy interpretation of language and persuasion. In H. Giles & R. St. Clair (Eds.), *The social and psychological contexts of language* (pp. 199-229). London: Lawrence Erlbaum Associates.

Burgoon, M., Parrott, R., Burgoon, J., Coker, R., Pfau, M., & Birk, T. (1989). Patients' perceptions of physicians compliance-gaining communication. *Health Communication, 2,* 28-41.

Burgoon, M., & Stewart, D. (1975). Toward a message-centered theory of persuasion: Empirical investigations of language intensity I. The effects of sex of source, receiver, and language intensity on attitude change. *Human Communication Research, 1,* 241-248.

Cann, A., Sherman, S. J., & Elkes, R. (1975). Effects of initial request size and timing of the second request on compliance: The foot-in-the-door and the-door-in-the-face. *Journal of Personality and Social Psychology, 32,* 774-782.

Cody, M. J., & McLaughlin, M. L. (1980). Perceptions of compliance-gaining situations: A dimensional analysis. *Communication Monographs, 47,* 132-148.

Dillard, J. P., & Burgoon, M. (1985). Situational influences in the selection of compliance-gaining messages: Two tests of the predictive utility of the Cody-McLaughlin typology. *Communication Monographs, 52,* 289-304.

Dillard, J. P., Hunter, J. E., & Burgoon, M. (1984). A meta-analysis of two sequential request strategies for gaining compliance: Foot-in-the-door and door-in-the-face. *Human Communication Research, 10,* 461-488.

Eakins, B. W., & Eakins, R. G. (1978). *Sex differences in human communication.* Boston: Houghton-Mifflin.

Engleman, E. G. (1974). Attitudes toward women physicians: A study of 500 clinic patients. *Western Journal of Medicine, 120,* 95.

Festinger, L. (1957). *A theory of cognitive dissonance.* Palo Alto, CA: Stanford University Press.

Hall, J. (1992). Linguistic markers of association as persuasive devices in mediated appeals. Unpublished doctoral dissertation, University of Arizona, Tucson.

Hovland, C.I., & Weiss, W. (1952). The influence of source credibility on communication effectiveness. *Public Opinion Quarterly, 15,* 635-650.

Infante, D. A., & Wigley, C. J. (1986). Verbal aggressiveness: An interpersonal model and measure. *Communication Monographs, 53,* 61-69.

Jones, S. B., & Burgoon, M. (1975). Toward a message-centered theory of persuasion: Empirical investigations of language intensity II. The effects of irrelevant fear and language intensity of attitude change. *Human Communication Research, 1,* 248-251.

Kanouse, D., & Hanson, L.R. (1972). Negativity in evaluations. In E.E. Jones, D.E. Kanouse, H.H. Kelley, R.E. Nisbett, S. Valins, & B. Weiner (Eds.), *Attribution: Perceiving the causes of behavior,.* Morristown, NJ: General Learning Press.

Kellermann, K. (1984). The negativity effect and its implication for initial interaction. *Communication Monographs, 51,* 37-55.

Klingle, R. S. (1994). Physician communication over time and patient compliance: A reinforcement expectancy interpretation of strategy effectiveness. Unpublished doctoral dissertation, University of Arizona, Tucson.

Marwell, G., & Schmitt, D. R. (1967a). Compliance-gaining behavior: a synthesis and model. *Sociological Quarterly, 8,* 317-328.

Marwell, G., & Schmitt, D. R. (1967b). Dimensions of compliance-gaining behavior: An empirical analysis. *Sociometry, 30,* 350-364.

McGuire, W. J. (1969). The nature of attitudes and attitude change. In G. Lindzey & E. Aronson (Eds.), *The handbook of social psychology* (Vol. 3, pp. 136-314). Reading, MA: Addison-Wesley.

McPeek, R. W., & Edwards, J. D. (1975). Expectancy disconfirmation and attitude change. *Journal of Social Psychology, 96,* 193-208.

Miller, G. R., Boster, F., Roloff, M., & Seibold, D. (1977). Compliance-gaining message strategies: A typology and some findings concerning effects of situational differences. *Communication Monographs, 44,* 37-51.

Miller, G. R., Boster, F., Roloff, M., & Seibold, D. (1987). MBRS Rekindled: Some thoughts on compliance gaining in interpersonal settings. In M. E. Roloff & G. R. Miller (Eds.), *Interpersonal processes: New directions in communication research* (pp. 89-116). Newbury Park: Sage.

Miller, G. R., & Burgoon, M. (1973). *New techniques of persuasion.* New York: Harper and Row.

Miller, M. D., & Burgoon, M. (1979). The relationship between violations of expectations and the induction of resistance to persuasion. *Human Communication Research, 5,* 301-313.

Pool, I., & Shulman, I. (1959). Newsmen's fantasies, audiences, and newswriting. *Public Opinion Quarterly, 23,* 145-158.

Rosenberg, P. R. (1979). Catch-22-The medical model. In E. C. Shapiro & L. M. Lowenstein (Eds.), *Becoming a physician: Development of values and attitudes in medicine* (pp. 81-92). Cambridge, MA: Ballinger.

Scanzoni, J. H. (1975). *Sex roles, life styles, and childbearing.* New York: The Free Press.

Communication and Personality: Improving the Predictive Fit

Thomas M. Steinfatt

During the period from 1950 to roughly the mid-1970s, much of the research in interpersonal communication concentrated on the person in the communication situation. The factors the person brought into the situation in terms of personality, and the way the communication process influenced the person, especially in terms of attitude change, were two overriding concerns of research. Many data sets involved a measure of personality in some fashion (Bettinghaus, Miller, & Steinfatt, 1970; Steinfatt, 1972, 1973, 1977, 1987; Steinfatt & Miller, 1971, 1974; Steinfatt, Miller, & Bettinghaus, 1969, 1974; Steinfatt & Seibold, 1979; Steinfatt, Seibold, & Frye, 1974). The personality measures in these studies usually predicted as expected, but with smaller effect sizes than anticipated.

Prior to the 1960s, aside from occasional negative results and the usual cautions concerning the interpretation of results, little criticism appeared in the literature regarding the predictive power of personality. Meehl and Hathaway (1946) had discussed concerns with subjects who were "faking good" or "faking bad," Cronbach (1946, 1950) discussed the problem of response sets, and Edwards (1953, 1957) discussed a property of test items he called social desirability. But these were discussions set in terms of the normal problems associated with measurement in any scientific inquiry.

In 1964, Vernon suggested that all was not well in predicting behavior from personality; he was joined in 1968 by Peterson, and in the 1970s by Endler (1973, 1975). DeFleur and Westie (1958), Deutscher (1966), and McGuire (1969) voiced similar concerns with respect to attitude/behavior relationships. Others (Bem, 1965; Mischel, 1969; Nisbett and Ross, 1980;

Shweder, 1975) suggested that the notion of consistent personality, attitudes, and values are mainly internal attributions based on perceptions of our own actions. These concerns were based largely on the inconsistency of empirical results across situations, as for example in Gillis and Woods (1971), where personality theories suggested that consistency should be found.

A number of partial answers to the problem of low correlations of personality measures with predicted behaviors have been suggested, including concerns with demand characteristics (Orne, 1962), the bias introduced by volunteers (Rosenthal & Rosnow, 1969; Rosnow & Rosenthal, 1966; Rosnow & Rosenthal, 1970), and evaluation apprehension (Rosenberg, 1969). These are reviewed in Kruglanski (1975). Others have concentrated on the lack of consistency of predicted behaviors across situations and on personality/situation interactions (Ajzen, 1987, 1988; Endler, 1981; McClelland, 1981; Zucker, Aronoff, and Rabin (1984). Related approaches are reviewed in Dreger (1972) and in Steinfatt & Infante (1976). A general review of these concerns may be found in Merydith and Wallbrown (1991), and related work in Craik, Hogan, and Wolfe (1993).

Though lessened in impact from the 1960s, communication research in the 1980s continued to show interest in the relationship of personality to communication. One example is McCroskey and Daly's *Personality and Interpersonal Communication* (1987), which summarized the major work in the area of individual differences research in communication. An individual difference variable not summarized in McCroskey and Daly (1987) is the need for approval, which originated in the work of Allen Edwards on social desirability (1953, 1957). While there are three basic measures of personality—ratings, observations of behavior, and self-reports—most individual difference variables employed in communication research are measured using self-report as the primary method. All self-report measures are subject to faking. The respondent can answer in a way designed to achieve a "good" score, if it can be discovered what a "good" score is. The respondent may form a hypothesis about the purpose of the measure, and this hypothesis often may be that the researcher is looking for "bad" or socially undesirable characteristics in the respondent. Or, the respondent simply may answer self-report items in a way that makes the respondent appear in the best possible light. Thus Edwards (1953) hypothesized: "If the behavior indicated by an inventory item is socially desirable, the subject will tend to attribute it to himself; if it is undesirable, he will not" (1953, p. 90).

For example, the Machiavellianism scales, particularly Mach IV, have been criticized for the social desirability present in many items, and Mach V is an attempt to remove the social desirability present in Mach IV (Geis,

1978). Reported correlations of social desirability with many of the sub-scales of the Minnesota Multiphasic Personality Inventory (MMPI) were so high that major revisions were required in both the theory of, and the interpretations given to, scores on these subscales (Edwards, 1970). While the correlations were artificially inflated due to item overlap with subscales of the MMPI, it has been suggested that "an individual's scores on most other personality instruments could be predicted with impressive accuracy [from social desirability]" (Crowne and Marlowe, 1964, p. 15). Since a common definition of psychopathology is a deviation from socially desirable standards of behavior, Heilbrun (1964) argued that social desirability scores were a measure of psychological health.

MEASURING SOCIAL DESIRABILITY

Edwards's method of calculating social desirability is discussed in detail by Edwards (1970, pp. 88-105). His scale has a split-half reliability of .83. He asked one group of subjects to rate 140 MMPI personality items, representing 14 of Murray's (1938) needs, on how socially desirable each item was. A second group then responded to the items on the personality inventory as they were intended to be. The correlation between the probability of selecting an item and its social desirability was .87 across the items. Two explanations are possible. Subjects could be trying to make a good impression, but it could be that behaviors judged desirable are also the most common behaviors. In fact, it would be surprising for this not to be the case in most societies. When 98 percent of Edwards' subjects claimed "I like to be loyal to my friends," were they trying to give a good impression or were they stating their self-perceptions accurately? It is difficult to tell the difference on an item which is both a very common behavior and at the same time also socially desirable.

Crowne and Marlowe (1960) produced the Marlow-Crowne Social Desirability Scale (M-C) which was designed to solve this problem. Each item on the scale was selected such that the behavior concerned was socially approved and had minimal psychopathological implications, but also had a low frequency of occurrence. One such item was, "No matter who I am talking to, I'm always a good listener." Only 15 percent of all subjects rate themselves above average as a listener, yet being a good listener is a socially desirable trait. Crowne and Marlowe believed that social desirability was not simply a way of responding to test items but a more general personality characteristic of an individual reflecting a need for social approval. The

M-C scale has KR20 and test-retest reliabilities of .88, and may be found in Strickland (1977). Sample items from their scale are:

I never hesitate to go out of my way to help someone in trouble.

I'm always willing to admit it when I make a mistake.

I don't find it particularly difficult to get along with loud-mouthed, obnoxious people.

SOCIAL DESIRABILITY AND COMMUNICATION

Several studies have found direct relationships between social desirability and communication behavior. Marlowe and Crowne (1961) asked subjects to spend 25 minutes on the boring spool-packing task used by Festinger and Carlsmith (1959) in their classic dissonance experiment. The experimenter introduced himself as a psychologist and acted aloof and important in playing a high authority role. In response to this high authority source, high-need-for-approval subjects rated the task as significantly more enjoyable and more important scientifically, said they learned more from the task, and expressed a greater desire to participate in a similar experiment than did low-need-for-approval subjects. These results could reflect a high need for approval, or a high need for conformity, since the authority figure of the experimenter could represent social pressure as well as social approval. But subjects scoring high on the Baron Independence of Judgment Scale (Baron, 1971), a measure of social conformity, differed from low scorers only on the question of how much was learned from the experiment. Marlowe and Crowne interpreted these results as demonstrating the influence of social desirability on behavior when an authoritative source makes requests of high need for approval subjects.

Rosenfeld (1967) found that persons high in need for approval consistently smile more often over repeated interactions with others than do persons low in need for approval, regardless of instructions to half of his 18 subjects to attempt to demonstrate a desire to disaffiliate from the confederate. Crowne and Marlowe (1964) related high need for approval to subjects' responses on a perceptual judgment task in an Asch-type situation. Two clusters of dots were presented for one second to a group including the subject and four confederates. Subjects were to state which cluster had more dots after listening to the confederates give their unanimously incorrect judgment. Each judgment was unambiguous and relatively easy.

High-need-for-approval-subjects yielded to the confederates' incorrect judgments on 59 percent of the trials, significantly more than the 34 percent
yielding by subjects with low social desirability scores. Thus, messages
from groups of persons equal in status to the subject are also more persuasive for high-need-for-approval subjects, as are high status sources. Other
Asch-type communication effects are reviewed by Steinfatt (1977, pp. 165-
173). Millham and Jacobson (1978) provide a general review of the literature on social desirability.

Despite a number of attempts, very few studies have reported a direct
relationship between social desirability and communication behaviors, or
indeed for behavior in general. Contributing to this paucity of published
results concerning social desirability may be the tendency for non-significant
results to go unpublished and unreported. The utility of social desirability
has usually been in the analysis of test items (Edwards) or of the motivation
of individuals (Crowne and Marlowe). Across the studies reviewed by
Millham and Jacobson (1978), situational factors indicative of the increased
probability of activation of social desirability and the need for approval are:
(a) increases in the perceived importance of the situation, (b) decreases in
the subject's self concept, and (c) clarity to the actor with respect to how
social approval could be obtained through a volitional act.

GENERAL RELATIONSHIP OF SOCIAL DESIRABILITY TO COMMUNICATION

Two main relationships between social desirability and individual differences have been proposed. Edwards (1953) conceived of social desirability as
a property of the scale and sought to determine the extent of social desirability in different scales through correlational methods. In contrast, Crowne
and Marlowe (1960) discuss social desirability as a need for approval, a property of the individual rather than of the scale. Their discussion of social desirability revolves around the tendency of individuals to conform to the wishes
expressed through communication by others, particularly authoritative and
powerful others. Each of these approaches is represented in current concerns
with item desirability bias in communication research (Burleson & Waltman,
1993; Burleson et al., 1988; Hamilton & Hunter, 1993; Hunter, 1988;
Kellermann, 1993; VanLear, 1993). Specifically, Hamilton & Hunter (1993)
have suggested that the Marlowe-Crowne Social Desirability Scale is multidimensional and thus inappropriate for use as a need for approval scale since
the subscales they identify are more unidimensional than M-C and thus
potentially have greater predictive possibilities.

This chapter proposes a third alternative: social desirability is a property of the individual which provides a measure of the relative desire of the individual to present him or herself in a socially desirable light *in his or her immediate situation*, as opposed to the willingness to provide relatively truthful, self-disclosive responses. Thus, the third alternative adopts Crowne and Marlowe's (1960) view of social desirability as a property of the individual, but rather than relating this property to attempts to seek approval *outside* of the immediate data gathering situation, looks on social desirability as a measure of *the subject's need to find approval within the current data gathering situation itself.* Whether this property is an enduring characteristic of the individual over time is an interesting but essentially irrelevant question to the third view: a high social desirability score indicates that the data the individual has provided on other self-report measures completed at the same time are indicative of a desire to appear socially desirable, as opposed to a desire to respond truthfully to self-report scales. A low social desirability score indicates that the data from other self-report measures completed at the same time are relatively valid indicators of the subject's perceptions of his or her own internal states. This alternative is consistent with the three situational factors of activation for social desirability: increased perceived importance of the situation, decreased self concept, and clarity of attainment of social approval. The former two are inherent in self-report measures. Presumably, the items to which the subject is responding are capable of revealing the inner states of the individual. This is both important and potentially demeaning to a subject with doubts of self worth. Clarity of attainment of social approval in the situation appears to be under the subject's control: respond to the test items in a socially desirable manner.

Observation of the functioning of the Marlowe-Crowne Social Desirability Scale in data sets obtained from diverse populations led to the third alternative. While its bivariate r with the predicted variable was often low, M-C was usually the major predictor of communication behavior in multiple regression equations where other predictors had far more theoretical relevance. Further, when high scorers on M-C were eliminated from the data sets, the predictive ability of the theoretically relevant predictors increased dramatically. Based on these observations, an attempt was made to determine the stability of this result across different communication behaviors, and to determine an optimal cutoff score for eliminating non-predictive data from the data sets.

METHOD

SUBJECTS

Subjects were from five groups. The first group consisted of 147 undergraduates from a large southern state university—80 females and 67 males; 7 Black, 6 Hispanic, 134 Anglo—with an average age of 20.8. The second group was composed of 40 MBA students at a small private northern university—12 females and 28 males; 38 Anglo and 2 Asian—with average age of 23.4. Group three consisted of 123 first-line supervisors, computer operators, nuclear power personnel, and field engineers, from utilities in the northeastern United States—109 males and 14 females; 109 Anglo, 8 Hispanic, and 6 Black—with average age of 38.6. The fourth group included 63 undergraduates at a large southwestern state university—30 males and 33 females; 23 Anglo, 23 Hispanic, 12 Native American, 5 Black—with an average age of 22.1. The fifth group was 40 public and private school administrators and teachers on St. Croix and St. Thomas, U.S. Virgin Islands—25 female, 15 male; 36 Black, 3 Anglo, 1 Asian—with an average age of 39.2. The data from these 413 subjects were combined for the analyses reported below.

PROCEDURE

Over the period of a semester, term, or training session, a battery of personality scales (PS), individual difference measures (ID), and communication style measures (CS) were completed by subjects. These subjects also participated in a number of communication related tasks and received scores for their communication task performance (CTP). Participation in the PS, ID, and CS data collection was voluntary and was accurately represented as an assessment of the individual's standing on various personality, individual difference, and communication style measures. A five-point response scale was used for all measures. No mention was made of the names nor purposes of the measures prior to their completion, and the individuals were assured that the results of the tests would be made known to them in an understandable form at or after the end of the semester/term/training session. For ease of interpretation to subjects, all variables were linearly scaled to run from 0 to 100. Subjects also understood that the results of the tests in anonymous form would be used in communication research. Communication task performance (CTP) was measured in class as a part of required exercises for the groups.

MATERIALS

The PS, ID, and CS measures administered and reported here were: (1) Norton's CS Instrument, (2) Situational Leadership, (3) Budner's Intolerance of Ambiguity Scale, (4) Levenson's Locus of Control Scale, (5) Rokeach's Dogmatism Scale, (6) The UCLA Loneliness Scale, (7) Snyder's Self-Monitoring Scale, (8) Mach IV, (9) the Marlowe-Crowne Social Desirability Scale, (10) the Gough-Sanford Rigidity Scale, (11) the PRCA-24, (12) Haney's Uncritical Inference Test, (13) Rokeach's Terminal Value Scale, (14) Norton's Open Communicator Measure, (15) Lawrence's Assertive/Aggressive Measure, (16) Crockett's Cognitive Complexity Measure, (17) Infante's Argumentativeness Scale, (18) Infante's Verbal Aggressiveness Scale, and (19) Blake and Mouton's Managerial Grid Measure (Bass, 1990; Lawrence, 1970; McCroskey and Daly, 1987; Norton, 1983; Robinson, Shaver, and Wrightsman, 1991).

Measures of CTP obtained throughout the semester and analyzed here included multiple measures of five communication variables: (1) Group leadership in running a computerized company, observed by two judges; competence in group interaction; outcomes for the computerized company; scores on a project planning exercise in communication in a three-person group; and judged competence in a corporate communication simulation. These scores were combined using equal weights to form a single outcome measure for group interaction competence for each subject. (2) Judgments of content, adaptation, organization, and language by two observers, and nonverbal visual and oral ratings by three judges on a videotaped presentation, were combined to form a single outcome measure for public speaking. (3) The total score on the Watson-Barker Listening Test, Form A, was used as a measure of listening. (4) Ratings by three judges of the focus, development, organization, and authorship of a three-page writing assignment in persuasive communication, and a writing mechanics score on a standardized test of editing a poorly written page, were combined to form a measure of writing competence. (5) Competence in dyadic conversation was measured by combining the judgments of the other participant with the judgments of two judges of an eight-minute videotaped segment of the conversation.

DATA ANALYSIS

All variables containing subscales, for example Machiavellianism, were analyzed as subscales—e.g., flattery, deceit, cynicism, and immorality. The data were analyzed through multiple regression analysis (MRA). No theoretically important set of predictors was forced for this analysis. A separate analysis was run for each of the five communication variables. These analyses consisted of three parts:

> **Part 1:** All predictors except Marlowe-Crowne (M-C) were entered and a backward stepwise procedure used until only significant predictors remained. A forward stepwise procedure was then used with M-C still disallowed as a predictor, until no additional predictor could achieve significance.
>
> **Part 2:** M-C was forced as an additional predictor.
>
> **Part 3:** Five additional analyses were run on each of the five variables. Subjects with M-C scores above the 90th percentile were dropped from the first analysis. The second through fifth analyses used subjects with M-C scores at or below the 80th, 70th, 60th, and 50th percentiles, respectively. For all analyses, predictors were retained only if they were both significant and accounted for at least 3% of the variance.

RESULTS

All analyses discussed below have all variables individually significant at .05 and each contributing a minimum of 3% to the variance accounted for. Variables are listed in the order of their betas, with the highest beta first. Several multiple R's are given for each variable: one for the entire subject set in the initial analysis without M-C as a predictor, one for the same data and predictor set with M-C included, and one or more for the truncated data sets in the five subsequent analyses. All R's reported are adjusted for number of predictors.

(1) Group interaction competence. The bivariate r with social desirability was .05. With social desirability forced out of the equation, the deceit subscale of Mach IV, intolerance of ambiguity, assertiveness, dogmatism, the group apprehension subscale of PRCA-24, and the uncritical inference score combined for an R of .66. With social desirability forced in with these predictors, R increased to .88 with social desirability the main predictor. R increased to .75 when the top 10% of the M-C scorers were removed from the data set, and to .81 when the top 20% were removed. R's for the 30%, 40%, and 50% removal cases ranged between .73 and .77.

(2) Public speaking. The bivariate r with social desirability was -.31. With social desirability forced out of the equation, two Norton variables

(impression leaving and animated/expressive), rigidity, aggressiveness, and situational leadership combined for an R of .50. With social desirability forced in with these predictors, R increased to .84, with social desirability the main predictor. R increased to .69 when the top 10% of the M-C scorers were removed from the data set, and to .82 when the top 20% were removed. R's for the 30%, 40%, and 50% removal cases ranged between .74 and .79.

(3) Listening. The bivariate r with social desirability was -.20. With social desirability forced out of the equation, two Norton variables (attentive and communicator image), aggression, and relationship values combined for an R of .45. With social desirability forced in with these predictors, R increased to .61, with social desirability the main predictor. R increased to .53 when the top 10% of the M-C scorers were removed from the data set, and to .62 when the top 20% were removed. R's for the 30%, 40%, and 50% removal cases ranged between .56 and .58.

(4) Writing competence. The bivariate r with social desirability was -.18. With social desirability forced out of the equation, two of Norton's style variables, intolerance of ambiguity, locus of control, flattery (of Mach IV), rigidity, and uncritical inference combined for an R of .69. With social desirability forced in with these predictors, R increased to .75, but social desirability was not the main predictor. R increased to .72 when the top 10% of the M-C scorers were removed from the data set, and to .75 when the top 20% were removed. R's for the 30%, 40%, and 50% removal cases ranged between .69 and .75.

(5) Competence in dyadic conversation. The bivariate r with social desirability was .04. With social desirability forced out of the equation, dogmatism, flattery, and deceit (of Mach IV), group apprehension (PRCA-24), dominant and contentious/argumentative (Norton), combined for an R of .54. With social desirability forced in with these predictors, R increased to .81, with social desirability the main predictor. R increased to .65 when the top 10% of the M-C scorers were removed from the data set, and to .80 when the top 20% were removed. R's for the 30%, 40%, and 50% removal cases ranged between .75 and .76.

DISCUSSION

The bivariate r's between social desirability and the predicted variables were not high. Their absolute values average .16, with   -.31 the largest r. This finding seems reasonable. The predictive relationship between social desirability and the CTP variables is not direct and is not predicted to be direct. The third alternative states that social desirability is a measure of the relative desire of the individual to present him or herself in a socially desirable light in his or her immediate situation. Marlowe-Crowne items were intermixed with the items of the individual difference measures on each administration. Thus by the third interpretation, subjects scoring highly on Marlowe-Crowne should be more likely to give socially desirable rather than truthful responses to most items at that administration, thus providing less valid individual differences data than would lower scoring subjects. The measures of communication task performance were obtained at different times and in different settings than the social desirability data. Again by the third interpretation, these CTP measures would not be expected to correlate highly with social desirability. This is exactly the pattern observed.

Considering specific CTP measures, there is little theoretical reason to predict that a desire to appear in conformity with social norms would be directly related to listening ability, or to competence in writing. While the desire to do well in these tasks might be enhanced by social desirability, there is no reason to expect this desire to translate into actual ability. Much the same may be said for the ability to give a presentation. The expression of socially desirable views in a public speech should not necessarily translate into a competent performance. Thus, the bivariate r's for these two CTP measures with social desirability is expected to be low. The data confirm this. A direct relationship of social desirability with group interaction and dyadic conversation CTP variables is more likely, but complex. Group interaction competence is the sum of four variables. Two of these, the computerized outcomes and the project planning, are objective measures that do not fit one of the criteria for activation of social desirability, which is the clarity of volitional attainment. It is not clear whether the other two meet the volitional attainment criterion since they are interactional measures but were judged on objective scales unavailable to the subjects. While the bivariate r's between social desirability and the former two subscales of the composite group interaction variable are -.23 and -.25, respectively, these r's for the latter two are .36 and .44, respectively. This finding seems consistent with the criteria for activation of social desirability, and with the third interpretation of social desirability. While competence in dyadic conversation might be considered a test case where social desirability should be a direct predictor of the variable, the nature of the interactions makes that less likely. The content of these interactions was friendly and non-competitive. Thus, the criterion of increased perceived importance of the situation may not be fulfilled. And the dyadic conversation measure was obtained at a different time and place from the social desirability measures in opposition to the third interpretation.

In sum, the relationship between social desirability and the CTP measures is not direct and should not be expected to be direct with the possible exception of two subscales of the group interaction variable. On these subscales the bivariate correlations are higher, as expected. The relationship between social desirability and the prediction of communication behavior is strong but indirect as suggested by the preceding analysis. Social desirability mediates between the individual difference variables and the behavioral variables they predict.

The best measure of the importance of a predictor in MRA is not the bivariate r between the predictor and predicted measures, but the size of the beta, the standardized regression coefficient. The betas between social desirability and the CTP measures are on the order of 1.5 to 2.5 times the size of the effects of the other individual difference predictors. This pattern suggests the possibility of a role as a suppressor for social desirability, an effect not often reported in the study of social behavior. A variable may serve as a major predictor in MRA in a number of ways other than through the size of its bivariate r with the predicted measure. A classical suppressor effect occurs when the r between the predicted variable and the predictor is low, the beta weight is high, and the predictor is highly correlated with at least some other predictors. When this occurs, as it does for social desirability, it indicates the possibility that the variable in question is strongly associated with the error portion of the variance in one or more of the other predictors (McNemar, 1962, pp. 186-187). When this happens, the suppressor variable frees the other predictors to work by statistically removing large portions of the error variance associated with those predictors. One predictor serves as a statistical suppressor for another predictor whenever the correlation of the first predictor with the dependent measure is less than the product of the correlation of the second predictor with the dependent measure, times the correlation between the two predictors (Cohen & Cohen, 1983, p. 94). This test for suppression assumes that all predictors have previously been oriented so that they correlate positively with the predicted variable. For each CTP measure, its correlation with social desirability is less than the product of the correlation of each significant predictor with that CTP measure times that predictor's correlation with social desirability.

That is, $r_{sd.CTP} < [r_{i.CTP} \times r_{i.sd}]$ for all i and all CTP, where i is a significant predictor of a specific CTP. In each case, social desirability has a low correlation with the dependent variable, relatively high correlations with the other significant predictor variables (from between .38 to .70), a negative regression weight, and the beta coefficients of the predictors are larger than their bivariate r's with the predictors. Thus, social desirability appears to be serving as a suppressor variable for the individual difference measures of this study.

While the relationship between social desirability and the CTP measures is not a direct relationship, it is very strong. Multiple R's between the predictor set and the CTP measures account for between 20% to 48% of the variance when social desirability is not present, and the average variance accounted for is 33%. This finding is in agreement with the findings of many studies that have attempted to predict behavior from self-report individual differences measures. The addition of social desirability to the prediction equation increased the variance accounted for far out of proportion to what would be expected from its low bivariate r's and uncertain theoretical relationship with the CTPs. The average variance accounted for increased to 61% when M-C was added to the predictors. The average variance accounted for also increased to 57.8% when the top 20% of M-C scorers were removed from the data set. And in each case M-C fails to be a significant predictor after these 20% are dropped from the analysis. This result suggests that it is the reduction in the error variance within the scores of these high M-C scorers that was largely responsible for the increase in prediction when social desirability was included as a predictor.

It seems likely that an individual who fabricates on one test might do so on another test taken at the same time. The individual is attempting to present him or herself in a socially desirable light, in his or her immediate situation, by responding in what he or she believes to be a socially desirable manner to the test items presented, in opposition to giving truthful responses. The specific nature of what constitutes socially desirable behavior may not be entirely clear in a given social situation. But specific test items are relatively clear and unambiguous and can more easily be judged for social desirability. This may be why social desirability acts as a suppressor rather than as a direct effect. Given such an effect, social desirability may serve as an index of general veracity during a given test-taking episode, with high scores on social desirability indicating that the subject is not providing accurate data. If so, and if the individual difference measures involved are good predictors of the CTP measures, provided that the self-reports they are based on are accurate, then analyzing only the scores of subjects attempting to represent accurately their own internal states should also improve the predictive ability of the predictor set.

In that case, one question concerns where to set the cutoff point for veracity. The M-C mean score was 45.3 on a 100-point scale. For each of the dependent variables reported here, eliminating M-C scorers who were above the 80th percentile produced optimal increases in prediction. Nothing was gained in removing scorers below this percentile. A score of 59.2 occurred at the 80th percentile in these data on the 100-item M-C scale. While taking ten percent interval jumps is hardly precise measurement, the data reported here suggest that a good beginning might be to regard scores of 60 or greater on a 100-point M-C scale as an indication that the remaining data generated by a subject in that data-gathering episode should be regarded with great suspicion and perhaps discarded. The motivation of the high M-C scoring respondent may be regarded as one which subscribes to social norms, rather than to present an accurate representation of one's internal states. Using a set score level, such as 60, assumes that scores on M-C are relatively consistent across testing and experimental situations and subjects. If one does not wish to make this assumption, suspicion of the scores of the top 20% of M-C scorers on any given administration of M-C used as a veracity index might be another possibility. In any case, more research is needed to determine the placement of such a criterion across studies, if such a value can be found.

Several criticisms can be leveled at these suggestions. The treatment of the five CTP variables as if they were uncorrelated is one. The correlations among these variables range from -.23 to .39. Future studies might profitably replicate portions of this research using a multivariate approach with predicted variables to see if any substantial differences in interpretation are obtained. As in any research involving large variable sets, the power and stability-of-estimate problems presented by a limited number of subjects are always present. While 413 subjects is not a small sample, the large number of variables entered into the statistical analyses reported here suggests the need for replication with still larger samples. The decision not to specify a set of theoretical predictors for each of the five CTP variables might be criticized as taking advantage of chance in the stepwise analyses. In other analyses of these data concerned with identifying stable relationships between theoretical predictors and communication behaviors, specifying a set of theoretical predictors would be appropriate. Since the concern here was with the effects of social desirability as an indicator of veracity, the stepwise approach seems warranted. Hamilton & Hunter's (1993) concerns with the multidimensionality of the Marlowe-Crowne Social Desirability Scale suggest that research attempting to study the relationship of M-C to veracity should compare the predictive results of M-C with the predictive results of its subscales, with an eye toward improving prediction in subscales that show promise.

A simple relationship between social desirability and communication behaviors might be intuitively appealing, but that is not what the data of this study suggest. The relationship is not simple and direct. Social desirability, in this study, did not correlate directly with general communication behavior. Nor should it be expected to. Instead, social desirability was proposed as a strong predictor of veracity in self-report data. That appears to be exactly its role. Including social desirability as a predictor when self-report individual difference measures are used in the prediction of communication behaviors, appears to strongly enhance the predictive ability of the individual difference measures.

The results for social desirability in these data provide for an optimistic assessment of the future of personality research in communication. The personality variables employed here were relatively weak predictors of communication behaviors when social desirability was not included among them. But with social desirability included, they were strong predictors of such behavior. Social desirability also served to provide a method and rationale for the exclusion of data from specific subjects when the truthfulness of that data is important. In any applications which involve the discarding of data from specific subjects based on social desirability scores, the usual cautions should be observed concerning subject mortality effects and confidentiality of results. The rationales for much of the theorizing in personality have strong implications for the study and prediction of communication behavior. Lessened interest in personality variables within communication in the past two decades has concerned the ability of personality variables to predict and explain other communication variables and behaviors.

Perhaps this chapter will interest future researchers in attempting to prove or refute the results presented here and the consequent value of a personality approach to the study of communication.

REFERENCES

Ajzen, I. (1987). Attitudes, traits, and actions: Dispositional prediction of behavior in personality and social psychology. In L. Berkowitz (Ed.), *Advances in experimental social psychology* (Vol. 20, pp. 1-63). New York: Academic Press.

Ajzen, I. (1988). *Attitudes, personality, and behavior.* Chicago: Dorsey.

Baron, R. A. (1971). *Human social behavior: A contemporary view of research.* Homewood, IL: Dorsey.

Bass, B. M. (1990). *Bass & Stogdill's handbook of leadership: Theory, research, and managerial applications.* New York: Free Press.

Bem, D. J. (1965). An experimental analysis of self persuasion. *Journal of Experimental Social Psychology, 1,* 199-218.

Bettinghaus, E., Miller, G., & Steinfatt, T. (1970). Source evaluation syllogistic content, and judgments of logical validity by high and low dogmatic persons. *Journal of Personality and Social Psychology, 16,* 238-244.

Blake, R. R. (1985). *The managerial grid III.* Houston: Gulf.

Burleson, B. R., & Waltman, M. S. (1993, May). *Assessing the validity of message behavior checklists: Some conceptual and empirical requirements.* Paper presented at the meeting of the International Communication Association, Washington, DC.

Burleson, B. R., Wilson, S. R., Waltman, M. S., Goering, E. M., Ely, T. K., & Whaley, B. B. (1988). Item desirability effects in compliance gaining research: Seven studies documenting artifacts in the strategy selection procedure. *Human Communication Research, 14,* 429-486.

Cohen, J., & Cohen, P. (1983). *Applied multiple regression/correlation analysis for the behavioral sciences, second edition.* Hillsdale, N.J.: Lawrence Erlbaum.

Craik, K. H., Hogan, R., & Wolfe, R. N. (1993). *Fifty years of personality psychology.* New York: Plenum.

Cronbach, L. J. (1946). Response sets and test validity. *Educational and Psychological Measurement, 6,* 475-494.

Cronbach, L. J. (1950). Further evidence on response sets and test design. *Educational and Psychological Measurement, 10,* 3-31.

Crowne, D. P., & Marlowe, D. (1960). A new scale of social desirability independent of psychopathology. *Journal of Consulting Psychology, 24,* 349-354.

Crowne, D. P., & Marlowe, D. (1964). *The approval motive: studies in evaluative dependence.* New York: Wiley.

DeFleur, M. L., & Westie, F. R. (1958). Verbal attitudes and overt acts: An experiment on the salience of attitudes. *American Sociological Review, 23,* 667-673.

Deutscher, I. (1966). Words and deeds. *Social Problems, 13*, 235-254.

Dreger, M. L. (1972). *Multivariate personality research*. Baton Rouge, LA: Claitor's Publishing Division.

Edwards, A. L. (1953). The relationship between the judged desirability of a trait and the probability that the trait will be endorsed. *Journal of Applied Psychology, 37*, 90-93.

Edwards, A. L. (1957). *The social desirability variable in personality research*. New York: Dryden.

Edwards, A. L. (1970). *The measurement of personality traits by scales and inventories*. New York: Holt, Rinehart, and Winston.

Endler, N. S. (1973). The person versus the situation—a pseudo issue? A response to Alker. *Journal of Personality, 31*, 287-303.

Endler, N. S. (1975). The case for person-situation interactions. *Canadian Psychological Review, 16*, 12-21.

Endler, N. S. (1981). Persons, situations, and their interactions. In Rabin, A. I., Aronoff, J. Barclay, A. M., & Zucker, R.A. (Eds.), *Further Explorations in personality* (pp. 114-159). New York: Wiley.

Festinger, L., & Carlsmith, J. M. (1959). Cognitive consequences of forced compliance. *Journal of Abnormal and Social Psychology, 58*, 203-210.

Geis, F. (1978). Machiavellianism. In H. London and J. E. Exner, Jr. (Eds.), *Dimensions of personality* (pp. 305-363). New York: Wiley

Gillis, J. S., & Woods, G. T. (1971). The 16PF as an indicator of performance in the Prisoner's Dilemma Game. *Journal of Conflict Resolution, 15*, 393-402.

Hamilton, M. A. & Hunter, J. E. (1993, May). *Need for approval and the inhibiting effect of hostility on conformity*. Paper presented at the meeting of the International Communication Association, Washington, DC.

Heilbrun, A. B. (1964). Social learning theory, social desirability, and the MMPI. *Psychological Bulletin, 61*, 377-387.

Hunter, J. E. (1988). Failure of the social desirability response set hypothesis. *Human Communication Research, 15*, 162-168.

Infante, D. (1987). Aggressiveness. In McCroskey, J., & Daly, J. (Eds.), *Personality and Communication* (pp. 157-193). Beverly Hills: Sage.

Kellermann, K. (1993, May). *Differences in behavioral acceptability for different compliance gaining goals*. Paper presented at the meeting of the International Communication Association, Washington, DC.

Kruglanski, A. W. (1975). The human subject in the psychology experiment: Fact and artifact. In L. Berkowitz (Ed.), *Advances in experimental social psychology* (Vol. 8, pp. 101-147). New York: Academic Press.

Lawrence, P. S. (1970). *The assessment and modification of assertive behavior*. Unpublished master's thesis, Arizona State University, Tempe.

Marlowe, D., & Crowne, D. P. (1961). Social desirability and response to perceived situational demands. *Journal of Consulting Psychology, 25*, 109-115.

McClelland, D. C. (1981). Is personality consistent? In Rabin, A. I., Aronoff, J. Barclay, A. M., & Zucker, R.A. (Eds.), *Further explorations in personality* (pp. 87-113). New York: Wiley.

McCroskey, J., & Daly, J. (1987). *Personality and Communication.* Beverly Hills: Sage.

McGuire, W. J. (1969). The nature of attitudes and attitude change. In G. Lindzey & E. Aronson (Eds.), *The handbook of social psychology*, 2nd ed. (Vol. 3, pp. 136-314). Reading, MA: Addison-Wesley.

McNemar, Q. (1962). *Psychological statistics.* New York: Wiley.

Meehl, P. E., & Hathaway, S. R. (1946). The K factor as a suppressor variable in the MMPI. *Journal of Applied Psychology, 30*, 525-564.

Merydith, S. P., & Wallbrown, F. H. (1991). Reconsidering response sets, test-taking attitudes, dissimulation, self-deception, and social desirability. *Psychological Reports, 69*, 891-905.

Millham, J., & Jacobson, L. I. (1978). The need for approval. In H. London and J. E. Exner, Jr. (Eds.), *Dimensions of personality* (pp. 365-390). New York: Wiley.

Mischel, W. (1969). Continuity and change in personality. *American Psychologist, 24*, 1012-1028.

Murray, H. A. (1938). *Explorations in personality.* New York: Oxford University Press.

Nisbett, R. E., & Ross, L. (1980). *Human inference: Strategies and shortcomings of social judgment.* Englewood Cliffs, NJ: Prentice-Hall.

Norton, R. (1983). *Communicator style: Theory, applications, and measures.* Beverly Hills: Sage.

Orne, M. T. (1962). On the social psychology of the psychological experiment: With particular reference to demand characteristics and their implications. *American Psychologist, 17*, 776-783.

Peterson, D. R. (1968). *The clinical study of social behavior.* New York: Appleton-Century-Crofts.

Robinson, J. P., Shaver, P. R., & Wrightsman, L. S. (1991). *Measures of personality and social psychological attitudes.* San Diego: Academic Press.

Rosenberg, M. J. (1969). The conditions and consequences of evaluation apprehension. In R. Rosenthal and R. C. Rosnow (Eds.), *Artifact in behavioral research* (pp. 280-350). New York: Academic Press.

Rosenfeld, J. M. (1967). Some perceptual and cognitive correlates of strong approval motivation. *Journal of Consulting Psychology, 31*, 507-512.

Rosenthal, R., & Rosnow, R. C. (1969). *Artifact in behavioral research.* New York: Academic Press.

Rosnow, R. C., & Rosenthal, R. (1966). Volunteer subjects and the results of opinion change studies. *Psychological Reports, 19*, 1183-1187.

Rosnow, R. C., & Rosenthal, R. (1970). Volunteer effects in behavioral research. *New Directions in Psychology, 4*, 211-269.

Shweder, R. A. (1975). How relevant is an individual difference theory of personality? *Journal of Personality, 43*, 455-485.

Steinfatt, T. (1972). Communication in the Prisoner's Dilemma and in a Creative Alternative Game. *Proceedings: National Gaming Council's Eleventh Annual Symposium, Report #143.* Baltimore: Center for Social Organization of Schools, The Johns Hopkins University, 212-224.

Steinfatt, T. (1973). The Prisoner's Dilemma and a Creative Alternative Game: The effects of communication under conditions of real reward. *Simulation and Games: The International Journal of Theory, Design, and Research, 4*, 389-409.

Steinfatt, T. (1977). *Human communication: An interpersonal introduction.* Indianapolis: Bobbs-Merrill.

Steinfatt, T. (1987). Personality and communication: classical approaches. In J. McCroskey and J. Daly (Eds.), *Personality and interpersonal communication* (pp. 42-126). Beverly Hills: Sage.

Steinfatt, T., & Infante, D. (1976). Attitude-behavior relationships in communication research. *Quarterly Journal of Speech, 62*, 267-278.

Steinfatt, T., & Miller, G. (1971, December). *Suggested paradigms for research in conflict resolution.* Paper presented at the meeting of the Speech Communication Association, San Francisco.

Steinfatt, T., & Miller, G. (1974). Communication in game theoretic models of conflict. In G. Miller and H. Simons (Eds.), *Perspectives on communication in social conflict* (pp. 14-75). Englewood Cliffs, NJ: Prentice Hall.

Steinfatt, T., Miller, G., & Bettinghaus, E. (1969, April). *Source credibility, logical content, and judgments of validity in high and low dogmatic persons.* Paper presented at the meeting of the Central States Speech Association, St. Louis, MO.

Steinfatt, T., Miller, G., & Bettinghaus, E. (1974). The concept of logical ambiguity and judgments of syllogistic validity. *Speech Monographs, 41*, 317-328.

Steinfatt, T., & Seibold, D. (1979). The creative alternative game: exploring interpersonal influence processes. *Simulation and Games: The International Journal of Theory, Design, and Research, 10*, 429-457.

Steinfatt, T., Seibold, D., & Frye, J. (1974). Communication in game simulated conflicts: two experiments. *Speech Monographs, 41*, 24-35.

Strickland, B. R. (1977). Approval motivation. In Blass, T. (Ed.), *Personality variables in social behavior* (pp. 315-356). Hillsdale, NJ: Erlbaum.

VanLear, A. C. (1993, May). *Social desirability bias in communication research: Communication competence, style, and personal relationships.* Paper presented at the meeting of the International Communication Association, Washington, DC.

Vernon, P. E. (1964). *Personality assessment: A critical survey.* New York: Wiley.

Zucker, R. A., Aronoff, J., and Rabin, A. I. (1984). *Personality and the prediction of behavior.* Orlando, FL: Academic Press.

Conceptualizing Deception as a Persuasive Activity

James B. Stiff

My first exposure to the study of deceptive communication occurred in a graduate seminar with Gerry Miller in the fall of 1982. In the early weeks of the seminar we read a paper that G.R. was preparing for an upcoming conference. The paper, entitled, "Telling It Like It Isn't And Not Telling It Like It Is: Some Thoughts On Deceptive Communication," outlined a framework for studying deceptive communication that conceptualized deception as a persuasive process. The foundation of this conceptual framework was a definition of deceptive communication as "message distortion resulting from deliberate falsification or omission of information by a communicator with the intent of stimulating in another, or others, a belief that the communicator himself or herself does not believe" (Miller, 1983, pp. 92-93). Miller's explication of this definition clarified the conceptual connection between deception and persuasive communication. Miller argued that "deceptive communication strives for persuasive ends; or, stated more precisely, deceptive communication is a general persuasive strategy that aims at influencing the beliefs, attitudes, and behaviors of others by means of deliberate message distortions" (1983, p. 99).

This conceptualization marked a departure from traditional approaches to deception that emphasized situational contexts—interpersonal deception, deceptive advertising, polygraph exams—toward an approach that emphasized the influence of these messages on targets of deception. This conceptualization also responded to Miller and M. Burgoon's (1978) call for studies of persuasion that moved beyond traditional message- or issue-centered activities and focused on more person-centered activities (see Chapter 2).

In the decade since Miller's conceptualization of deception as persuasion, the study of deceptive communication has gained prominence among communication scholars and today several programs of research examine the production, evaluation, and effects of deceptive messages (for a review, see Miller & Stiff, 1993). If one considers the sheer volume of research on the persuasive aspects of deceptive messages, then Miller's conceptualization of deceptive communication has been quite influential. However, if the goal of communication inquiry is a general theory of communication (Berger, 1991), then a more useful benchmark for judging the success of Miller's (1983) conceptual marriage of deceptive communication to the broader area of social influence is the development of theories that accommodate broadly based definitions of persuasion, including deceptive communication.

In recent years, much of my research and the research Gerry Miller and I conducted together reflects Miller's view of deception as social influence. For the most part, our investigations have examined how people evaluate truthful and deceptive messages and draw conclusions about the veracity of message sources. A careful review of these investigations reflects the prominent influence that general theories of persuasion have had on our thinking about the deception process. This chapter describes many of these investigations and, in the process, examines the conceptual contributions that persuasion theory and deception research have to offer one another. Specifically, three theoretical concepts that are well known to persuasion scholars—information integration, heuristic processing, and expectancy violations—will be introduced, and the influence of these concepts on our thinking about deceptive communication will be examined. The chapter concludes with a discussion of the conceptual and methodological contributions that recent investigations of deceptive communication have to offer persuasion scholars.

INFORMATION INTEGRATION AND VERACITY JUDGMENTS

Targets of deceptive messages are faced with the onerous task of evaluating and integrating different types of information contained in a source's verbal and nonverbal behavior and in the message environment—i.e., normative judgments. Proper evaluation and integration of these cues are essential for accurate veracity judgments, and the difficulty of this task is underscored by research consistently demonstrating that people are unable to accurately detect deception in others (Miller & Stiff, 1993).

In an effort to explain people's inability to detect deception, researchers have sought to estimate the relative importance people assign to various sources of information and the relationship of information sources to message veracity. Findings from several of these investigations provide unequivocal support for the conclusion that people rely heavily on nonverbal cues when judging message veracity, even though most nonverbal cues are not reliable indicators of deception (Miller & Stiff, 1993).

For example, in one study we examined the nonverbal correlates of *deceptive messages* and compared them with the verbal and nonverbal correlates of people's *veracity judgments*. Although none of the ten nonverbal cues coded was correlated with actual message veracity, participants relied on seven of these nonverbal cues to make veracity *judgments*. The correlations with veracity judgments were moderate in size for three nonverbal cues (blinks, hand gestures, and response latency), and quite strong for four other cues (smiles, posture shifts, pauses, and response duration) (Stiff & Miller, 1986). Moreover, findings were consistent with those from three other studies in which the nonverbal cues related to *actual* truth and deception differed from the cues related to people's *judgments* of deception. Thus, one explanation for people's inability to make accurate judgments of deception may stem from the importance people assign to nonverbal cues, which appear to be less reliable indicators of actual deception than verbal content cues (Miller & Stiff, 1993).

Although these investigations provided evidence of the primacy of nonverbal cues in judgments of honesty and deceit, they provided few insights about how people integrate verbal and nonverbal message cues with cues in the message environment to make judgments about deception. Initially, investigations of the *relative* importance that people assign to verbal and nonverbal cues examined the influence of various modes of message presentation on judgmental accuracy. In one early study, people who were exposed to written or audiotaped message presentations of truthful and deceptive messages were significantly more accurate judges of deception than those who were exposed to a live message presentation (Maier & Thurber, 1968). Maier and Thurber speculated that the presence of visual nonverbal cues in the live condition may have distracted observers from attending to the verbal and vocal behaviors of message sources. Similar findings from two other studies (Bauchner, Brandt, & Miller, 1977; Hocking, Bauchner, Kaminski, & Miller, 1979) fueled speculation that visual cues distracted observers from evaluating the vocal and verbal cues, which were thought by researchers to be more valid indicators of deception.

Although these studies produced similar findings, they were all limited by a common methodological flaw; the mode of message presentation in these studies was confounded with both the quantity and type of information contained in the messages. For example, Maier and Thurber manipulated message modality by creating live, audiotaped, and written versions of truthful and deceptive messages. The live messages contained visual, vocal, and verbal sources of information; the audiotaped messages contained vocal and verbal information; and the written messages contained only the verbal content of these messages. Consequently, these studies were unable to determine whether the low detection accuracy in the live conditions was due to the distracting effects of visual cues, the amount of information contained in the message, or the mode of message presentation. It was argued that these experimental confounds could potentially explain the overriding effects of visual cues on veracity judgments (Stiff et al., 1989).

To examine the viability of the distraction explanation, an experiment was conducted in which the mode of message presentation was held constant, and verbal, vocal, and visual qualities of a source's message were varied. The verbal, vocal, and visual cue manipulations were designed to reflect the types of behaviors commonly found in truthful and deceptive messages. For example, in the truthful verbal conditions, trained actors provided clear, consistent, plausible, and concise responses to an interviewer's questions. In the deceptive verbal condition these responses were less clear, consistent, plausible, and concise. Similar manipulations were created for visual and vocal correlates of deception (Stiff, et al., 1989). Videotapes of these interviews were shown to observers who were asked to judge the veracity of the interviewee and to evaluate qualities of the verbal message content.

Consistent with prior studies, observers' judgments were heavily influenced by the visual cue manipulation. Observers exposed to interviews that manipulated visual cues associated with deception rated the source as significantly more deceptive than observers exposed to the truthful visual cue manipulation. Vocal and verbal cue manipulations had little effect on veracity judgments. Although findings underscored the value that observers apparently ascribe to visual cue information in deceptive transactions, they also disconfirmed the distraction explanation of this effect. While observers relied prominently on visual cues, these cues had no effect on evaluations of verbal message content. If the presence of deceptive visual cues was distracting, it would have prevented observers from accurately identifying characteristics of verbal content.

In an effort to explain the primacy of nonverbal information in influencing people's veracity judgments, two situational cues were examined that were thought to affect the relative weight observers assigned to verbal and nonverbal information. The first situational cue examined was the degree of familiarity that observers had with the context of the deceptive interaction (Stiff et al., 1989). It was speculated that the primacy of nonverbal cues in prior deception detection studies may have been due to the lack of familiarity that participants had with the context of the deceptive interaction. In unfamiliar situations people have little basis for making judgments about the truthfulness of verbal message content and, as a result, they rely primarily on nonverbal cues to make veracity judgments. Thus, it was hypothesized that when the context of a deceptive interaction was unfamiliar to observers, observers would base their veracity judgments on culturally held beliefs about what a liar "looks like" instead of characteristics of verbal content. However, when the situational context was familiar, it was hypothesized that observers would base their judgments on verbal content cues.

Once again, actors were employed to manipulate verbal and visual behavior in response to an interviewer's questions. In addition, two interview contexts were created—one in which the events depicted in the interview were familiar to our observers and one in which the depicted events were unfamiliar. Videotapes of these interviews were shown to observers who made judgments about the interviewee's veracity. Findings provided partial support for the hypothesis. In the familiar situation, people relied exclusively on verbal content cues to make judgments. In the unfamiliar situation, however, observers' judgments were influenced by both visual and verbal cue manipulations (Stiff et al., 1989).

One explanation for this unanticipated finding may be that observers in the unfamiliar situation felt less confident basing their judgments exclusively on verbal cues and relied on visual cues as well. Regardless of the explanation, these findings are consistent with two prior studies in which situational factors influenced the relative importance of verbal and nonverbal information in people's judgments (Krauss, Apple, Morency, Wenzel, & Winton, 1981; Zuckerman, Amidon, Bishop, & Pomerantz, 1982).

A second situational cue examined was the availability of normative information about the judgments of others. Many everyday situations require people to make veracity judgments in a group setting. In these situations, verbal and nonverbal information from message sources is often accompanied by knowledge about the judgments of others. For example, in jury deliberations, jurors are cognizant of each other's judgments. Social normative influences like these have been shown to be quite influential on individual judgments and may be most influential in situations where uncertainty is high (Deutsch & Gerard, 1955). For example, in situations where a source's verbal and nonverbal behaviors are congruent,—i.e., truthful verbal and truthful nonverbal behaviors, or deceptive verbal and deceptive nonverbal behaviors—uncertainty about the source's veracity should be low. However, in situations where verbal and nonverbal cues are incongruent, uncertainty about the source's veracity should be high. Thus, it was hypothesized that when verbal and nonverbal cues were congruent, observers would rely primarily on those cues to make veracity judgments. However, when these cues were incongruent, people's veracity judgments would be influenced by social normative information available to them (Hale & Stiff, 1990; Stiff, Hale, Garlick, & Rogan, 1990).

Using the same research paradigm, actors manipulated combinations of verbal and visual cues that were correlates of truth and deception as they responded to interview questions. These interviews were videotaped and shown to observers who were given either positive, negative, or no normative information. Observers in the positive normative information were told that most people who had seen the videotapes judged the source to be truthful, while those in the negative normative information condition were told that most observers judged the source as deceptive. In both studies, people's judgments were guided by visual cue information, regardless of the congruence between the verbal and visual cues, or the presence of social normative information. Thus, although the strengths of the visual, verbal, and social normative information manipulations were quite similar, the visual cue information manipulation had an overriding influence on people's judgments. Verbal cues and social normative information had little influence on veracity judgments.

Taken together, findings from these investigations provide strong evidence of the primacy of nonverbal cues in people's judgments of deceptive communication. People assign greater importance to visual nonverbal information than they do to verbal content cues and vocal nonverbal cues. Although situational characteristics like familiarity may affect the relative strength of their influence, visual cues exert a prominent influence on people's veracity judgments (Miller & Stiff, 1993).

Although none of these investigations were specifically designed to test Information Integration Theory (Anderson, 1981), this avenue of deception research has clearly been influenced by Anderson's thinking about how people combine different sources of information in making veracity judgments. The crux of this theory is a description of how people *evaluate* and *integrate* information when making judgments about attitude objects.

According to Information Integration Theory, two factors constitute the evaluation of information; *scale value* represents people's perception of the valence of the information and *weight* reflects the relative importance of that information. Once information is evaluated, it is integrated through an averaging process with existing information to determine people's attitudes.

Applied in deceptive transactions, Information Integration Theory can explain the primacy of nonverbal cues in veracity judgments. Prior research on nonverbal correlates of deception suggests that some nonverbal cues are positively related to judgments of deception and others are negatively related to these judgments (Miller & Stiff, 1993; Stiff & Miller, 1986). Observers in these experiments conducted the type of evaluations described by Information Integration Theory. The positive and negative correlations between verbal and nonverbal behaviors and veracity judgments reflect the *scale value* evaluations that observers make, while the strength of these correlations reflects the *weight* that people assign to these different cues. Once they are evaluated, these individual sources of information are integrated to form a judgment of veracity.

Evidence of the primacy of visual nonverbal cues, however, suggests a somewhat different integration formula than the averaging model depicted in Information Integration Theory. Although many visual, vocal, and non-verbal cues are similarly correlated with deceptive judgments when considered separately, when considered in combination, visual cues appear to dominate the veracity judgment process. Nevertheless, people's judgments about a source's behavior reflect the same conceptual processes depicted in Information Integration Theory.

In addition to this conceptual connection, tests of information integration processes provided the methodological framework for studies of deception detection. Indeed, investigations of visual cue primacy (Hale & Stiff, 1990; Stiff et al., 1990; Stiff et al., 1989) were patterned after Anderson's tests of Information Integration Theory. For example, Anderson (1973) created positive, negative, and neutral messages about well-known presidents. Participants read combinations of these messages and evaluated the favorableness of the president. Consistent with Information Integration Theory, Anderson found that the informational value of these messages was averaged to form overall assessments of the president described in the communication.

Our studies of nonverbal cue primacy used a similar method. Messages were created that contained different combinations of truthful and deceptive verbal, vocal, and visual cue information. Participants in our study observed these message presentations and evaluated the source's veracity

(Stiff et al., 1989). In two other studies, observers were presented with social normative information and then exposed to the message manipulations (Hale & Stiff, 1990; Stiff et al., 1990). Although little evidence of information averaging was found, Anderson's procedure for manipulating informational content of messages was essential to the investigation of the relative effects of visual, vocal, verbal and situational cues on veracity judgments.

COGNITIVE HEURISTICS AND VERACITY JUDGMENTS

Social-cognitive theories of persuasion have also influenced our thinking about the process of deception detection. One prominent theory, The Heuristic Model of Persuasion (Chaiken, 1987), described two distinct approaches to processing persuasive message information. *Systematic message processing* involves careful evaluation and scrutiny of message content. When people engage in systematic processing, they pay careful attention to the substance of a message, evaluating claims and supporting evidence for validity and consistency. *Heuristic processing*, on the other hand, requires relatively little cognitive effort. Instead, receivers invoke simple decision rules to judge the validity of a message. These decision rules are called *heuristics* and are substituted for more mindful message processing. Recognizing that people are often "minimalist information processors" (Tversky & Kahneman, 1974), the Heuristic Model of Persuasion posits that many distal persuasion cues are processed by means of simple schemas or decision rules that have been learned on the basis of past experiences and observations (Chaiken, 1987, p. 4). Decision rules like "expert sources are probably correct" and "more is better" are just two examples of the types of heuristics that may guide people's judgments about a persuasive appeal.

The Heuristic Model of Persuasion posits that systematic processing depends on the ability and motivation of message receivers to scrutinize message content. When people lack the ability or motivation necessary for systematic processing, they use heuristics to make judgments about the persuasive message. However, systematic processing does not preclude simultaneous use of heuristics to judge messages. Indeed both types of processing often occur simultaneously because the heuristic processing requires little cognitive effort.

Considerable evidence has been gathered to support the validity of the Heuristic Model of Persuasion (Chaiken, 1987), and we decided to apply Chaiken's thinking to the study of deception in interpersonal relationships.

Early studies of relational deception found that people are no more accurate at detecting deception perpetrated by a relational partner than they are at detecting deception perpetrated by a stranger (Comadena, 1982; Miller et al., 1981). The concept of a truth bias has been offered as one explanation for low detection accuracy rates among relational partners (McCornack & Parks, 1986).

As originally conceived, the truth bias is a tendency of people to judge a relational partner's behavior as truthful. McCornack & Parks (1986) argued that as relationships become more intimate, people develop a level of trust in their partner that leads them to judge a partner's behavior as truthful. Thus, the truth bias was introduced as a behavioral bias, a tendency to judge a partner as truthful, which reflects the presumption of honesty that accompanies the development of many relationships.

In a recent study we reconceptualized the truth bias construct (Stiff, Kim, & Ramesh, 1992). We argued that a behavioral measure of truth bias represents a:

> mean (or typical) response that does not permit an analysis of how the bias varies from situation to situation. Conceptualized behaviorally, the notion of a truth bias suggests that a person can have the bias one minute and be without it the next if he or she becomes suspicious for any reason. In essence, the approach of McCornack and Parks confounds the concept of a bias with its behavioral consequences (Stiff et al., 1992, pp. 327-328).

Instead, we suggested conceptualizing the truth bias as a cognitive heuristic. This approach permits a distinction to be drawn between the cognitive processes that guide veracity judgments and the judgments themselves.

Conceptualized as a cognitive heuristic, the truth bias implies that as relationships become more intimate, partners develop a simple decision rule for judging each other's behavior—i.e., "My partner has been truthful in the past, therefore he or she is being truthful now." This decision rule substitutes for careful scrutiny of a partner's messages and becomes chronically accessible through constant activation (Stiff et al., 1992). Operation of the truth bias is consistent with Chaiken's (1987) conception of heuristic message processing and suggests a causal process in which relational intimacy is positively related to the truth bias, which in turn is positively related to judgments of truthfulness and negatively related to detection accuracy.

Although the truth bias heuristic is available in well-developed relationships, it was speculated that situational characteristics of deceptive transactions may serve to offset the operation of this heuristic and lead people to engage in more active message processing (see Buller, Strzyzewski, & Comstock, 1991). For example, it was argued that suspicion aroused during an interaction would reduce reliance on the truth bias heuristic and result in more active scrutiny of a source's message. Consistent with Chaiken's (1987) concept of systematic processing, it was hypothesized that aroused suspicion would be negatively related to the truth bias heuristic and judgments of truthfulness (Stiff et al., 1992).

Findings from our study were consistent with our reconceptualization of the truth bias as a cognitive heuristic. Relational partners in our study participated in an interview in which one partner responded truthfully or deceptively to the questions of the other. When the truth bias was operating, people made truthful judgments of their partner's behavior. However, when suspicion about their partner's veracity was aroused by the experimenter, people engaged in more systematic processing. That is, people who were highly suspicious asked interview questions that reflected greater cognitive involvement with the interview than people who were not suspicious (Stiff et al., 1992).

Our investigation of relational deception was guided by Chaiken's Heuristic Model of Persuasion and, consistent with this model, we found evidence of systematic and heuristic processing in deceptive transactions. Heuristic processing was reflected in the use of the truth bias heuristic while systematic processing was apparent in the questions asked by interviewers who were made to be suspicious of their partner's veracity.

EXPECTANCY VIOLATIONS AND VERACITY JUDGMENTS

Thus far, we have examined the influence of Information Integration Theory and the Heuristic Model of Persuasion on studies of deceptive communication. Recently, a third approach to studying persuasive communication, Language Expectancy Theory, has guided investigations of deception and deception detection. Several models of expectancy violations have been developed to explain people's evaluation of message presentations. Adopting an attributional approach, Eagly and her colleagues invoked the concept of expectancy violations to explain the persuasive influence of message sources when they advocate positions counter to the expectations of message receivers (Eagly, Chaiken, & Wood, 1981). In addition, J. Burgoon and her colleagues have developed a model of nonverbal expectancy violations (J. Burgoon & Hale, 1988) and examined their effects in social influence situations (Stacks & J. Burgoon, 1981). Preceding these two approaches, however, was the development of Language Expectancy Theory to explain the persuasive effects of language intensity (M. Burgoon, 1975; M. Burgoon & Miller, 1985; see Chater 2). Although all three models of expectancy violations have a number of common principles, the application of Expectancy Theory to explain language effects in persuasion (M. Burgoon & Miller, 1985) is most closely related to investigations of deceptive messages.

Burgoon & Miller observed that "cultural and social forces shape our patterns of ordinary language and determine normative and non-normative usage. As communicators mature, they not only learn the mechanics of language but also *what* to say and how to say it" (1985, p. 200). This view of language development led to one overarching proposition and two corollary propositions about language expectations and their influence on persuasion:

> **Proposition 1:** People develop expectations about language behaviors which subsequently affect their acceptance or rejection of persuasive messages.
> **Proposition 1a:** Use of language that negatively violates normative expectations about appropriate communication behavior inhibits persuasive effectiveness.
> **Proposition 1b:** Use of language that positively violates expectations by conforming more closely than anticipated to normative expectations of appropriate communication behavior facilitates persuasive effectiveness (M. Burgoon & Miller, 1985, p. 201).

Applied in deceptive transactions, Language Expectancy Theory suggests that people form expectations about "what truthful behavior looks and sounds like" and when these expectations are violated, they judge a source's behavior to be deceptive. Conversely, when a source's behavior conforms to these expectations people are likely to judge the source as truthful. Studies that examine the verbal and nonverbal correlates of veracity judgments are implicitly concerned with people's expectations about truthful behavior. For example, we identified several verbal and nonverbal cues that were correlated with judgments of deception (Stiff & Miller, 1986) and by implication, these cues reflect people's expectations of truthful message presentations.

Although nonverbal behaviors have received the lion's share of attention from scholars of deception, recent investigations have begun to focus attention on verbal characteristics of truthful and deceptive messages. For example, Information Manipulation Theory (McCornack, 1992) and the development of Criteria Based Content Analysis (Undeutsch, 1989; Wegener, 1989) are representative of a growing body of literature on the examination of people's expectations about the *verbal* characteristics of truthful and deceptive messages.

CONVERSATIONAL NORMS AS EXPECTATIONS

Information Manipulation Theory is derived from Grice's (1989) "cooperative principle" of interaction. This principle suggests that people engaged in cooperative interaction are *expected* to fulfill certain conversational maxims. For example, Grice's relevance maxim suggests that interactants are expected to contribute information that is relevant to the preceding utterances in the interaction. The *quality, quantity,* and *manner* maxims reflect similar expectations that people have about cooperative interaction.

Information Manipulation Theory posits that deceptive interactions are by nature non-cooperative. Accordingly, this theory predicts that deceptive messages should contain more violations of Grice's conversational maxims than truthful messages. McCornack et al. (1992) conducted an initial test of this theory by creating segments of hypothetical messages that violated one of Grice's four conversational maxims. These messages were presented to research participants who then judged the veracity of the message source. Consistent with their predictions, McCornack et al. found that messages containing violations of one of these maxims were rated as more deceptive than the message that fulfilled all four conversational maxims.

This study was limited by the use of hypothetical scenarios to examine the effects of violations of Grice's (1989) conversational maxims on veracity judgments. To alleviate this concern, we examined the verbal content of truthful and deceptive interviews and coded interviewee responses for violations of the relevance and quantity maxims (Stiff, Corman, & Raghavendra, 1993). Four categories of replies were created—those that violated only the relevance maxim, those that violated only the quantity maxim, those that violated both the relevance and quantity maxims, and those that violated neither the relevance nor the quantity maxim.

Investigation of these interviews failed to provide support for Information Manipulation Theory. Contrary to McCornack's (1992) predictions, *truthful* messages contained more violations of these two conversational maxims than deceptive messages. Moreover, we found that violations of these maxims were unrelated to interviewer's veracity judgments (Stiff et al., 1993). We speculated that deceivers in our study might have felt more constrained to appear cooperative, and hence may have been less comfortable violating the conversational maxims. A second possibility bears mentioning. It may be that Grice's (1989) reasoning is incorrect. Indeed, our finding that truthful messages contained more violations of conversational maxims than deceptive messages did may suggest that the conversational constraints imposed by these maxims are too cumbersome for many natural interactions. Instead, people may feel constrained to fulfill these conversational maxims only when they are most concerned about appearing cooperative— i.e., in deceptive situations.

While these preliminary studies produced contradictory findings, both provided evidence that people have expectations about the verbal characteristics of truthful messages, and violations of these affect veracity judgments. Although there is some debate about the specific nature of these expectations and the persuasive effects of violating them, these investigations reflect an important extension of M. Burgoon and Miller's (1985) Language Expectancy Theory (see Chapter 2).

EXPECTATIONS ABOUT CHILDREN'S TESTIMONY

Further evidence of the expectations people form about truthful and deceptive messages comes from studies of the credibility of children's testimony. Recently, child psychologists and child abuse specialists have begun to develop procedures for assessing the validity of children's testimony about sexual abuse. Because the credibility of children's testimony often plays a pivotal role in the outcome of sexual abuse trials, German researchers have proposed Criteria Based Content Analysis (CBCA) as a method of assessing the validity of children's statements (Undeutsch, 1989; Wegener, 1989). This method, which evolved from years of experience with child abuse cases, proposes that truthful descriptions of sexual abuse will contain specific characteristics that are not contained in fabricated accusations of abuse (Raskin & Esplin, 1991; Steller & Koehnken, 1989).

The content categories of CBCA reflect the expectations that child abuse specialists have about the truthful testimony of children. For example, one content category suggests that truthful allegations may contain recollections of specific statements made by the alleged abuser, statements that spatially or temporally frame the abuse incident, and statements that describe unexpected complications during the incident (Raskin & Esplin, 1991). Recent investigations of CBCA suggest that the expectations reflected in these content categories are valid. Truthful statements, or statements with a high probability of being true (based on investigative information and case outcomes), contain significantly more of these types

of descriptions than deceptive statements, or statements with a high probability of being deceptive (Boychuk, 1991; Raskin & Esplin, 1991). In one
study, characteristics matching each of five content categories were present in 95% of the forensic interviews in which there was a high probability that the child's accusation was truthful, but in only 30% of the
interviews in which there was a high probability that the child was communicating deceptively.

This research provides insights about the expectations people have for
children's testimony, and the effects that violations of these expectations
can have on judgments about the validity of such testimony. This program
of study, together with research regarding expectations for verbal and nonverbal truthful and deceptive behavior, suggests that Expectancy Theory
might hold a great deal of promise for the study of deception in a wide
range of transactional contexts.

SOME CONCLUDING COMMENTS

Has the conceptual marriage of deceptive communication to the larger
body of persuasion research been successful? If the three avenues of
research described in this chapter are any indication, then the answer to
this question is most certainly yes. Three prominent theories of persuasive
communication—Information Integration Theory (Anderson, 1981), the
Heuristic Model of Persuasion (Chaiken, 1987), and Expectancy Theory
(M. Burgoon & Miller, 1985)—have clearly guided thinking about the
process of deception detection. Although the theoretical link between
deception and these theories is explicit in some studies and implicit in others, persuasion theory has made significant contributions to our understanding of deceptive communication. One additional point bears mentioning.
Because this chapter has examined the influence of persuasion theory on
studies of deception, one might begin to wonder whether the area of deceptive communication can contribute to our understanding of more general
persuasive activities. In closing, let me suggest two ways that studies of
deceptive communication can contribute to persuasion research.

First, many deception studies have examined the role of verbal and nonverbal behaviors in the message production process. For example, Greene
and his colleagues have considered the influence of cognitive processes and
planning on the production of verbal and nonverbal behaviors (Greene,
O'Hair, Cody, & Yen, 1985). Although persuasion scholars have shown a
keen interest in message production processes (Dillard, Segrin, & Hardin,

1989; O'Keefe, 1988), these studies have focused primarily on the verbal content of such messages and paid relatively little attention to accompanying nonverbal behavior. Because verbal and nonverbal behavior are inextricably woven in many persuasive transactions, studies of verbal and nonverbal deceptive behavior have much to offer scholars who are interested in persuasive message production.

A second example of the potential contributions of deception research to persuasion scholars stems from the study of deception as a transactional process. Indeed, recent studies of the mutual influence that sources and targets of deceptive messages have on the outcomes of these transactions may pave the way for more interactive studies of persuasive communication. For example, we found that highly suspicious interviewers asked more cognitively involving questions than less suspicious interviewers and that the level of cognitive involvement in interviewer questions was positively related to the response latencies of interviewees. Because response latencies in our study were positively correlated with judgments of deceptiveness, questions asked by highly suspicious interviewers directly affected the nonverbal behaviors they relied on to make judgments of deception (Stiff, Corman, & Raghavendra, 1991). Our emphasis on the interactive nature of these transactions was apparent in another study in which we examined the sequence and timing of interviewer's probes on subsequent nonverbal behavior (Stiff, Corman, Krizek, & Snider, 1994).

Together, these studies adopt a transactive approach to deception that may inform the study of general persuasive activity. For example, studies of sequential request strategies (i.e., the foot-in-the-door, door-in-the-face, and low-ball techniques) examine the timing and influence of request-refusal sequences on the compliance of persuasive targets (see Cialdini, 1987; Dillard, 1991). This body of research on interpersonal influence may benefit from deception research that examines the interactive influences of sources and targets in deceptive transactions.

The conceptual and methodological contributions that persuasion and deception research have to offer one another provide strong evidence of the utility of Miller's (1983) conceptualization of deception as a persuasive activity. Indeed, the success of this conceptual marriage suggests that it may be time for deception scholars to abandon the development of theories of "deceptive communication" and instead focus attention on the application and extension of general persuasion theories in the context of deceptive transactions.

REFERENCES

Anderson, N.H. (1973). Information integration theory applied to attitudes about U.S. Presidents. *Journal of Educational Psychology, 64*, 1-8.

Anderson, N.H. (1981). *Foundations of information integration theory.* San Diego, CA: Academic Press.

Bauchner, J.E., Brandt, D.R., & Miller, G.R. (1977). The truth/deception attribution: Effects of varying levels of information availability. In B.R. Ruben (Ed.), *Communication yearbook 1* (pp. 229-243). New Brunswick, NJ: Transaction Books.

Berger, C.R. (1991). Communication theories and other curios. *Communication Monographs, 58*, 101-113.

Boychuk, T.D. (1991). *Criteria-based content analysis of children's statements about sexual abuse: A field-based validation study.* Unpublished doctoral dissertation, Arizona State University, Tempe.

Buller, D.B., Strzyzewski, K.D., & Comstock, J. (1991). Interpersonal deception: I. Deceivers' reactions to receivers' suspicions and probing. *Communication Monographs, 58*, 1-24.

Burgoon, J.K., & Hale, J.L. (1988). Nonverbal expectancy violations: Model elaboration and application to immediacy behaviors. *Communication Monographs, 55*, 58-79.

Burgoon, M. (1975). Empirical investigations of language intensity: III. The effects of source credibility and language intensity on attitude change and person perception. *Human Communication Research, 1*, 251-256.

Burgoon, M., & Miller, G.R. (1985). An expectancy interpretation of language and persuasion. In H.Giles and R. St. Clair (Eds.), *Recent advances in language communication, and social psychology* (pp. 199-229). London: Lawrence Erlbaum.

Chaiken, S. (1987). The heuristic model of persuasion. In M. P. Zanna, J. M. Olson, & C. P. Herman (Eds.), *Social influence: The Ontario symposium* (Vol. 5, pp. 3-39). Hillsdale, NJ: Lawrence Erlbaum.

Cialdini, R.B. (1987). Compliance principles of compliance professionals: Psychologists of necessity. In M.P. Zanna, J.M. Olson, & C.P. Herman (Eds.), *Social influence: The Ontario Symposium* (Vol. 5, pp. 165-184). Hillsdale, NJ: Lawrence Erlbaum.

Comadena, M.E. (1982). Accuracy in detecting deception: Intimate and friendship relationships. In M. Burgoon (Ed.), *Communication yearbook 6* (pp. 446-472). Beverly Hills, CA: Sage.

Deutsch, M., & Gerard, H.B. (1955). A study of normative and informational social influence upon individual judgment. *Journal of Abnormal and Social Psychology, 51*, 629-636.

Dillard, J.P. (1991). The current status of research on sequential-request compliance techniques. *Personality and Social Psychology Bulletin, 17*, 283-288.

Dillard, J. P., Segrin, C., & Hardin, J.M. (1989). Primary and secondary goals in the production of interpersonal influence messages. *Communication Monographs, 56,* 19-38.

Eagly, A.H., Chaiken, S., & Wood, W. (1981). An attribution analysis of persuasion. In J.H. Harvey, W.J. Ickes, & R.F. Kidd (Eds.) *New directions in attribution research* (Vol. 3, pp. 37-62). Hillsdale, NJ: Lawrence Erlbaum.

Greene, J.O., O'Hair, D., Cody, M.J., & Yen, C. (1985). Planning and control of behavior during deception. *Human Communication Research, 11,* 335-364.

Grice, H.P. (1989). *Studies in the way of words.* Cambridge, MA: Harvard University Press.

Hale, J.L., & Stiff, J.B. (1990). Nonverbal primacy in veracity judgments. *Communication Reports, 3,* 75-83.

Hocking, J.E., Bauchner, J., Kaminski, E.P., & Miller, G.R. (1979). Detecting deceptive communication from verbal, visual, and paralinguistic cues. *Human Communication Research, 6,* 33-46.

Krauss, R.M., Apple, W., Morency, N., Wenzel, C., & Winton, W. (1981). Verbal, vocal, and visible factors in judgments of another's affect. *Journal of Personality and Social Psychology, 40,* 312-320.

Maier, N.R.F., & Thurber, J. (1968). Accuracy judgments of deception when an interview is watched, heard, and read. *Personnel Psychology, 21,* 23-30.

McCornack, S.A. (1992). Information manipulation theory. *Communication Monographs, 59,* 1-16.

McCornack, S.A., & Parks, M.T. (1986). Deception detection and relational development: The other side of trust. In M.L. McLaughlin (Ed.), *Communication yearbook 9* (pp. 377-389). Beverly Hills, CA: Sage.

Miller, G.R. (1983). Telling it like it isn't and not telling it like it is: Some thoughts on deceptive communication. In J.I. Sisco (Ed.), *The Jensen lectures: Contemporary communication studies* (pp. 91-116). Tampa: University of South Florida Press.

Miller, G.R., Bauchner, J.E., Hocking, J.E., Fontes, N.E., Kaminski, E.P., & Brandt, D.R. (1981). "... and nothing but the truth": How well can observers detect deceptive testimony? In B.D. Sales (Ed.), *Perspectives in law and psychology: Vol. 2. The jury judicial, and trial process* (pp. 145-179). New York: Plenum.

Miller, G.R., & Burgoon, M. (1978). Persuasion research: Review and commentary. In B.D. Ruben (Ed.) *Communication yearbook 2* (pp. 29-47). New Brunswick, NJ: Transaction.

Miller, G.R., & Stiff, J.B. (1993). *Deceptive communication.* Newbury Park, CA: Sage.

O'Keefe, B.J. (1988). The logic of message design: Individual differences in reasoning about communication. *Communication Monographs, 55,* 80-103.

Raskin, D.C., & Esplin, P.W. (1991). Assessment of children's statements of sexual abuse. In J. Doris (Ed.), *The suggestibility of children's recollections: Implications for eyewitness testimony* (pp. 153-164). Washington, DC: American Psychological Association.

Stacks, D.W., & Burgoon, J.K. (1981). The role of nonverbal behaviors as distractors in resistance to persuasion in interpersonal contexts. *Central States Speech Journal, 32,* 61-72.

Steller, M., & Koehnken, G. (1989). Criteria-based statement analysis. In D.C. Raskin (Ed.), *Psychological methods in criminal investigation and evidence* (pp. 217-245). New York: Springer.

Stiff, J.B., Corman, S.R., Krizek, R., & Snider, E. (1994). Individual differences and changes in nonverbal behavior: Unmasking the changing faces of deception. *Communication Research, 21,* 555-581.

Stiff, J.B., Corman, S.R., & Raghavendra, S. (1991, May). *Exploring the process of deception detection.* Paper presented at the annual meeting of the International Communication Association, Chicago.

Stiff, J.B., Corman, S.R., & Raghavendra, S. (1993, February). *Conversational norms and judgments of veracity.* Paper presented at the annual meeting of the Western States Communication Association, Albuquerque.

Stiff, J.B., Hale, J.L., Garlick, R., & Rogan, R.G. (1990). Effect of cue incongruence and social normative influences on individual judgments of honesty and deceit. *The Southern Communication Journal, 55,* 206-229.

Stiff, J.B., Kim, H.J., & Ramesh, C. (1992). Truth biases and aroused suspicion in relational deception. *Communication Research, 19,* 326-345.

Stiff, J.B., & Miller, G.R. (1986). "Come to think of it ...":Interrogative probes, deceptive communication, and deception detection. *Human Communication Research, 19,* 326-345.

Stiff, J.B., Miller, G.R., Sleight, C., Mongeau, P.A., Garlick, R., & Rogan, R. (1989). Explanations for visual cue primacy in judgments of honesty and deceit. *Journal of Personality and Social Psychology, 56,* 555-564.

Tversky, A., & Kahneman, D. (1974). Judgment under uncertainty: Heuristics and biases. *Science, 185,* 1124-1131.

Undeutsch, U. (1989). The development of statement reality analysis. In J.C. Yuille (Ed.), *Credibility assessment* (pp. 101-120). Dordrecht, The Netherlands: Kluwer.

Wegener, H. (1989). The present state of statement analysis. In J.C. Yuille (Ed.), *Credibility assessment* (pp. 121-134). Dordrecht, The Netherlands: Kluwer.

Zuckerman, M., Amidon, M.D., Bishop, S.E., & Pomerantz, S.D. (1982). Face and tone of voice in the communication of deception. *Journal of Personality and Social Psychology, 43,* 347-357.

Commentary on Compliance-Gaining Message Behavior Research

Franklin J. Boster

Arguably, in the last 15 years the study of compliance-gaining message behavior has held the attention of communication scholars as much as, if not more than, any other single topic in the discipline. I am aware of more than 100 papers, addressed directly to the issue, that have been published in this time frame, and approximately two-thirds of them have been published by communication scholars in communication journals. Furthermore, diverse interests within communication have found compliance-gaining message behavior of importance. Although the area is dominated by interpersonal communication scholars, admittedly taking some liberties with this term, those students of communication education, health communication, intercultural communication, mass communication, and organizational communication have found the study of compliance-gaining message behavior pertinent to their research agenda as well.

The broad appeal is not difficult to understand. One reason is that the phenomenon intersects many, if not most, of the contexts that form the subdisciplines of the field of communication. To illustrate, in the course of any 24-hour period we may attempt to get our teenage daughter to study more, a graduate student to complete a deferred grade, and our dean to increase support to the graduate program. In the same period we may be inundated with messages designed to have us purchase a plethora of products and services, a politician may solicit our money for a reelection campaign, and our physician may attempt to get us to exercise more frequently. Such examples provide numerous research opportunities for communication scholars with a variety of contextual interests. A second reason is that the outcomes of compliance-gaining attempts can, and often do, have important *consequences;* and given the conventional wisdom that the messages employed in compliance-gaining attempts are crucial to the success of these attempts, the appeal of compliance-gaining as an area of study for communication scholars gains clarity.

And typically, studying compliance is something that we have done well. Despite a substantial amount of methodological criticism, it is my general impression that this literature is marked by interesting hypotheses, rigorous designs, and sophisticated statistical analyses. Although interesting hypotheses, rigorous designs, and sophisticated statistical analyses do not ensure that a phenomenon will be understood clearly, they do indicate that the scholars working in this area attend carefully to their craft, and this scrutiny has produced benefits. Presently, there are a number of thought-provoking results in the literature, and their importance will increase if a principle to organize them is discovered.

Given that the relatively optimistic tone of the preceding paragraphs is warranted, it may strike the reader as curious that the number of compliance-gaining studies published is waning (Berger, 1994). It is my hypothesis that the decreased publication rate of compliance-gaining studies is a result of a paradox not uncommon to the social sciences. Specifically, the literature is replete with data, yet there are insufficient data. I shall elucidate this paradox subsequently, but prior to doing so I will advance a second hypothesis. The aforementioned paradox results from and, in turn, produces a second paradox. Specifically, the topic, compliance-gaining message behavior, is both too broad and too narrow to facilitate knowledge generation effectively and easily. I shall turn to explaining the initial paradox, and return to the second one toward the end of this chapter.

The fact that there are over 100 published data-based studies of compliance-gaining message behavior testifies to the veracity of the first clause of the paradox. There can be little disagreement that this literature comprises a substantial data base, and that making sense of it has proven to be a difficult task. Most scholars working in the area would agree that the primary problem is theory. Put simply, there is no theory, or set of competing theories, to explain the existing data adequately. The point is made in a more interesting manner by Maclean, "...unless you have some good idea of what you are looking for and how to find it, you can approach infinity with nothing more than a mishmash of little things you know about a lot of little things" (1992, p. 262).

In my opinion we are unnecessarily brutal in our self-criticism for this sin of omission. I am not convinced that our theories are so poor. Nevertheless, even if one disagrees, there are at least two circumstances conducive to constructing theories from data, neither of which happen to fit the present state of the compliance-gaining literature. Certainly such circumstances make theory development more difficult. The first condition is one in which there is an empirical regularity, usually a bivariate relationship, built around a reasonably common experimental paradigm that suggests alternative explanations. An example is the choice shift phenomenon that has fascinated scholars of group dynamics for more than 30 years, and which has generated numerous theoretical explanations. Because of the regularity of the relationship(s) in such instances (e.g., groups produce more extreme decisions than individuals in choice shift experiments) there is little need for additional data until one discovers a method by which alternative explanations can be tested against one another, thereby creating the possibility of eliminating one of them.

The second condition is a literature built around a reasonably common experimental paradigm in which there are contradictions in a relationship between or among variables. The social facilitation effect, also of considerable interest to group dynamics scholars, is an excellent example of this phenomenon. This effect was anything but regular. Instead, some experiments reported that the presence of others facilitated performance, and others reported that the presence of others inhibited performance. Because the type of experiment that could resolve the contradiction was unclear, researchers ignored the issue until Zajonc's seminal theoretical paper in 1960 made sense of the contradiction, and suggested an experiment that could test his theory. Soon alternative explanations were generated, and empirical tests of alternative explanations of the effect resumed.

The compliance-gaining message behavior literature is dissimilar from these cases in several important ways. First, there is no one particular relationship between or among variables upon which scholars focus. Understandably, the independent variables examined differ widely across experiments, so that I believe it is fair to characterize the data-base as scattered. Second, although the common focus is on the dependent variable, even here there are differences; in some cases message selection is examined, in others message generation, and in yet others message behavior. Thus, the experimental paradigm is not as common as it is with the choice dilemma task, so often characteristic of choice shift research, or the audience and coaction contexts so frequently employed in social facilitation studies, although the possibility remains that compliance-gaining message behavior is not as robust to changes in experimental paradigm as are the choice shift and social facilitation effects; thus, the paradox. There are too few data because no particular relationship has been examined with sufficient frequency to conclude that there either is or is not a regularity. Put another way, it would be impossible to perform a meaningful meta-analysis of any bivariate relationship in this literature. On the other hand, there are too many data because it is a truly daunting task for any theorist to make sense of a data-base when one is unsure if there are empirical regularities, and if there are, what they might be.

In the pages that follow I examine with greater specificity the compliance-gaining message behavior literature. This examination begins with an overview of some early studies, followed by some comments on substantive research and theory in the area. It concludes with some suggested directions for subsequent scholarship.

The reader should be forewarned that I do not propose to write a comprehensive commentary of the sort that one might find in the pages of a journal devoted to the publication of reviews. This arena is one to which Santayana's admonition, "The great difficulty in education is to get experience out of the idea," applies. I have found that getting personal experience out of these paragraphs is not simply difficult, but rather impossible. Thus, the mention of my bias at this juncture should serve as a forewarning induction for the reader.

I will not attempt to provide a systematic review of theories, or a thorough review of the empirical findings, that comprise this body of knowledge; instead being content with highlighting some results the implications of which I find to be important. And, although I might hope that the majority of scholars working in the area would agree with my suggested directions, I have no illusions that they will embrace them either now or in the distant future. Rather, this chapter is a commentary in the sense of being a personal narrative.

BRIEF HISTORICAL NOTE

In the Spring of 1974 I participated in a graduate seminar in which I was exposed to the Marwell and Schmitt (1967) work on compliance-gaining. That study suggested several possibilities for further study, and in the Summer of 1974 a project to study the effect of situational parameters on compliance-gaining message choices was launched. A paper from this project was published (Miller, Boster, Roloff, & Seibold, 1977), and almost immediately it had a substantial impact, a fact that was recognized when in 1989 we received the Charles H. Woolbert Research Award from the Speech Communication Association for "Scholarship of Exceptional Originality and Influence." Although I might disagree with the exceptional originality portion of the award, the influence portion was certainly accurate. Roloff quickly followed with two papers (Roloff & Barnicott, 1978, 1979), Michael Cody and his colleagues published several articles (Cody & McLaughlin, 1980; Cody, McLaughlin, & Jordan, 1980; Cody, McLaughlin, & Schneider, 1981; McLaughlin & Cody, 1980), and convention programs were filled with compliance-gaining manuscripts.

Of course, our article was not the only factor influencing the number of compliance-gaining research projects. At the same time, Delia and his students and colleagues at the University of Illinois were tackling many of the same issues, albeit in a slightly different manner. In psychology both Falbo (e.g., Falbo & Peplau, 1980) and Kipnis (e.g., Kipnis, Schmidt, & Wilkinson, 1980) were pursuing similar interests—the former focusing on sex differences, the latter on organizational influence. Clearly, the study of compliance-gaining message behavior was rapidly becoming a hot topic. This trend escalated in the next decade, especially in communication, as scholars sought to assess the impact of every individual difference variable and situational parameter imaginable on compliance-gaining message behavior.

Meanwhile, we also found some time to examine dimensions of messages and situations, argue the merits of various methodological approaches to the study of the topic, and even discuss theory occasionally. Toward the end of the decade, and into the 1990s, however, the number of compliance-gaining projects decreased markedly, as Berger (1994) has noted.

I have already mentioned one hypothesis for this decline, and alluded to another. It is also of some importance to consider two hypotheses that I think are incorrect. I do not believe that the study of compliance-gaining has decreased because our attention has been deflected by other issues. And, I do not believe that the study of compliance-gaining has decreased because we have resolved all of the major questions that concern compliance-gaining message behavior. The surfeit of studies performed in the 1980s did, however, both generate interesting research questions and suggest some possible resolutions. In the next section I examine some of these questions and results.

A SELECTIVE REVIEW OF THE COMPLIANCE-GAINING LITERATURE

For some of us with interests in traditional persuasion research, i.e., experimental public address, the study of compliance-gaining was liberating for at least two reasons. First, the study of persuasion had restricted us to an examination of the change, reinforcement, or shaping of beliefs, values, or attitudes (cf. Bettinghaus & Cody, 1987), but the study of compliance-gaining broadened the focus to allow us to study the ways in which messages help or hinder us in getting our way, regardless of whether attitudes are affected.

It is of some interest to note in this regard that the phrase, "compliance-gaining," employed by Marwell and Schmitt differs from earlier usage. To scholars like Festinger (1953), French (1956), and Kelman (1961) the general terms employed to describe social influence were conformity, social power, or opinion change. Compliance referred to a specific type of social influence in which the source of the power of the influencing agent was her or his ability to control the target's ability to reach her or his goals. Kelman (1961) actually referred to this process as compliance, French (1956) split the process into two sub-processes, reward power and coercive power, and Festinger (1953) preferred the cumbersome expression, "public conformity without private acceptance." Clearly, Marwell and Schmitt (1967) were not using the term "compliance" in this way, but rather intended it to have the broader meaning now commonly assigned to the phrase "social influence" or the term "conformity."

Second, although it did not have to be that way, persuasion was studied typically in a passive communication context, one in which a speaker presented a message to an audience from whom no feedback was received. Marwell and Schmitt's compliance-gaining situations were not of this ilk. Rather, they involved common sorts of encounters in which one attempted to influence another who was likely to provide feedback in the form of compliance-resisting messages, e.g., trying to get a raise from one's supervisor, striving to convince one's son to study more frequently, enlisting the aid of a roommate in learning a foreign language, attempting to sell encyclopedias.

Moving into the realm of interpersonal influence changed the research question from, "What effect does this message have on attitudes?" to "What do persons say when they want to get their way?" The latter question is an important one, but then again so is the first one. Unfortunately, the former was too often forgotten in the pursuit of the latter. In any case the modified focus generated a number of interesting research questions in addition to the one mentioned above, and a brief digression reviewing some of them illustrates the point.

One limitation of the typical compliance-gaining message behavior experiment is that it is static. As a reaction to this restriction there have been several studies that attempted to examine at least portions of the sequential flow of compliance-gaining messages in a communication transaction. For example, both deTurck (1985) and Lim (1990) examined how the initiator of a compliance-gaining encounter responded when the target did not comply with the initial message recommendation. Conversely, McLaughlin, Cody, and Robey (1980), O'Hair (1991), and Metts, Cupach, and Imahori (1992) investigated the ways in which the target resists the initiator's compliance-gaining messages. In the same spirit Youngs (1986) studied the conditions under which one type of compliance-gaining message, threat, tended to spiral in compliance-gaining encounters.

Because of the important impact of situational variables on compliance-gaining message behavior several scholars have made inquiries into the dimensions of compliance-gaining situations (Cody & McLaughlin, 1980; Cody, Woelfel, & Jordan, 1983; Dillard & Burgoon, 1985; Hertzog & Bradac, 1984). Others have inspected unused compliance-gaining messages (Hample & Dallinger, 1985). Yet others have analyzed persons' perceptions of others' compliance-gaining message behavior (Infante, Anderson, Martin, Herington, & Kim, 1993). Most of these questions, and certainly the primary question ("What do persons say when they want to get their way"), have been studied in a variety of ways. These methodological approaches may be grouped into two major categories, those employing self-reports and those employing direct observation of action. Self-report methods may be sub-divided into structured questionnaire procedures and interview procedures. These methods will be discussed briefly in turn.

Marwell and Schmitt's (1967) initial study involved providing respondents with a structured questionnaire. This questionnaire contained a series of compliance-gaining scenarios each of which was accompanied by a list of 16 messages. The respondent's task was to rate on a six-point scale how likely he or she would be to employ each of these messages, how effective each message would be in gaining the compliance of the target, the extent to which the respondent preferred to use each message, and an estimate of how well the respondent could execute that message. Although every respondent made some of these ratings, not every respondent made all four of them. Marwell and Schmitt (1967) reported data pertinent only to the first question, likelihood of using each message; and to my knowledge, the results for the other three sets of ratings have never been published.

There have been a number of variations on this theme. For instance, the Marwell and Schmitt study was a repeated measures design; all respondents made ratings for each compliance-gaining scenario. Subsequently, several compliance-gaining experiments have opted for an independent groups design in which each respondent makes ratings in only one experimental condition (Sillars, 1980; Williams, 1980). For Marwell and Schmitt compliance-gaining situations were considered to be a random factor; whereas, typically in communication studies researchers have attempted to control, and measure the impact of, situational variables (e.g., Miller et al., 1977), in some cases employing more than one scenario per experimental condition to estimate the impact of the treatment (Hample & Dallinger, 1987; Williams, 1980). Marwell and Schmitt reviewed the compliance-gaining literature, derived 16 compliance-gaining strategies from it, and wrote one message per strategy, each message designed specifically for a given compliance-gaining situation. Others have allowed respondents to generate messages from which they induced strategies (Falbo, 1977; Wiseman & Schenck-Hamlin, 1981). In other variations multiple messages per strategy have been constructed (Dillard & Burgoon, 1985; Williams, 1980), strategy definitions have been presented rather than specific messages (Burgoon, Dillard, Doran, & Miller, 1982; Burgoon, Dillard, Koper, & Doran, 1984), and dichotomous response scales have been employed (Dillard & Burgoon, 1985; Williams, 1980). Despite this surfeit of variations of the basic Marwell and Schmitt procedure, there is no reason at this time to believe that any of them produce substantial differences in persons' self-reports (e.g., see Boster, Stiff, & Reynolds, 1985 concerning the lack of inductive-deductive differences).

Alternatively, interview procedures take the form of presenting respondents with relatively detailed descriptions of the target of influence and the goal of the influence attempt, and then asking them to generate messages designed to obtain conformity from the target (Clark, 1979; Clark & Delia, 1976). As with the Marwell and Schmitt procedure there are a number of variations in the interviewing method. Also similar to the Marwell and Schmitt procedure these variations do not appear to produce major differences in these self-reports (e.g., the respondent-coded versus experimenter-coded differences in O'Keefe & Delia, 1979). There is evidence consistent with the hypothesis that these two self-report procedures, message selection and message generation respectively, produce different substantive results (e.g., Clark, 1979). Debate on the relative merits of the two procedures (Boster, 1988; Burleson & Wilson, 1988; Burleson, Wilson, Waltman, Goering, Ely, & Whaley, 1988; Hunter, 1988; Seibold, 1988), however, has been largely unproductive, at least in the sense that both methods continue to be used.

Rather than rehashing the entire debate I shall simply state my position on the issue. First, although I do not endorse such a view, I believe that it is fair to say that the criterion employed by most scholars to judge the utility of these self-report procedures is the extent to which they correspond to the compliance-gaining behavior that one would exhibit were one actually in such a situation. The concern is, I believe, that the consequences of one's action are of no importance to the respondent when producing self-reports, but are of considerable import when actually engaging in a compliance-gaining interaction, and that this difference may produce differences in compliance-gaining messages. The most important, and most unclear, term in the statement of this position is "correspond." If by correspond one means that the words and the order in which they appear on a checklist, or in a message generated during an interview, match exactly what one says during an actual compliance-gaining encounter, then there would be few, if any, instances of correspondence for either self-report method. Trying to make such predictions would be an absurd enterprise, similar to a physicist trying to predict the path a leaf takes when it falls from a tree in the autumn, or the exact spot that a boulder hits the Tempe Police Department when it rolls down from the top of Tempe butte.

A less restrictive sense of correspond is that what one says in a compliance-gaining encounter matches a general qualitative category that appears on a checklist or that emanates from a content analysis of interview data, such as a threat or a promise. Despite the fact that there are few data to evaluate my claim, i.e., which match behavior in natural compliance-gaining settings with self-reports, I suspect that there would be little correspondence found in such a research enterprise, although one might obtain some predictive accuracy with an extremely long list or with an interview situation isomorphic with the context in which behavior was observed. Moreover, I suspect that even if correspondence were found, the results would be less than satisfying. There are numerous hypotheses concerning the impact of messages on the important consequences of influence attempts, such as the target's resulting affect toward the source or the extent to which the message gains the target's compliance. In the main, these hypotheses suggest that it is the *quantitative* (e.g., verbal aggressiveness, perspective taking, etc.), rather than the categorical or qualitative (e.g., promise, threat, etc.), features of messages that affect these important consequences. If these hypotheses are correct, then even an ability to predict the categorical attributes of compliance-gaining message behavior accurately would be of little value to those studying social influence.

Endorsing this point of view leads to a third sense of correspondence as some quantitative dimension(s) of behavioral response(s) that is predictable from knowledge of some quantitative dimension of the self-report responses. It is equally clear that a spate of such quantitative dimensions could be measured from observing the same set of compliance-gaining behavior. An important task is to decide which dimensions of behavior to measure, and which type of self-report procedure to employ in predicting the relevant behavioral dimension. For example, it might not be a bad guess to employ Clark and Delia's (1976) interview procedure and coding scheme to predict the extent to which one's compliance-gaining behavior takes the perspective of the target (e.g., Applegate, 1982). Furthermore, employing responses to the Marwell and Schmitt procedure to predict the extent of verbal aggression in a target's compliance-gaining behavior might prove to be a useful exercise.

But, regardless of one's position on the relative merits of the self-report methods, if their utility is limited by their ability to predict compliance-gaining action, or behavior, then it is reasonable to question whether or not it would be profitable to dispense with them and directly observe action in compliance-gaining encounters. There are, however, at least two reasons for retaining them. First, self-report responses may serve to mediate the relationship between individual difference variables or situational parameters and compliance-gaining behavior. In this sense these responses could play a role similar to that of attitudes in the theory of reasoned action. Second, collecting behavioral data may be difficult, and if self-reports are able to serve as a proxy for behavior, at least under certain conditions, then scholars may accomplish their experimental goals much more easily by employing them.

The first point awaits rigorous experimental scrutiny; the second is less compelling as a result of the development of a number of relatively simple methods of observing compliance-gaining behavior. These methods consist of placing participants, or a participant and a confederate, in conflict situations, and observing the resulting message behavior. Examples include the Revealed Creative Alternative game (Chmielewski, 1982), negotiating the distribution of points on an experimental task (Boster & Stiff, 1984), a game in which participants negotiate the price of an automobile (Boster, Levine, & Kazoleas, 1993; Scudder, 1988), attempting to get a target to complete a survey (Boster & Lofthouse, 1986), and attempting to get a target to participate in an experiment (Wilson, Cruz, Marshall, & Rao, 1993).

Despite the typical strategy of linking performance with extra course credit some of these procedures may lack experimental realism (e.g., Boster & Stiff, 1984), and others may lack mundane realism (e.g., Boster & Lofthouse, 1986). Furthermore, some procedures severely restrict participants' message options (Chmielewski, 1982; Boster & Stiff, 1984). And, the nature of some of the procedures precludes performing certain experimental inductions, e.g., trying to vary the intimacy of the relationship using the Boster and Lofthouse (1986) procedure would be impossible. Nevertheless, behavioral methods, such as those mentioned above, have consequences for the respondents and, thus, avoid one of the questions raised about self-reports.

These methods of measuring the dependent variable are important because, when examining the impact of situational parameters and individual difference variables on what persons say to get their way, the method may affect the outcome. For example, in an examination of the impact of self-interest, a situational induction, by Clark (1979) there was an effect on message generation, the interviewing procedure, but not on message selection, the questionnaire procedure. Boster and Stiff (1984) reported subsequently that self-interest had an effect on message behavior in their point allocation negotiation experiment, although Boster and Lofthouse (1986) found self-interest to have no effect on their behavioral measure. Assuming that sampling error could not account for these differences, one might conclude from the admittedly sparse interviewing data that as self-interest increases greater pressure is exerted on the target in the form of statements of action (Clark, 1979), from the message selection data that self-interest has no effect on compliance-gaining message selection (Burgoon, Dillard, Doran, & Miller, 1982; Clark, 1979; Miller, 1982; Williams, 1980), and from the behavioral studies that the data are mixed.

In the main, however, the impact of most situational parameters is assessed within, not between, experimental paradigms. Perhaps the most wide-ranging examination of this issue was a program of research performed by Cody and his colleagues (Cody & McLaughlin, 1980; Cody, Woelfel, & Jordan, 1983; Cody, Greene, Marston, O'Hair, Baaske, & Schneider, 1986) in which respondents' perceptions of situational variation were associated with responses on a message selection task. Questions can be raised about this approach. For example, the fact that persons can distinguish features of compliance-gaining situations does not ensure that the features they distinguish affect their compliance-gaining message responses. Moreover, compared with carefully constructed experimental inductions this approach may not generate the variance in respondents' perceptions of situational parameters necessary to produce a substantial effect.

I have written previously (Boster, 1985) that the Cody strategy may be a fruitful point at which to begin one's inquiry into the effect of situational differences on compliance-gaining behavior, but if studies of this ilk have produced consistent results they are not yet apparent (cf. Cody et al., 1986 to Dillard & Burgoon, 1985). This state of affairs is not unique to this set of six or seven situational dimensions, but rather is common across studies of most situational parameters (e.g., see Dillard & Burgoon, 1985, p. 291).

One result that has been remarkably consistent, however, involves *other-benefit inductions*. There is a tendency for persons to be more aggressive and persistent in their compliance-gaining attempts when they attempt to influence a target for her or his own good (high other-benefit), or at least the situation is such that it can be so construed, than when such circumstances are absent (low other-benefit). My colleague John Hunter refers to this finding as the Torquemada Effect, named after the Spanish Grand Inquisitor of the 15th Century. Reportedly, Torquemada, concerned that the souls of non-Christians would live in eternal torment (high other-benefit), transmitted a direct request to his captives offering to them the option of converting to Christianity, a move that he believed would procure a slot in Heaven for them. Failure to comply with this direct request was followed by a stronger message (and subsequent action); namely, burning at the stake, an act designed to purify the soul before death and thereby to procure the much coveted Heavenly slot for the victim/benefactor. Hence, one way of viewing the auto da fe is as a particularly zealous attempt to influence others when their compliance would have been in their own best interest, their own best interest being defined, of course, by Torquemada.

Less extreme versions of this dimension of situational differences abound. For instance, attempting to influence one's child to study more often, a friend to increase the frequency of his visits to the physician, or an acquaintance to hail a taxi rather than trying to drive inebriated are all likely to be situations in which one seeks compliance, at least to a considerable extent, for the benefit of the target. In contrast, there is likely little benefit to the target when you attempt to convince a cousin to buy a used car with severe and unknown (to the target) mechanical problems, a colleague to allow you to exchange his currency when visiting a foreign country (coupled with your intent to swindle him in the subsequent transaction), or an acquaintance to loan money to you.

There are four data sets pertinent to evaluating the impact of other-benefit on compliance-gaining responses. My reanalysis of the Marwell and Schmitt (1967) data (Boster, 1977) indicated that their experimental stimuli included two high benefit-other and two low benefit-other situations, and that persons' message ratings were higher in the high benefit-other condition ($r = .36$). Because this finding could have resulted from a confound between other- and self-benefit, a replication eliminating this problem was conducted (Williams, 1980) in which similar results were found ($r = .28$). Subsequently, Stiff and I (Boster & Stiff, 1984) found that when other-benefit was high, persons were more likely to send messages advocating that the other allocate more points to them than when other-benefit was low ($r=.48$). Lofthouse and I (Boster & Lofthouse, 1986) discovered that persons were more persistent in their initial compliance-gaining attempts when other-benefit was high than when it was low ($r=.29$). Hence, in two different compliance-gaining message selections and two different compliance-gaining message behavior experiments very similar results were obtained. The mean correlation in these studies is in the mid .30 range, an effect size comparable to those produced in some of the classic demonstrations of the importance of situational factors (Funder & Ozer, 1983), and the variance in the correlations could likely be eliminated by controlling methodological factors such as sampling error, measurement error, and strength of experimental induction more carefully.

Although these four studies are in no sense definitive, their grim implications for social interaction merit additional research attention. For example, under certain circumstances, and to some extent, the message behavior exhibited in high other-benefit conditions may be effective. Nevertheless, in these circumstances the target of the compliance-gaining attempt may perceive such action as condescending, so that even if compliance is in some sense truly in the target's best interest, the compliance-gaining encounter may generate resentment that mars subsequent interaction with the target. And, high other-benefit may serve to justify, to oneself and others, extremely persistent and punitive message behavior and perhaps later action. In this way one may attempt, perhaps successfully, to convince oneself, others, or both of the righteousness of inhuman behavior.

The effect of individual difference variables on compliance-gaining message behavior has been less affected by method than by other factors. For instance, generally, respondents high in dogmatism produce higher message selection ratings than those low in dogmatism (Roloff & Barnicott, 1979; Williams, 1980). In contrast, however, Boster and Levine (1988) found this effect in one compliance-gaining situation, but not in another. The behavioral data are also mixed. For example, dogmatism had an impact on one of Boster and Stiff's (1984) measures, but not the other.

Such individual difference effects are not totally unexpected. In his presidential address to the American Psychological Association, Cronbach (1957) suggested that because different types of persons tend to respond to any given situation differently, treatment by subjects interactions would likely be stronger predictors of behavior than would either situational or individual difference variables alone, or combined additively, a notion echoed by communication scholars (e.g., Cody et al., 1985). Clearly, the Boster and Levine (1988) data are consistent with Cronbach's thinking.

On the other hand, recent evidence indicates that the nature of individual difference effects may be more complex than what Cronbach envisioned. Levine, Kazoleas, and I recently noticed that individual difference variables may combine nonadditively with *each other* to affect compliance-gaining messages behavior (Boster, Levine, & Kazoleas, 1993). Specifically, for persons low in verbal aggressiveness, high argumentatives were more persistent than low argumentatives, but for persons high in verbal aggressiveness, high argumentatives were less persistent than low argumentatives.

As noted previously making sense of a set of studies containing so many paradoxical and contingent results is difficult without an organizing principle. Although no single such principle exists, there are several theories of the compliance-gaining process, and there is some common ground as well as differences that mark them. Before examining a sample of these ideas, however, it is important to be clear about their subject matter. One could develop a theory of how self-reports, either message selection or message generation, are produced. Hunter and Boster's (1987) model, for example, can be read in this manner. Alternatively, one could develop a theory of how self-reports are related to compliance-gaining action, the various conceptions of correspondence mentioned earlier being examples. A third theoretical domain involves specifying how compliance-gaining acts affect important social outcomes, such as whether or not one gets one's way or the resulting sentiment of the target for the source. Primarily, this domain is the concern of social influence and sociometry theorists. A fourth possibility is to consider the ways in which compliance-gaining behavior is generated, keeping in mind that interest in different dimensions of action may produce different theories. It is theories of this type that will be discussed in the following several paragraphs.

In the main, these theories have in common the premise that compliance-gaining message behavior is guided by perceptions of its consequences. The consequences deemed to be important differ somewhat from theorist to theorist, but the amount of agreement is pronounced. For example, implicit in Marwell and Schmitt's (1967) rationale for asking respondents to rate effectiveness, preference, and competence in execution for each message, as well as the use item, is the notion that effectiveness, personal moral preferences, and perceptions of one's communicative competence are important consequences that determine message selection. Similarly, it is stated explicitly in the Miller et al. paper (1977, p. 38) that effectiveness and resulting target affect are important determinants of message selection.

Subsequent theoretical treatments were clearly consistent with this line of reasoning. Sillars (1980) argued that compliance value (effectiveness) and relational value (target affect) were the two primary determinants of message selection. Chmielewski (1982) mentioned attitude toward the strategy (effectiveness) and social norms, or a concern with others' (i.e., other than the influencing agent or the target) perceptions, as central explanatory constructs. Baxter (1984) suggested that effectiveness and politeness, or concern with the target's face (target affect), were the two most important determinants of message selection. In Smith's (1984) elucidation of contingency rules theory, environmental contingency rules can be construed as being intertwined closely with perceptions of the effectiveness of the message, image-maintenance rules being related to both target affect and social norms, and self-identity rules being related closely with Marwell and Schmitt's (1967) thinking about personal moral consequences of one's action. Finally, Meyer (1990) defined a compliance-gaining strategy as a cognitive representation that includes elements of effectiveness, target affect, and a concern with how well one might execute a compliance-gaining message.

Taken together these theories articulate at least four consequences of a compliance-gaining message believed to determine its likelihood of being employed: (1) the likelihood that it results in obtaining the target's compliance (effectiveness), (2) the extent to which it results in the target liking or disliking the influencing agent (target affect), (3) the impressions formed by others as a result of observing the influencing agent's message behavior (other affect), and (4) one's personal feelings as a result of using such a message(s) (self affect). Rarely are the theorists specific about how these variables combine to affect the compliance-gaining message employed, Chmielewski (1982) and Dillard (1990) being somewhat exceptional in this regard, but given the linear models typically employed in analyzing data collected to test the theories, one can assume safely that any message that maximized the sum of these perceived consequences would be predicted to be the message used by the influencing agent. Chmielewski (1982) is specific about this prediction; Dillard (1990) believes that effectiveness is primary, a belief often inconsistent with the data I have observed.

Generally, these theories are not dynamic; they do not specify clearly how and why influence attempts change over time. Some have speculated that compliance-gaining messages will become more negative as a function of the target's rejection of influence attempts, and Chmielewski (1982) suggested that this phenomenon results from concern with target affect decreasing as a function of rejection. But, in the main, change has not been the focus of compliance-gaining message theory.

There have been more abstract explanations for the importance of perceived consequences on compliance-gaining message behavior. For example,

Miller (1990) clearly believed that, in general, behavior is a function of its consequences, and invoked reinforcement history as an explanation of compliance-gaining message behavior. Dillard (1990) took the more popular (at present) cognitive approach, and suggested that a sequence of goals and plans best explained subsequent compliance-gaining action (see Chapter 1). Miller's critique of the goals position is persuasive, although not unassailable. The goals-plan-action sequence does, however, smack of a university speech course that prescribes a dated model of critical thinking, and examples of bargaining about the price of a bottle of wine evoke images of sterile academics sitting in an ivory tower sharing some Brie and chatting about whether or not the theater is really dead. All of that is far removed from Iowa pool halls in the 1950s, and probably far removed from most human behavior in the 1990s as well. It may be that Santayana's characterization of the fanatic, one who redoubles his efforts when he forgets his aims, is more characteristic of typical compliance-gaining message behavior than a TOTE unit (Miller, Galanter, & Pribram, 1960). Not infrequently we are thrust into situations in which we are surprised to find the soon-to-be target engaging in objectionable action, or we encounter unexpected rejection of what we think to be a reasonable direct request. The situation demands an immediate response before the moment is lost. There is little time for planning. Whether past plans, heuristics, and the like explain the matter more satisfactorily than reinforcement histories is a moot point, perhaps similar to whether one refers to bread dipped in meat juices as Steak a la Napoleon or as sop.

CONCLUSION: A MODEST PROPOSAL

> Nevertheless I have somewhat against thee, because thou hast left thy first love. Remember therefore from whence thou art fallen, and repent...(John's letter to the Church at Ephesus, Rev. 2: 4-5).

Imagine that someone, other than one who does compliance-gaining studies, was to question us about our research. The one question I dread is, "What impact do these messages (that we are trying to predict) have on the consequences of which you are so aware, and believe to be important?" My reason for dreading this question would be that an honest answer would have to be, "Not much." Follow up questions such as, "Why not?" or "Aren't you people supposed to know a lot about social influence?" (see the quotation from Revelation above) would be equally embarrassing.

I could provide some defense, discussing certain aspects of the classical persuasion literature, or citing examples such as experiments by Shepherd and O'Keefe (1984) or Regan (1971). Nonetheless, I could not be very informative in an area in which I should be able to provide useful answers. With this realization comes the second paradox that I mentioned earlier in this essay, the study of compliance-gaining is at once too narrow and too broad to facilitate knowledge generation effectively. It is too broad for the reason mentioned earlier, i.e., the diffuse nature of the literature. It is too narrow because it does not test the effects of compliance-gaining messages on important outcomes of communicative transactions.

It is my contention that incorporating outcomes, or consequences, in compliance-gaining experiments would be beneficial in a number of ways. As an example consider one of my favorite experiments, a study by Regan (1971). Subjects made ratings of various paintings in the presence of a confederate who was also engaged in this task. In the control condition the confederate walked out of the laboratory with the subject upon completion of the experiment, and asked the subject to purchase some raffle tickets. In the experimental condition the confederate left the laboratory during a break in the experiment, returned with two sodas, and gave one to the subject. Upon completion of the experiment the confederate again asked the subject to purchase raffle tickets. By virtue of the fact that the paper was published, some of the results can be guessed easily, but others are not so obvious. The obvious finding was that subjects bought more raffle tickets, by a factor of two, in the experimental condition than in the control condition. The surprising result was that compared with the price of the soda, the average subject spent *five times* more in the purchase of raffle tickets in the experimental condition. Moreover, in the experimental condition there was *no* correlation between ratings of liking for the confederate and the number of tickets purchased.

This study is extremely informative for the student of compliance-gaining for a number of reasons. One reason is that the message strategy employed in Regan's experimental condition, pregiving using Marwell and Schmitt's (1967) term, becomes defined more clearly. To Marwell and Schmitt (1967) pregiving entailed rewarding the target before requesting compliance. Regan's pregiving strategy involved rewarding the target followed by a *direct request* for compliance. Clearly, any number of other types of requests could be made in the second stage of the pregiving strategy, e.g., altercasting, and awareness of this fact helps elucidate the pregiving strategy as a family of strategies in which some sort of request follows rewarding the target.

Second, given that this particular type of pregiving strategy was very effective in gaining the target's compliance, one must ask whether or not other messages of this family would be as effective, and under what conditions such effects would be obtained. For example, would any obligation-inducing message produce such high rates of compliance? Would a reward followed by a message making the obligation explicit produce counter-forces, such as reactance, that would render the strategy less effective? Would the Regan pregiving strategy be as effective with intimates as with strangers? Third, the fact that in the experimental condition liking had no impact on compliance addresses another one of the important consequences of compliance-gaining messages; namely, target affect. Again, questions such as those raised above are pertinent.

Informed by experiments like Regan's, subsequent compliance-gaining experiments would profit from examining the types of persons who employ obligation-inducing messages, the conditions under which they do so, and the impact they have on important outcomes. In such an experimental paradigm, messages are conceived as either mediating or moderating (or both) the relationship between situational and individual difference variables and compliance-gaining consequences. The compliance-gaining message behavior data provide information about messages employed frequently in various contexts and by various types of persons. The effectiveness of these messages becomes an important social influence question. Social influence results provide information concerning message consequences, and suggest the messages upon which the compliance-gaining message behavior portion of subsequent experiments might profitably focus.

REFERENCES

Applegate, J.L. (1982). The impact of construct system development on communication and impression formation in persuasive contexts. *Communication Monographs, 49*, 277-289.

Baxter, L.A. (1984). An investigation of compliance-gaining as politeness. *Human Communication Research, 10*, 427-456.

Berger, C. (1994). Power, dominance, and social interaction. In M.L. Knapp & G.R. Miller (Eds.). *Handbook of interpersonal communication* (2nd ed., pp. 450-507). Newbury Park, CA: Sage.

Bettinghaus, E.P., & Cody, M.J. (1987). *Persuasive communication*. New York: Holt, Rinehart and Winston.

Boster, F.J. (1977). *An empathy model of compliance-gaining message selection*. Unpublished doctoral dissertation. Michigan State University, East Lansing.

Boster, F.J. (1985). Argumentation, interpersonal communication, persuasion, and the process(es) of compliance gaining message use. In J.R. Cox, M.O. Sillars, & G.B. Walker (Eds.), *Argument and social practice: Proceedings of the fourth SCA/AFA conference on argumentation* (pp. 578-591). Annandale, VA: SCA.

Boster, F.J. (1988). Comments on the utility of compliance gaining message selection tasks. *Human Communication Research, 15*, 166-177.

Boster, F.J., Levine, T.R., & Kazoleas, D.C. (1993). The impact of argumentativeness and verbal aggressiveness on strategic diversity and persistence in compliance gaining behavior. *Communication Quarterly 41*, 405-414.

Boster, F.J., & Lofthouse, L.J. (1986, May). *Situational and individual difference determinants of the persistence and content of compliance gaining behavior: A test of the generalizability of some compliance gaining message choice findings*. Paper presented at the annual meeting of the International Communication Association, Chicago.

Boster, F.J., & Stiff, J.B. (1984). Compliance gaining message selection behavior. *Human Communication Research, 10*, 539-556.

Boster, F.J., & Stiff, J.B., & Reynolds, R.A. (1985). Do persons respond differently to inductively-derived and deductively-derived lists of compliance gaining message strategies? A reply to Wiseman and Schenck-Hamlin. *Western Journal of Speech Communication, 19*, 177-187.

Burgoon, M., Dillard, J.P., Doran, N., & Miller, M.D. (1982). Cultural and situational influences on the process of persuasive strategy selection. *International Journal of Intercultural Relations, 6*, 85-100.

Burgoon, M., Dillard, J.P., Koper, R., & Doran, N. (1984). The impact of communication context and persuader gender on persuasive message selection. *Women's Studies in Communication, 7*, 1-12.

Burleson, B.R., & Wilson, S.R. (1988). On the continued undesirability of item desirability: A reply to Boster, Hunter, & Seibold. *Human Communication Research, 15*, 178-191.

Burleson, B.R., Wilson, S.R., Waltman, M.S., Goering, E.M., Ely, T.K., & Whaley, B.B. (1988). Item desirability effects in compliance-gaining research: Seven studies documenting artifacts in the strategy selection procedure. *Human Communication Research, 14*, 429-486.

Chmielewski, T.L. (1982). A test of a model for predicting strategy choice. *The Central States Speech Journal, 33*, 505-518.

Clark, R.A. (1979). The impact of self interest and desire for liking on the selection of communicative strategies. *Communication Monographs, 46*, 257-273.

Clark, R.A., & Delia, J.G. (1976). The development of functional persuasive skills in childhood and early adolescence. *Child Development, 47*, 1008-1014.

Cody, M.J., Green, J.O., Marston, P.J., O'Hair, H.D., Baase, K.T., & Schneider, M.J. (1985). Situational perception and message strategy selection. In M.L. McLaughlin (Ed.), *Communication yearbook 9* (pp. 390-420), Beverly Hills, CA: Sage.

Cody, M.J., & McLaughlin, M.L. (1980). Perceptions of compliance-gaining situations: A dimensional analysis. *Communication Monographs, 47*, 132-148.

Cody, M.J., McLaughlin, M.L., & Jordan, W.J. (1980). A multidimensional scaling of three sets of compliance-gaining strategies. *Communication Quarterly, 28*, 34-46.

Cody, M.J., McLaughlin, M.L., & Schneider, M.J. (1981). The impact of relational consequences and intimacy on the selection of interpersonal persuasion tactics: A reanalysis. *Communication Quarterly, 29*, 91-106.

Cody, M.J., Woelfel, M.L., & Jordan, W.J. (1983). Dimensions of compliance-gaining situations. *Human Communication Research, 9*, 99-113.

Cronbach, L.J. (1957). The two disciplines of scientific psychology. *American Psychologist, 12*, 671-684.

Delia, J.G., Kline, S.L., & Burleson, B.R. (1979). The development of persuasive communication strategies in kindergartners through twelfth-graders. *Communication Monographs, 46*, 241-256.

deTurck, M.A. (1985). A transactional analysis of compliance-gaining behavior: Effects of noncompliance, relational contexts, and actor's gender. *Human Communication Research, 12*, 54-78.

Dillard, J.P. (1990). A goal-drive model of interpersonal influence. In J.P. Dillard (Ed.), *Seeking compliance: The production of interpersonal influence messages* (pp. 41-56). Scottsdale, AZ: Gorsuch Scarisbrick.

Dillard, J.P., & Burgoon, M. (1985). Situational influences on the selection of compliance-gaining messages: Two tests of the predictive utility of the Cody-McLaughlin typology. *Communication Monographs, 52,* 289-304.

Falbo, T. (1977). Multidimensional scaling of power strategies. *Journal of Personality and Social Psychology, 35,* 537-547.

Falbo, T., & Peplau, L.A. (1980). Power strategies in intimate relationships. *Journal of Personality and Social Psychology, 38,* 618-628.

Festinger, L. (1953). An analysis of compliant behavior. In M. Sherif & M.O. Wilson (Eds.), *Group relations at the crossroads* (pp. 232-256). New York: Harper.

French, Jr., J.R.P. (1956). A formal theory of social power. *Psychological Review, 63,* 181-194.

Funder, D.C., & Ozer, D.J. (1983). Behavior as a function of the situation. *Journal of Personality and Social Psychology, 44,* 107-112.

Hample, D., & Dallinger, J.M. (1985). Unused compliance gaining strategies. In J.R. Cox, M.O. Sillars, & G.B. Walker (Eds.), *Argument and social practice: Proceedings of the fourth SCA/AFA conference on argumentation* (pp. 675-691). Annandale, VA: Speech Communication Association.

Hample, D., & Dallinger, J.M. (1987). Cognitive editing of argument strategies. *Human Communication Research, 14,* 123-144.

Hertzog, R.L., & Bradac, J.J. (1984). Perceptions of compliance-gaining situations: An extended analysis. *Communication Research, 11,* 363-391.

Hunter, J.E. (1988). Failure of the social desirability response set hypothesis. *Human Communication Research, 15,* 162-168.

Hunter, J.E., & Boster, F.J. (1988). A model of compliance gaining message selection. *Communication Monographs, 54,* 63-84.

Infante, D.A., Anderson, C.M., Martin, M.M., Herington, A.D., & Kim, J. (1993). Subordinates' satisfaction and perceptions of superiors' compliance-gaining tactics, argumentativeness, verbal aggressiveness, and style. *Management Communication Quarterly, 6,* 307-326.

Kelman, H.C. (1961). Processes of opinion change. *The Public Opinion Quarterly, 25,* 57-78.

Kipnis, D., Schmidt, S.M., & Wilkinson, I. (1980). Intraorganizational influence tactics: Explorations in getting one's way. *Journal of Applied Psychology, 65,* 440-452.

Lim, T. (1990). The influence of receivers' resistance on persuaders' verbal aggressiveness. *Communication Quarterly, 38,* 170-188.

Maclean, N. (1992). *Young men and fire.* Chicago: The University of Chicago Press.

Marwell, G., & Schmitt, D.R. (1967). Dimensions of compliance-gaining behavior: An empirical analysis. *Sociometry, 30,* 350-364.

McLaughlin, M.L., Cody, M.J., & Robey, C.S. (1980). Situational influences on the selection of strategies to resist compliance-gaining attempts. *Human Communication Research, 7*, 14-36.

Metts, S., Cupach, W.R., & Imahori, T.T. (1992). Perceptions of sexual compliance-resisting messages in three types of cross-sex relationships. *Western Journal of Communication, 56*, 1-17.

Meyer, J.R. (1990). Cognitive processes underlying the retrieval of compliance-gaining strategies: An implicit rules model. In J.P. Dillard (Ed.), *Seeking compliance: The production of interpersonal influence messages* (pp. 57-73). Scottsdale, AZ: Gorsuch Scarisbrick.

Miller, G.A., Galanter, E., & Pribram, K.H. (1960). *Plans and the structure of behavior.* New York: Holt, Rinehart, and Winston.

Miller, G.R. (1990). Final considerations. In J.P. Dillard (Ed.), Seeking compliance: The production of interpersonal influence messages (pp. 189-200). Scottsdale, AZ: Gorsuch Scarisbrick.

Miller, G.R., Boster, F.J., Roloff, M.E., & Seibold, D.R. (1977). Compliance-gaining message strategies: A typology and some findings concerning effects of situational differences. *Communication Monographs, 44*, 37-51.

Miller, G.R., & Steinberg, M. (1975). *Between people.* Chicago: Science Research Associates, Inc.

O'Hair, M.J., Cody, M.J., & O'Hair, D. (1991). The impact of situational dimensions on compliance-resisting strategies: A comparison of methods. *Communication Quarterly, 39*, 226-240.

O'Keefe, B.J., & Delia, J.G. (1979). Construct comprehensiveness and cognitive complexity as predictors of the number and strategic adaptation of arguments and appeals in a persuasive message. *Communication Monographs, 46*, 231-240.

Regan, D.T. (1971). Effects of a favor and liking on compliance. *Journal of Experimental Social Psychology, 7*, 627-639.

Roloff, M., & Barnicott, Jr., E.F. (1978). The situational use of pro- and anti-social compliance-gaining strategies by high and low machiavellians. In B.D. Ruben (Ed.), *Communication yearbook 2* (pp. 193-205). New Brunswick, NJ: Transaction Books.

Roloff, M., & Barnicott, Jr., E.F. (1979). The influence of dogmatism on the situational use of pro- and anti-social compliance-gaining strategies. *Southern Speech Communication Journal, 45*, 37-54.

Scudder, J.N. (1988). The influence of power upon powerful speech: A social-exchange perspective. *Communication Research Reports, 5*, 140-145.

Seibold, D.R. (1988). A response to "Item desirability in compliance-gaining research." *Human Communication Research, 15*, 152-161.

Shepherd, G.J., & O'Keefe, B.J. (1984). The relationship between the developmental level of persuasive strategies and their effectiveness. *The Central States Speech Journal, 35*, 137-152.

Sillars, A.L. (1980). The stranger and the spouse as target persons for compliance-gaining strategies: A subjective expected utility model. *Human Communication Research, 6*, 265-279.

Smith, M.J. (1984). Contingency rules theory, context, and compliance behaviors. *Human Communication Research, 10*, 489-512.

Williams, D.L. (1980). *The effects of beneficial situational characteristics, negativism, and dogmatism on compliance-gaining message selection.* Unpublished master's thesis, Arizona State University, Tempe, AZ.

Wilson, S.R., Cruz, M.G., Marshall, L.J., & Rao, N. (1993). An attributional analysis of compliance-gaining interactions. *Communication Monographs 60*, 352-372.

Wiseman, R.L., & Schenck-Hamlin, W. (1981). A multidimensional scaling validation of an inductively-derived set of compliance-gaining strategies. *Communication Monographs, 48*, 251-270.

Youngs, Jr., G.A. (1986). Patterns of threat and punishment reciprocity in a conflict situation. *Journal of Personality and Social Psychology, 51*, 541-546.

Interpersonal Influence: The View from *Between People*

Michael E. Roloff

O ver the last two decades, the study of interpersonal influence has flourished. Substantial literatures now exist on both interpersonal compliance gaining (Seibold, Cantrill, & Meyers, 1985; Boster, 1990) and conflict management (Roloff, 1987a). Despite this immense activity, there remain important unresolved issues. One of the most intriguing and persistent is focused on the way in which influence is conducted in relationships of varying degrees of intimacy. Early on, intimacy was thought to be a critical factor determining the kinds of influence strategies that would be employed (e.g., Miller & Steinberg, 1975; Roloff, 1976) and it became a standard variable used in compliance-gaining research (e.g., Miller, Boster, Roloff, & Seibold, 1977; Kaminski, McDermott, & Boster, 1977; Roloff & Barnicott, 1978a, 1978b; Sillars, 1980; Cody, McLaughlin, & Schneider, 1981; see Chapter 5). However, despite evidence that individuals differentiate among compliance-gaining situations based upon the intimacy between persuader and target (Cody & McLaughlin, 1980; Cody, Woelfel, & Jordan, 1983), intimacy proved to be a disappointing predictor of which compliance-gaining strategies are enacted. Indeed, Dillard and Burgoon (1985) concluded that their own "findings, in combination with earlier work, suggest that the role of intimacy in the compliance-gaining process is minimal" (p. 303).

Although Dillard and Burgoon's conclusion was justifiable given the available evidence, it may be overly pessimistic. In part, the small effect sizes and inconsistent directional effects often associated with intimacy may stem from inadequate attention to theory rather than its apparent inconsequential nature. Much of the early research was based upon a framework advanced by Miller and Steinberg (1975) in their book, *Between People*. They argued that relationships can be distinguished based upon the kinds of information that partners have about one another and that intimates have greater access to information about their partners that discriminates them from similar others. They speculated that intimates could rely upon their individuated data about their partners to construct more adaptive and effective strategies. Based upon this reasoning, researchers employed manipulations in which subjects were asked to imagine that they wanted to gain the compliance of a person who was described as an intimate (e.g., spouse) or a nonintimate (e.g., stranger). Respondents then indicated how likely they would be to employ a set of strategies.

In retrospect, this methodological approach is less than optimal. Although the relational categories used to induce intimacy seem valid and, when employed, manipulation checks verified such, the hypothetical nature of the context attenuated their validity. For example, unmarried undergraduates were asked to report how they would persuade their spouse. It is doubtful that subjects in this condition could draw upon information about their nonexistent spouse (let alone discriminating data) from which to choose strategies! Even in more realistic situations involving targeted friends or dating partners, it is unclear that subjects had access to information that was any more individuated than did subjects trying to gain compliance from a hypothetical stranger. Moreover, researchers provided little a priori explanation of how discriminating information might be related to the strategies from which subjects could choose.

Not only might this "loose" operationalization of Miller and Steinberg's notions have underestimated the impact of intimacy but it may have condemned their perspective to undue obscurity. I have found many of their ideas to be useful. Although the number of citations to it have diminished over the years, many of Miller and Steinberg's notions are implicit in my work. In preparing this chapter, I reread Miller and Steinberg's book and formed eight interrelated propositions that are particularly relevant to interpersonal influence. In the remaining portion of the chapter, I will discuss each and describe related research.

Proposition 1: The primary function of communication is to control one's environment so as to acquire needed resources (Miller & Steinberg, 1975, p. 62).

Miller and Steinberg clearly built their perspective on the principles of social exchange theory (Homans, 1961; Thibaut & Kelley, 1959). They recognized that individuals are not self-sufficient and that communication skills develop as a "tool" by which people might gain sustenance (cf. Harkness, 1990). From the outset of an interaction, communicators often have in mind a desired set of resource-based outcomes (see Chapter 1). Therefore, communication success can be determined by how well resulting outcomes correspond to the initial objectives. In some cases, total compliance with initial desires can be achieved whereas in others, an equitable compromise allocation of resources is sufficient.

I extended Miller and Steinberg's analysis by noting that there are two ways in which communication can serve as a "tool" for acquiring resources (Roloff, 1981, 1987b). First, an interaction may serve as a conveyance for resources. During the course of a conversation, resources such as love, status, and information are exchanged (Foa & Foa, 1974). Interactants view these transactions as following a norm of reciprocity in which resources of equivalent value and type are given and returned (Roloff & Campion, 1985). Moreover, satisfaction with an interaction is positively correlated with global perceptions that the exchanges contained therein are equitable (Dailey & Roloff, 1987).

Second, communication may serve as a device for negotiating an exchange agreement. The acquisition of assistance, information, and goods are prominent among the goals persuaders report that they routinely try to achieve (Rule, Bisanz, & Kohn, 1985). In some cases, this may be as simple as expressing a need or requesting a resource; but in other situations, negotiations become more complex as individuals have to communicate justifications, apologies, incentives, and perhaps make concessions (Roloff, 1987b). In doing so, communication is used to set up and coordinate an exchange.

Regardless of whether communication is a conduit for exchange or a means for negotiating one, Miller and Steinberg highlighted the pragmatic function of communication. Communication is a technology for acquiring what is needed for survival.

> **Proposition 2:** The greater the anticipated difficulty in acquiring needed resources from a target person, the greater the effort that will be expended in formulating a plan to control him or her (Miller & Steinberg, 1975, pp. 136-137).

Miller and Steinberg argued that communicators must devise means of controlling the attitudes and behaviors of others to maximize the likelihood of achieving resources. Rather than viewing control as negative, influence was presented as a neutral and often desirable feature of everyday life. However, Miller and Steinberg did not characterize most humans as being preoccupied with control. Typically, the acquisition of resources occurs in a smooth fashion with little planning or plotting. Only when individuals are uncertain that they can achieve needed resources do they expend great energy in strategy formulation (cf. Stutman & Newell, 1990; see Chapter 1).

This observation fits nicely with work on negotiation planning. Negotiators often put forth insufficient effort when preparing for bargaining and, as a result, overlook strategies that might yield better outcomes (Roloff & Jordan, 1992). Goals that are difficult but possible to achieve have an "energizing effect" on planning such that negotiators scrutinize the situation to a greater extent and are more likely to devise novel strategies.

Accordingly, negotiators who are committed to achieving moderately high levels of profit are more likely to discover the integrative potential of a situation (i.e., the possibility that opposing parties might both achieve their goals) and to formulate a logrolling strategy (i.e., hold firm on one's own high priority issues while conceding on those of greater priority to the opponent) to capitalize on it (Roloff & Jordan, 1991). When bargainers seek modest profit goals, they overlook the integrative potential of the situation and rely upon simple concession-making to achieve their objectives. Since logrolling is a more effective strategy (Tutzauer & Roloff, 1988), insufficient planning effort is costly.

Hence, Miller and Steinberg believed that communicators expend only as much effort in planning as they anticipate they need to achieve their resources. In doing so, they miss opportunities to optimize their outcomes.

Proposition 3: Communicators formulate influence messages that anticipate the responses of their targets (Miller & Steinberg, 1975, p. 7).

Miller and Steinberg characterize the process of message design as being strategic in nature. Communicators try to predict how their targets might respond to their influence attempts and then construct linguistic elements to facilitate positive reactions and overcome negative ones. Once an interchange begins, interactants adapt message content to the responses they encounter.

Research verifies that communicators often try to anticipate the responses of their targets prior to confronting them (Honeycutt, Zagacki, & Edwards, 1990; Roloff & Jordan, 1991; Stutman & Newell, 1990). When seeking resources, requesters anticipate that targets might resist due to seven obstacles: (1) the target does not have the resources, (2) the target does not have adequate quantities of the resources, (3) the target has already committed the resources, (4) the request is inappropriate, (5) the requester should be responsible for his or her own needs, (6) the target simply does not want to comply, and (7) the target has no incentive to comply (Ifert & Roloff, 1993a). These categories can be clustered into two larger units based upon the perceived degree to which the obstacle primarily reflects inability to comply (obstacles 1, 2, 3) or unwillingness to do so (obstacles 4, 5, 6, 7). Requesters expect that inability obstacles are more likely to be encountered and expressed than are those reflecting unwillingness (Ifert & Roloff, 1993a). Communicators tailor the features of requests to overcome anticipated obstacles to compliance (Francik & Clark, 1985; Gibbs, 1986; Gibbs & Mueller, 1988; Roloff & Janiszewski, 1989). Moreover, when encountering resistance, persistent requesters adapt their messages to the type of expressed obstacle (Ifert & Roloff, 1993b).

Hence, Miller and Steinberg did not simply repeat the ideas of social exchange theorists. They added a unique, communication-based component focused on how messages are composed in order to enhance positive responses to requests.

> **Proposition 4:** The information upon which a communicator predicts a target's probable response to a message varies in the degree to which it distinguishes the target from similar others (Miller & Steinberg, p. 12).

When making predictions, Miller and Steinberg argued that interactants can draw upon three databases. First, they can access their knowledge of individuals who are members of the target's culture. Persons from the same culture share to a greater degree some habits, values, and rules of conduct than do members from different cultures (e.g., Argyle & Henderson, 1985).

Second, predictions may be based upon the target's membership in social groups. Within a culture, one finds variation—such as gender and age—across demographic groups in how social relations should be defined (Forgas & Dobosz, 1980; Wish, Deutsch, & Kaplan, 1976) and conducted (Argyle & Henderson, 1985; Knapp, Ellis, & Williams, 1980).

Finally, communicators may rely upon their knowledge of the unique characteristics of the target that differentiate him or her from members of the same culture or social groups. Indeed, individual males and females report that they often communicate in a manner that is different from the way in which they perceive members of their own gender typically act

(Gruber & White, 1986). These data are the most individualized since they are tied to prior observations of the proclivities of a particular target.

Regardless of the accuracy of their data, individuals have impressions of how different types of associations are conducted from which to base predictions (Argyle & Henderson, 1985; Forgas & Dobosz, 1980; Knapp, et al., 1980; Wish & Kaplan, 1977; Wish, et al., 1976). Although information tied directly to observation of the target's behavior would seem to be the most accurate basis from which to predict a target's response, Miller and Steinberg speculate that communicators often ignore it in favor of more general stereotypes.

Krueger and Rothbart (1988) found evidence supporting this reasoning. Subjects estimated a target person's behavior based upon categorical information about the person (gender and occupation) and accounts of specific actions that the person had enacted that were to some degree similar to the behavior to be predicted. Results indicated that categorical information influenced predictions to a greater extent than did specific actions *unless* the specific actions appeared to be *consistently* enacted by the target. When making predictions, knowing that a target engaged in a behavior on a *single* occasion is insufficient to override knowledge of the target's demographics.

Like Miller and Steinberg, Krueger and Rothbart (1988) argued that there is typically a trade-off between the bandwidth of a social category (number of units falling within the category) and the fidelity with which it predicts specific behavior. Demographic categories such as age and gender are quite broad and their substantial within category variation may render them relatively useless when predicting the specific actions of a particular individual.

On the other hand, knowledge that a single specific action occurred may not be any more useful as a predictor of future occurrences. In effect, its bandwidth is too narrow (i.e., inadequate sampling of prior behaviors). Because it is difficult to sample adequately the relevant prior behaviors of all of their targets of influence, communicators may rely primarily on their knowledge of social categories for most of their predictions.

Thus, Miller and Steinberg reasoned that the type of data from which predictions are made might be tied to the general class of individuals to which the target belongs or might be based upon impressions of the unique qualities of the target. In their view, true interpersonal communication is distinguishable from other forms in its reliance on individualized information rather than categorical data.

Proposition 5: Individuals vary both in the ability to accurately predict the unique way in which a target will respond to a message and in the ability to compose a message which will be tailored to those individualized reactions (Miller & Steinberg, 1975, p. 175).

Miller and Steinberg stressed the importance of empathic skills to communication success. To achieve desirable outcomes, a communicator must be sufficiently perceptive in order to identify the key target characteristics that shed light on probable responses and then formulate a message that will increase the likelihood of a positive response. In essence, the successful communicator engages in audience analysis. Miller and Steinberg (1975) argued that the first step toward becoming an empathic and successful communicator "lies in monitoring one's own behavior and developing careful communication habits" (p. 184).

Research suggests that their position is well taken. Elliott (1979) studied individuals who varied in their predispositions to monitor and adapt their own behavior to situational cues. High and low self-monitors were allowed to plan for a communication in which they were asked to create a true or fabricated impression of their attitude toward legalization of marijuana. Prior to the encounter, they could purchase personality, attitudinal, or biographical information about their communication partners.

Regardless of the type of impression they were to create, high self-monitors were more likely than low self-monitors to purchase personality information; and when preparing a lie, they were more likely to supplement this material with attitudinal and biographical information. Furthermore, regardless of whether the goal was to create an accurate or fabricated self-presentation, high self-monitors were perceived to be more socially competent, friendly, and believable than were low self-monitors. In essence, high self-monitors sought more information about their targets (and especially so when they intended to deceive) and apparently were more successful at accomplishing their goals than were low self-monitors.

However, translation skills may be deficient even when a communicator possesses perceptual skills. For example, Hewes, Roloff, Planalp, and Seibold (1990) distinguished between impact skills and influence skills. The former allow an individual to identify environmental stimuli, to assign meaning to them, and to decide whether or not to react. The latter constitute the ability to bring to bear communication in the service of whatever goals might be activated as a result of one's identification and interpretation of stimuli. Hewes et al. note that a communicator may fail to accomplish his or her goal due to either faulty impact skills (i.e., does not accurately assess relevant stimuli) or the inability to act on accurate perceptions of environmental cues.

In an unpublished study, Robert Bell and I (1993) employed a similar analysis to investigate the inability of lonely individuals to accomplish their communication goals. Lonely persons appear to suffer from communication skill deficits. When seeking to initiate a relationship, they devise plans that are judged by others to be less effective (Berger & Bell, 1988) and not surprisingly, enact less effective self-presentations (Bell & Roloff, 1991). However, it is unclear whether their deficit arises from misconstruing the situation or their inability to act upon their perceptions.

Recently, Segrin (1993) reported that lonely individuals are more socially sensitive than are their non-lonely counterparts and he speculates that lonely persons suffer from encoding rather than decoding problems. To test this notion, Bell and I (1993) asked individuals varying in loneliness to describe the obstacles they would confront when seeking a resource from either a stranger or a friend and then we asked them to compose a help-seeking message. Because lonely people view their relationships as being of lower quality, we predicted that they would anticipate more obstacles to compliance than would non-lonely subjects. In effect, their targets are under less obligation to help them given that even their friendships are not especially intimate. Indeed, we found that lonely subjects view their relationships as less intimate (particularly with a friend) than do non-lonely subjects, and lonely individuals anticipate more obstacles to compliance.

Since lonely individuals seem to be keenly aware of the obstacles they confront, we reasoned that they should increase the amount of persuasive discourse in their help-seeking messages. In effect, they must include more incentives and explanations in their messages to overcome the greater obstacles facing them. This was not the case. For the most part, the amount of persuasive discourse in the messages of lonely and non-lonely subjects did not differ and in a few instances, lonely individuals included less.

Unfortunately, our research does not inform as to the source of the lonely person's inability to translate perceptions into messages. It is possible that lonely people are unaware of how to persuade others. Hence, they cannot bring to bear prior knowledge of the type of discourse that will work. Alternatively, they may be unmotivated to try to persuade others to help them. Because of prior failures, they may not put forth sufficient effort into message composition. For example, lonely individuals in our study constructed less elaborate messages after the target refused to help than did non-lonely subjects.

Regardless, Miller and Steinberg's observation about empathy seems valid. Communicators differ in their ability to discern individualized cues about targets and to create messages that conform to their observations.

Proposition 6: Because of their greater knowledge of each other, intimates develop communication rules that are are often different from those of nonintimates (Miller & Steinberg, p. 55).

Miller and Steinberg argued that communication is a rule-governed activity and that some interaction patterns are predictable from these socially derived conventions. They also asserted that the nature of these rules may vary with the intimacy of the relationship between interactants. Nonintimates follow communication rules imposed by the culture or groups to which the interactants belong. Through socialization, individuals learn how to converse with others who are also members of their social category, including those about whom they have minimal knowledge. On the other hand, intimates may modify and even abandon broader-based conversational conventions. The greater trust and personal information acquired during relational development allow them to relax certain conversational constraints and to enact a broader range of communication behavior.

Similarly, I noted that the nature of the norm of reciprocity varies across relationships of varying intimacy (Roloff, 1987b). Although receipt of a resource obligates a return, reciprocation in intimate relationships is more flexible. Because close associations are need-based and trusting, intimates may return needed but different types of resources or somewhat less valuable ones than they originally received. Also, they have a longer period of time in which to reciprocate. Conversely, nonintimates have less information about one another's needs and reliability and, therefore, their exchanges are more likely to conform to an equity criterion (cf. Mills & Clark, 1982).

Consistent with Miller and Steinberg's perspective, I reasoned that the different ways in which reciprocation occurs in intimate and nonintimate associations should affect the discourse contained in requests for resources (Roloff, 1987b). Because intimates have greater understanding of each other's needs and are more obligated to act on them than are nonintimates, individuals in close relationships expend less effort in persuading each other to provide assistance. Indeed, Roloff, Janiszewski, McGrath, Burns, and Manrai (1988) found that compared to nonintimates, intimates compose requests to borrow a resource that are less elaborate, containing fewer explanations as to why the resource is needed, fewer questions about whether the target possessed the needed resource, and fewer inducements for the target to help. However, when encountering a refusal to help, intimates, more so than nonintimates, try to persuade the target to comply and are less likely to express forgiveness for the refusal.

There are limits to this pattern. Chris Janiszewski and I argued that the type of exchange being negotiated will alter the content of requests composed by intimates and nonintimates (Roloff & Janiszewski, 1989). Performing a *favor* typically requires the target to sacrifice a resource to the requester while *lending* a resource involves a short-term inconvenience (i.e., the borrower is obligated to return the resource in a reasonable period and in good shape). Because of the greater costs associated with favors and the greater obligation to help within close relationships, intimates should view their requests as imposing more on the target than will nonintimates. After all, intimates should feel greater obligation to grant a costly request. To overcome this obstacle, intimates create more elaborate messages than do nonintimates.

Indeed, when seeking to borrow a resource, intimates enact fewer explanations for the need than do nonintimates but when seeking a favor, compose messages that contain more explanations than do nonintimates (Roloff & Janiszewski, 1989). Moreover, when encountering a resisting target, intimates seeking to borrow a resource respond with greater counterpersuasion and less forgiveness than do nonintimates but this pattern is completely reversed when intimates respond to a target who rejects a request for a favor.

Thus, Miller and Steinberg's observation is sound. Intimates tailor their communication to the situation in such a manner that it is different from that enacted by nonintimates.

> **Proposition 7:** When the need for resources is urgent, individuals will be more successful when making requests of intimates than nonintimates (Miller & Steinberg, 1975, p. 68).

Miller and Steinberg argued that some resources are readily available and, assuming that one has something for which to exchange, are attainable from both intimates and nonintimates. However, when a resource is costly or the need is urgent, requesters should turn to intimates about whom they have individualized information concerning how to persuade them and who are more obligated to provide assistance. Consistent with their assertion, Shapiro (1980) found that people in need are more likely to turn to intimates for assistance even when help would be costly to the target.

Moreover, Jordan and Roloff (1990) discovered that when directly asked, intimates are more likely than nonintimates to comply verbally with requests for favors and to borrow resources.

In effect, Miller and Steinberg characterized intimate relationships as being generally supportive. Indeed, diaries kept on everyday activities indicate that even in unhappy marriages, the number of positive things spouses do for one another greatly outnumber the negative ones (e.g., Birchler, Weiss, & Vincent, 1975).

> **Proposition 8:** An intimate's ability to exert control increases with his or her coercive potential (Miller & Steinberg, 1975, p. 117).

Although Miller and Steinberg recognized that close relationships are typically supportive, they also noted that intimates often achieve control by bringing to bear punishments, denying resources, or increasing their partner's costs. Moreover, Miller later argued that persuasive appeals to reason and emotion are often accompanied and made more effective by discourse that is indirectly coercive such as threats and identity attacks (Miller, 1980).

Even though Miller and Steinberg discussed coercion as an overt means of exercising control to achieve resources, their analysis implies that its mere potential may produce compliance. During relational development, individuals may learn that certain topics prompt coercive and often violent reactions from their partners. As a result, they avoid communicating about anything that might prompt such explosions. Denise Cloven and I (1993) asked individuals in dating relationships to list things about their partners that were irritating. Afterward, subjects indicated how many irritants they had told to their partner, whether the partner had ever been physically or verbally aggressive to them, and how aggressive they thought their partners would be if confronted with a complaint.

Not surprisingly, there was a positive correlation between having been the victim of a partner's aggression and expecting the partner to respond aggressively to future complaints. Interestingly, the partner's aggressive potential is positively correlated with withholding complaints about his or her dominating behavior but not other types of complaints (e.g., habits). Apparently, victims are able to discriminate grievances that can be safely expressed from those that are dangerous to communicate. Furthermore, perceiving that one's partner is uncommitted to the relationship or that he or she has high-quality alternative relationships increased withholding dominance complaints toward a potentially verbally aggressive partner. In effect, individuals withhold when they anticipate verbal punishment and fear their partner might leave the relationship for another.

In another study, we found that individuals are especially likely to withhold complaints when they perceive their own relational alternatives are inferior but that their partners have quality relational options (Roloff & Cloven, 1990). Furthermore, a partner's perceived alternatives can "chill" the expression of complaints, even though he or she has never overtly threatened to end the relationship. Apparently, the mere potential for losing the association is sufficient.

Miller and Steinberg cautioned against the use of coercion in intimate relationships. Even though it may successfully prevent the expression of grievances, withholding complaints denies valuable information for understanding problems and taking action. Hence, the coercive partner may erroneously perceive that the relationship is in "good health" since there are no expressed complaints. As the irritating behavior continues, the victimized partner may become dissatisfied with the relationship and exit.

SUMMARY

At the outset of this project, I was uncertain about what I would find when I reread Miller and Steinberg's tome. *Between People* is nearly 20 years old and was never revised. I was pleased to discover that my memories were not too distorted. Hidden amongst the clever cartoons, humorous anecdotes, and other textbook garnish is a set of ideas that I find to be a useful and provocative description of interpersonal influence. Admittedly, many of the notions are not thoroughly explicated but that is forgivable given the state of research at the time they were formulated and the sophistication of the student audience for whom the text was written.

Regardless, the book contains many interesting and, as of yet, unanswered questions about interpersonal influence. For example, research still does not inform us concerning how much individualized information intimates have about one another and whether/how they use it to tailor their influence messages. Although personality impressions of friends are more accurate than those of strangers (Funder & Colvin, 1988), individuals should be able to discriminate between the characteristics of two friends. If they can, then not only might the message elements of intimates differ from nonintimates, but there should be variation in the messages constructed for different targets with whom one has equally intimate relations.

Furthermore, it is unclear how communicators use individualized information in their messages. Although it seems reasonable that such data are used to predict obstacles to compliance, the linguistic manifestations of such forecasts might vary. It is possible that intimates employ such data as "small talk" during the prelude to a request or can use it to construct an appealing offer in exchange for a needed resource. More importantly, specialized knowledge may have no explicit linguistic manifestations at all. Rather, it may allow more careful editing as intimates avoid using arguments that might be met with resistance.

Despite its limitations, Miller and Steinberg's analysis provides an insightful and more comprehensive portrait of interpersonal influence than afforded by other perspectives. The logic contained therein has aged rather well.

REFERENCES

Argyle, M., & Henderson, M. (1985). The rules of relationships. In S. Duck & D. Perlman (Eds.), *Understanding personal relationships: An interdisciplinary approach* (pp. 63-84). Beverly Hills, CA: Sage.

Bell, R.A., & Roloff, M.E. (1991). Making a love connection: Loneliness and communication competency in the dating marketplace. *Communication Quarterly, 39,* 58-74.

Bell, R.A., & Roloff, M.E. (1993). *Inability to confront obstacles: The communication deficit of lonely individuals.* Unpublished manuscript.

Berger, C.R., & Bell, R.A. (1988). Plans and the initiation of social relationships. *Human Communication Research, 15,* 217-235.

Birchler, G.R., Weiss, R.L., & Vincent, J.P. (1975). Multimethod analysis of social reinforcement exchange between maritally distressed and nondistressed spouse and stranger dyads. *Journal of Personality and Social Psychology, 31,* 349-360.

Boster, F.J. (1990). An examination of the state of compliance-gaining message behavior research. In J.P. Dillard (Ed.), *Seeking compliance: The production of interpersonal influence messages* (pp. 7-20). Scottsdale, AZ: Gorsuch Scarisbrick.

Cloven, D.H., & Roloff, M.E. (1993). Aggressive potential and the expression of complaints: The chilling effect in intimate relationships. *Communication Monographs, 60,* 199-219.

Cody, M.J., & McLaughlin, M.L. (1980). Perceptions of compliance-gaining situations: A dimensional analysis. *Communication Monographs, 47,* 132-148.

Cody, M.J., McLaughlin, M.L., & Schneider, M.J. (1981). The impact of relational consequences and intimacy on the selection of interpersonal persuasion tactics: A reanalysis. *Communication Quarterly, 29,* 91-106.

Cody, M.J., Woelfel, M.L., & Jordan, W.J. (1983). Dimensions of compliance-gaining situations. *Human Communication Research, 9,* 99-113.

Dailey, W.O., & Roloff, M.E. (1987, May). *What do we want from information exchange? Profit? Equity? Neither?* Paper presented at the convention of the International Communication Association, Montreal, Canada.

Dillard, J.P., & Burgoon, M. (1985). Situational influences on the selection of compliance-gaining messages: Two tests of the predictive utility of the Cody-McLaughlin typology. *Communication Monographs, 52,* 289-304.

Elliott, G.C. (1979). Some effects of deception and level of self-monitoring on planning and reacting to a self-presentation. *Journal of Personality and Social Psychology, 37,* 1281-1292.

Foa, U.G., & Foa, E.B. (1974). *Societal structures of the mind.* Springfield, IL: Charles C. Thomas.

Forgas, J.P., & Dobosz, B. (1980). Dimensions of romantic involvement: Towards a taxonomy of heterosexual relationships. *Social Psychology Quarterly, 43,* 290-300.

Francik, E.P., & Clark, H.H. (1985). How to make requests that overcome obstacles to compliance. *Journal of Memory and Language, 24,* 560-568.

Funder, D.C., & Colvin, C.R. (1988). Friends and strangers: Acquaintanceship, agreement, and the accuracy of personality judgement. *Journal of Personality and Social Psychology, 55,* 149-158.

Gibbs, R.W., Jr. (1986). What makes some indirect speech acts conventional? *Journal of Memory and Language, 25,* 181-196.

Gibbs, R.W., Jr., & Mueller, R.A.G. (1988). Conversational sequences and preferences for indirect speech acts. *Discourse Processes, 11,* 101-116.

Gruber, K.J., & White, J.W. (1986). Gender differences in the perceptions of self's and others' use of power strategies. *Sex Roles, 15,* 109-118.

Harkness, C.D. (1990). Competition for resources and the origins of manipulative language. In J.P. Dillard (Ed.), *Seeking compliance: The production of interpersonal influence messages* (pp. 21-40). Scottsdale, AZ: Gorsuch Scarisbrick.

Hewes, D.E., Roloff, M.E., Planalp, S., & Seibold, D.R. (1990). Interpersonal communication research: What should we know? In G.M. Phillips & J.T. Wood (Eds.), *Speech communication: Essays to commemorate the 75th anniversary of the Speech Communication Association* (pp. 130-180). Carbondale, IL: Southern Illinois University Press.

Homans, G.C. (1961). *Social behavior: Its elementary forms.* New York: Harcourt Brace Jovanovich.

Honeycutt, J.M., Zagacki, K.S., & Edwards, R. (1990). Imagined interaction and interpersonal communication *Communication Reports, 3,* 1-8.

Ifert, D.E., & Roloff, M.E. (1993a, May). *Identifying influence subgoals: Anticipating obstacles to resource requests.* Paper presented at the convention of the International Communication Association, Washington, D.C.

Ifert, D.E., & Roloff, M.E. (1993b, November). *Responding to rejected requests: Persistence and response type as functions of obstacles to compliance.* Paper presented at the convention of the Speech Communication Association, Miami, FL.

Jordan, J.M., & Roloff, M.E. (1990). Acquiring assistance from others: The effect of indirect requests and relational intimacy on verbal compliance. *Human Communication Research, 16,* 519-555.

Kaminski, E.P., McDermott, S.T., & Boster, F.J. (1977, April). The use of compliance-gaining strategies as a function Machiavellianism and situation. Paper presented at the annual convention of the Central States Speech Association, Southfield, MI.

Knapp, M.L., Ellis, D.G., & Williams, B.A. (1980). Perceptions of communication behavior associated with relationship terms. *Communication Monographs, 47,* 264-278.

Krueger, J., & Rothbart, M. (1988). Use of categorical and individuating information in making inferences about personality. *Journal of Personality and Social Psychology, 55,* 187-195.

Miller, G.R. (1980). On being persuaded: Some basic distinctions. In M.E. Roloff & G.R. Miller (Eds.), *Persuasion: New directions in theory and research* (pp. 11-28). Beverly Hills, CA: Sage.

Miller, G.R., Boster, F., Roloff, M.E., & Seibold, D. (1977). Compliance-gaining message strategies: A typology and some findings concerning effects of situational differences. *Communication Monographs, 44,* 37-51.

Miller, G.R., & Steinberg, M. (1975). *Between people: A new analysis of interpersonal communication.* Chicago: Science Research Associates.

Mills, J., & Clark, M.S. (1982). Exchange and communal relationships, In L. Wheeler (Ed.), *Review of personality and social psychology* (Vol. 3, pp. 121-144). Beverly Hills, CA: Sage.

Roloff, M.E. (1976). Communication strategies, relationships, and relational changes. In G.R. Miller (Ed.), *Explorations in interpersonal communication* (pp. 173-196). Beverly Hills, CA: Sage.

Roloff, M.E. (1981). *Interpersonal communication: The social exchange approach.* Beverly Hills, CA: Sage.

Roloff, M.E. (1987a). Communication and conflict. In. C.R. Berger & S.H. Chaffee (Eds.), *Handbook of communication science* (pp. 484-536). Newbury Park, CA: Sage.

Roloff, M.E. (1987b). Communication and reciprocity within intimate relationships. In M.E. Roloff & G.R. Miller (Eds.), *Interpersonal processes: New directions in communication research* (pp. 11-38). Newbury Park, CA: Sage.

Roloff, M.E., & Barnicott, E. (1978a). The influence of dogmatism on the situational use of pro-and anti-social compliance-gaining strategies. *Southern Speech Communication Journal, 45,* 37-54.

Roloff, M.E., & Barnicott, E. (1978b). The situational use of pro- and antisocial compliance-gaining strategies by high and low Machiavellians. In B. Ruben (Ed.), *Communication yearbook 2* (pp. 193-208). New Brunswick, NJ: Transaction Books.

Roloff, M.E., & Campion, D.E. (1985). Conversational profit-seeking: Interaction as social exchange. In R.L. Street, Jr. & J.N. Cappella (Eds.), *Sequence and pattern in communicative behaviour* (pp. 161-189). London: Arnold.

Roloff, M.E., & Cloven, D.H. (1990). The chilling effect in interpersonal relationships: The reluctance to speak one's mind. In D.D. Cahn (Ed.), *Intimates in conflict: A Communication perspective* (pp. 49-76). Hillsdale, NJ: Erlbaum.

Roloff, M.E., & Janiszewski, C.A. (1989). Overcoming obstacles to interpersonal compliance: A principle of message construction. *Human Communication Research, 16,* 33-61.

Roloff, M.E., Janiszewski, C.A., McGrath, M.A., Burns, C.S., & Manrai, L.A. (1988). Acquiring resources from intimates: When obligation substitutes for persuasion. *Human Communication Research, 14,* 364-396.

Roloff, M.E., & Jordan, J.M. (1991). The influence of effort, experience, and persistence on the elements of bargaining plans. *Communication Research, 18,* 306-332.

Roloff, M.E., & Jordan, J.M. (1992). Achieving negotiation goals: The "fruits and foibles" of planning ahead. In L.L. Putnam & M.E. Roloff (Eds.), *Communication and negotiation* (pp. 21-45). Newbury Park, CA: Sage.

Rule, B.G., Bisanz, G.L., & Kohn, M. (1985). Anatomy of persuasion schema: Targets, goals, and strategies. *Journal of Personality and Social Psychology, 48,* 1127-1140.

Segrin, C. (1993, April). *The impact of dysphoria and loneliness on social perception skills.* Paper presented at the joint convention of the Central and Southern States Communication Associations, Lexington, KY.

Seibold, D.R., Cantrill, J.G., & Meyers, R.A. (1985). Communication and inter-personal influence. In M.L. Knapp & G.R. Miller (Eds.), *Handbook of interpersonal communication* (pp. 551-611). Beverly Hills, CA: Sage.

Shapiro, E.G. (1980). Is seeking help from a friend like seeking help from a stranger? *Social Psychology Quarterly, 43*, 259-263.

Sillars, A.L. (1980). The stranger and the spouse as target persons for compliance-gaining strategies: A subjective-expected utility model. *Human Communication Research, 6*, 265-278.

Stutman, R.K., & Newell, S.E. (1990). Rehearsing for confrontation. *Argumentation, 4*, 185-198.

Thibaut, J., & Kelley, H. (1959). *The social psychology of groups.* New York: John Wiley.

Tutzauer, F., & Roloff, M.E. (1988). Communication processes leading to integrative agreements: Three paths to joint benefits. *Communication Research, 15*, 360-380.

Wish, M., Deutsch, M., & Kaplan, S.J. (1976). Perceived dimensions of interpersonal relations. *Journal of Personality and Social Psychology, 33*, 409-420.

Wish, M., & Kaplan, S.J. (1977). Toward an implicit theory of interpersonal communication. *Sociometry, 40*, 234-246.

"You've Lost That Loving Feeling...": Romance Loss as a Function of Relationship Development and Escalation Processes

Michael Sunnafrank

Interpersonal attraction and relationships are largely created through social influence processes. Communicative attempts to positively influence attraction are obvious, particularly in cases involving desire to begin or escalate relationships with particular others (Miller & Steinberg, 1975). An important class of such situations involves attempts to create romantic relationships. This chapter examines a neglected aspect of these romantic influence attempts: the possibility that successful strategies for beginning and developing romantic love relationships may almost inevitably sow the seeds of relational discontent and romance loss.

At the outset, clarification of the type of personal relationship being examined here is necessary. Romantic love relationships include three necessary characteristics: partners in romantic relationships are psychologically intimate with one another (actively share important personal information and feelings with one another); experience amorous feelings and an intense desire to be with one another; and expect that some degree of mutual long-term commitment to the relationship exists or may develop. Sternberg (1986) proposes three similar components of love relationships: intimacy, passion, and decision/commitment. However, he characterizes romantic love as involving only the first two of these components and refers to a relationship that adds the decision/commitment component as consummate love. Sternberg does indicate that the decision/commitment of consummate love is something for which his romantic lovers would strive. Further, he proposes that romantic lovers are emotionally bonded. In the present formulation, such striving and emotional bonding are seen as reflecting an expectation by partners that a long-term commitment to the relationship may well develop. In fact, this expectation is seen as a beginning phase of long-term commitment. Given this, romantic love relationships are treated here as involving all three components.

Research on romantic love has proceeded along various lines including examination of characteristics that cause partners to be romantically attracted to one another (Berscheid & Walster, 1978), investigation of factors that distinguish between successfully and unsuccessfully developing romantic relationships (Duck, 1976; Kerckhoff & Davis, 1962; Miller & Sunnafrank, 1982), and investigation of perceptual biases in romantic relationships (Huston, Surra, Fitzgerald, & Cate, 1981; Waller, 1938). However, only limited research has examined the social influence processes involved in attempting to develop romantic relationships. Most evidence on these romantic influence attempts must be derived indirectly from research on interpersonal influence processes—which generally ignores romantic enticement—or from work on relationship development, dating, and courtship processes—which tends to lack a social influence focus.

Social influence processes involved in attempts to develop and escalate potential romantic relationships are clearly ripe for study. The goal of this chapter is to propose one focus such research should pursue. To preview my position, I start with the premise that most romantic relationships fail to attain the permanence for which one or both partners may have hoped, and that many which do achieve such permanence prove to be less satisfactory than the partners expected. While there are numerous factors that could contribute to these outcomes, an intriguing possibility is suggested by examining the social influence processes individuals employ in attempting to develop romantic relationships. Specifically, in their efforts to attract partners, individuals may engage in social influence strategies that create an impression of a promising relational future, as well as a very positive impression of who they will be and how they will act in that future. Individuals who succeed in creating such optimistic impressions will also be more likely to succeed in their goal of escalating the relationship toward more intimate levels; however, it is highly unlikely that such positive expectations will be fulfilled in the relational future. Such unrealized expectations may eventually produce disappointment, dissatisfaction, and destabilization in the relationship. This position is fleshed out below, along with a theoretical model, which attempts to account for this phenomenon.

Once that model is established, the chapter focuses on social influence processes that could produce this situation.

SOWING THE SEEDS OF RELATIONAL DISCONTENT

It is clear that the preponderance of romantic couples never accomplish the life-long romance partners may have once considered possible. The great majority of romantic relationships dissolve well before marriage or cohabitation is attempted. More than half of all romantic relationships which do produce a marriage or other cohabitation are subsequently terminated by the couples involved (*Statistical Abstracts*, 1992). Even relationships that produce a life-long partnership generally lose one or more of the qualities necessary to sustain romance (psychological intimacy, passionate and amorous desire to be united, commitment to the relationship).

There are, of course, various possible reasons for romance loss. Research efforts on relationship dissolution (Baxter, 1987; Cody, 1982; Cupach & Metts, 1986; Miller & Parks, 1982) point to many processes that might contribute to difficulties in maintaining romantic relationships. However, one important and neglected source of difficulty may lie in the processes involved in developing romantic relationships. During the formation of romantic relationships two potentially conflicting goals are pursued by partners as they attempt to screen and allure one another. In screening, partners evaluate one another to determine suitability for further relationship development. Success in achieving this goal would require fairly accurate person perception skills, and partners willing and able to engage in open and honest self-presentation. However, pursuit of the allurement goal could conflict directly with this need for accurate person perception and partner honesty. Allurement involves a process in which individuals attempt to entice desirable partners into developing and escalating a relationship that may evolve into romantic love. During these attempts, individuals generally portray a highly positive image of themselves and the relational future. It has long been recognized that in such a situation, communicative behaviors and other displays may be enacted which create a more positive and idealized picture of the individual and the relationship potential than is warranted (Waller, 1938).

An alternative to using allurement techniques, which provide an idealized image, would be to attempt to portray a realistic image of one's self and the relational future. Even if possible, this strategy would be unlikely to succeed in attracting a partner to participate in developing and escalating a romantic relationship. As several theories indicate, individuals are more likely to pursue a relationship that promises greater rewards (Altman & Taylor, 1973; Miller & Steinberg, 1975; see Chapter 6). This would seem particularly likely for romantic relationships, which require considerable amounts of partners' time and energy, and which would consequently cause partners to forego many other activities and relationships. If individuals do not engage in alluring behaviors that produce unrealistically high expectations, the excitement and motivation necessary to embark on an involving romantic relationship may be lacking.

Such allurement processes would be most likely to occur and be effective in positively influencing a partner's perceptions and in producing exaggerated expectations in relationships where individuals know little about one another, as in relationships between individuals who have recently met or who have previously been no more than nodding acquaintances. In such cases, partners would have little information immediately available, which would contradict the idealized portrayal and thereby reduce motivation to develop the relationship. Research findings on the development of romantic love are consistent with this position: it appears to be relatively rare for individuals to form romantic relationships with others whom they know well before the romance begins to develop. Relationship development patterns leading to marriage in the United States suggest that most couples who eventually marry begin casual dating within a few weeks of first meeting and that these relationships quickly escalate to more serious commitments (Huston, et al., 1981). This suggests that allurement processes that produce the exaggerated expectations likely in these quickly developing relationships may almost be a necessity in escalating relationships to romantic levels. Of course, the more unrealistic these expectations, the greater the likelihood of eventual disappointment and destabilizing encounters in the relational future.

A considerable amount of time may pass before partners realize their expectations are flawed. Individuals involved in romantic relationships tend to cooperate in maintaining the idealized image of their partner and often ignore or rationalize contradictory information (Huston, et al., 1981; Waller, 1938). Of course, this tendency to see the relationship and the partner through the rose-colored glasses of romantic love has been the theme of prose and poetry long before its documentation by social scientists. Still, the dissolution of the great majority of romances testifies to the fact that this idealized image frequently gives way to a much different view. In a subsequent section, various types of alluring behaviors will be examined along with the ramifications of such behaviors for increasing eventual disappointment and possible dissolution of romantic relationships. In order to examine these ram-ifications in detail, it is first necessary to specify a theoretical explanation of the phenomenon being examined.

A THEORY OF ROMANCE LOSS

The theoretical perspective taken on this phenomenon follows a long tra-dition of rewards-costs explanations of human behavior (Altman & Taylor, 1973; Homans, 1974; Miller & Steinberg, 1975; Roloff, 1981; Sunnafrank, 1986; Thibaut & Kelley, 1959; see Chapter 6). A basic assumption of these perspectives is that individuals prefer to receive the most positive outcomes possible and that they will direct their actions toward that end. Moreover, these perspectives generally propose that individuals scan new opportunities (strangers, situations) and attempt to forecast the outcome potential of these opportunities. In the case of new acquaintances, interpersonal behaviors such as decisions to approach or avoid the person, types of relationship to seek with the acquaintances, and how to interact to achieve the positive outcomes desired are determined by the results of these predictions (Altman & Taylor, 1973; Sunnafrank, 1986).

Once an individual is motivated to initiate or escalate a relationship, a key to doing so would be to motivate the chosen partner. A general approach individuals could use to determine how to motivate partners would be to apply something akin to the above rewards-costs reasoning. Individuals should perceive their partner would be motivated by the expec tation that pursuing the relationship would be a worthwhile thing to do. That is, the partner must come to expect that the potential for positive out-comes is high enough to justify a decision to escalate the relationship. In order to produce these highly positive partner expectations, individuals should act in ways calculated to provide their partner with positive out-comes and the expectation of future positive outcomes: they should engage in alluring behaviors.

This process can best be explained through adapting Thibaut and Kelley's (1959) concepts of comparison level (CL) and comparison level for alterna-tives (CLalt). In general terms, comparison level is the average outcome value individuals have come to expect from relationships. Satisfaction with and attraction to an existing relationship is determined by the degree to which outcomes from the relationship exceed or fall short of the CL. The CL is determined by the outcome experiences known to an individual (including direct, vicarious, and imagined outcome experiences), weighted by their saliency. Two potentially important saliency factors in determining the weighting of previous outcomes are the recency of the previous outcome experience and the type of relationship producing these outcomes. As Thibaut and Kelley (1959) propose, the recency factor indicates that more recent outcome experiences are given more weight in determining CL. Additionally, outcomes experienced in the same or similar types of relationships should be more salient in evaluating a particular relationship. This relationship type factor suggests that in evaluating outcomes from a romantic relationship individuals would be most likely to compare these outcomes to those they have come to expect from romantic relationships. Outcomes received in different types of relationships, such as work, roommate, and family relationships, would generally not be highly salient or relevant in evaluating romantic outcomes.

Comparison level for alternatives is employed when individuals must choose between alternative relationships or situations. The CLalt is normally set by the outcome value available to an individual in their best available alternative relationship. Individuals will attempt to develop a new alternative relationship only to the extent that it appears realistically to offer outcome values exceeding this level. Simply stated, individuals will choose the alternative which provides them the most positive outcomes. From this perspective, romantic relationships should only form between individuals when both perceive the partner to offer greater outcome potential than the best alternative relationship or situation available to them.

Given this, two related tasks confront an individual interested in motivating a partner into developing a potentially romantic relationship. First, the relationship with the individual must appear to offer greater outcome potential than does the partner's best alternative relationship (CLalt). Since development of romantic relationships requires considerable time and energy investment (Miller & Steinberg, 1975), the potential outcome value of developing such relationships must be enough beyond CLalt to justify these additional costs to the partner. The appearance of greater outcome potential would not only be required to entice the partner to forego the best alternative relationship in beginning relational escalation, but would continue to be necessary throughout the romance in order to keep the partner from leaving for a more attractive alternative.

Second, as the relationship begins and continues to develop, the partner must experience and expect outcome values beyond those expected from average relationship outcomes (CL). Relatively high motivation to develop a romantic relationship must be present for a partner to invest the time and energy such development requires. The more the relationship's outcome values exceed the partner's CL, the more motivated the partner will be to invest in continued development. This necessity to appear more promising than CLalt and to significantly exceed CL would explain individuals' propensities to engage in various alluring behaviors which may result in exaggerated partner expectations for the relational future. More realistic expectations may simply be insufficiently positive to significantly surpass CL and CLalt. The problem this eventually presents for relationships can be understood from an examination of the effects exaggerated expectations eventually have on the partner's CL.

As romantic relationships develop, individuals attain more information about the partners' personal preferences. This information allows individuals to adapt to these preferences and provide outcome experiences further exceeding the partners' CL. Increasingly positive relational experiences should continue as long as the partners continue discovering and adapting to one another's personal preferences, after which point the value of outcome experiences should level off. High levels of attraction, satisfaction, and motivation to continue the relationship should result from these high (relative to CL) outcome values.

These highly positive outcome experiences should eventually result in heightening each partners' CL. Increased CLs in this situation would be expected for two reasons. First, recall that an individual's CL is the average outcome value that he or she has come to expect from relationships and that the CL is determined by the individual's previous relational experiences. As a romantic relationship lengthens, the outcome partners experience in the relationship become an increasingly large part of each person's store of previous relational experiences. The highly positive experiences provided by these romantic relationships would therefore necessarily increase each partner's CL. Second, recall that outcome experiences are weighted by their saliency in determining CL. Both the recency and the relationship type saliency factors indicate that outcome experiences from a current romantic relationship would be weighted most heavily in determining the partners' respective CLs for evaluating the relationship. Recent experiences from the developing romance would clearly be among the most recent outcomes available to the partners and therefore be given greater weight. Moreover, the most similar type of relationship experiences would likely come from the current relationship's own past. This is particularly likely in relationships where partners presently have no other relationships of the same type, as is the case with exclusive romantic relationships. This process would likely require a long period of time, perhaps many months or years. Early in the relationship, recent outcome experiences from other sources should largely determine the CL. However, as the sheer number of outcome experiences in the current relationship increases over time, and as previous romantic relationships recede further into the past, the current relationship's influence on CL would dramatically increase.

The above reasoning provides a unique interpretation of the CL concept which suggests that exclusive romantic relationships come to dominate an individual's CL for evaluating romantic relationships. In so doing, long-term romantic relationships are largely evaluated against their own past successes. Rising CLs due to highly positive outcome experiences in the relationship's past would eventually tend to reduce each partner's attraction to and satisfaction with the relationship. Although the actual outcome experiences in the relationship might still be the same as in the past, their value would be lower relative to the rising CL. This relative reduction would also reduce the level of satisfaction, attraction, and motivation regarding the relationship. The psychological intimacy, amorous desire, and commitment required for romantic love would likely decline as a result.

Moreover, lowered attraction to and satisfaction with the relationship would be expected to produce a reduction in an individual's use of alluring behaviors to please and entice his or her relational partner. This would produce declining levels of outcome experiences for the partner which should produce reciprocal reactions from him or her. The resulting mutual decline in outcome values would be particularly precipitous in cases where one or both partners had engaged in allurement behaviors which were far removed from their normal behavior. In such cases, the outcomes experienced in the relationship would likely drop well below each partner's CL. Relational dissolution would often result from this experience. In other relationships which continue through this experience, it is possible that this pattern would reverse itself. The new lower outcome values would eventually decrease CL levels and some equilibrium between outcome experiences in the relationship and CL might be reached. However, even such equilibrium would be contrary to the continued existence of romantic love. The intense motivation and attraction of romantic love are produced by the degree to which the outcome values experienced in the relationship exceed CL. Once relative equilibrium between CL and these relational outcome values occurs, little or no such excess value would remain.

Of course, variation in relational satisfaction, attraction, and motivation will continue in enduring relationships. For example, relational events may periodically remind individuals of their unfulfilled higher expectations for the relationship. This would cause these previous outcome expectations to become at least temporarily salient to the individual's CL and some resurgence of dissatisfaction and disappointment would result. At other times, actual outcome experiences in the relationship might be temporarily raised beyond the CL by some special event. This could result in heightened satisfaction with and hope for the relationship. Aside from these temporary fluctuations, partners' outcome experiences in these long-lasting relationships should generally be what they have come to expect through their CLs. As Berscheid (1983) has noted, such meeting of relational expectations is antithetical to the intense emotional experience necessary for the continued existence of romantic love.

This analysis provides an explanation of romance loss as well as of dissatisfaction and dissolution patterns in romantic relationships. It could also be employed in examining beginning friendships, roommate relationships, and work relationships in which partner behaviors also produce high and somewhat unrealistic expectations for the relationships and subsequent dissatisfaction with long-term relational outcomes. However, three aspects of romantic relationship development make these relationships ideally suited to this explanation. First, such relationships tend to involve relatively intense developmental periods in which the relationship becomes exclusive and dominates the partners' lives and consequently their CLs. Second, romantic relationships tend to form between individuals who have little information about one another before the romance begins to quickly develop (Huston, et al., 1981; Berg & McQuinn, 1986). In such circumstances individuals would be little aware of who their partner is or what the partner is normally like, and partners could employ allurement strategies which might be far from their normal behavior with little likelihood of early detection. Third, romantic relationships tend to produce high levels of motivation and emotion for the individuals involved. These high motivation levels would be expected to result in an equally high likelihood that partners might engage in allurement to attract and escalate a relationship with the object of their desire.

ALLURING BEHAVIORS AND CONSEQUENCES

The following discussion provides specific examples of how alluring behaviors may result in instability in romantic relationships and contribute to romance loss. It is important to note that these are examples only and are not meant to provide a complete list of allurement techniques. It should also be noted that the following behaviors may sometimes have allurement as their primary goal while at other times allurement may be only a low-level secondary goal. For example, telling partners how highly you regard them (discussed as partner enhancement below) may be more an attempt to influence how partners feel about themselves than about you. In fact, social influence attempts frequently have multiple goals, some of which are not even readily apparent even to the influence agents (O'Keefe & Sheperd, 1987). Given this, the following behaviors are conceived of as reflecting alluring behaviors even though allurement may not always be a highly conscious goal of the actor (see Chapter 1).

PARTNER ENHANCEMENT

Partner enhancement refers to alluring behaviors that enhance the romantic partner's self-esteem. As such, it is simply a particular instance of the ingratiation tactic of other-enhancement (Jones and Wortman, 1973). One of the most powerful influences on an individual's attraction to another is the impression that the other is attracted to the individual and holds the individual in high regard (Sunnafrank, 1991). During the intense period of romantic relationship development, the tendency to idealize one's partner (Huston, et al., 1981; Waller, 1938) would frequently be communicated to that partner. These messages of liking, loving, and positive regard are conveyed between partners in numerous ways. Poems, letters, phone conversations, face-to-face interactions, and nonverbal messages all provide avenues by which individuals extol the many virtues of their partner and/or the extremely high attraction and devotion they feel toward the partner. Partners would likely develop a more positive perception of their own characteristics and greater self-respect as they begin to realize this idealized view of themselves.

This source of positive relational outcomes should be expected to diminish as relationships evolve. This is likely for two reasons. First, as individuals come to expect such behaviors from their partner, each additional partner-enhancing message would have less relative value, which should cause partner-enhancement messages to lose their effectiveness. Second, as individuals' own motivations regarding the relationship diminish (as predicted by the theoretical position discussed previously), they would be less inclined to idealize their partner. A reduction in partner-enhancement messages would logically follow. This reduction in value and/or frequency of messages conveying positive regard for romantic partners would represent a decrease in partner outcomes from the relationship. In extreme cases it might even be interpreted as rejection. Certainly the loss or decline of this source of relational rewards would produce serious relational difficulty.

SELF-DISCLOSURE

Self-disclosure can be employed in various ways to propel growth in romantic relationships. Among other outcomes, self-disclosure of personal information to a partner can signal liking, a willingness to develop the relationship, trust of the partner, and a desire to receive reciprocal disclosures from the partner (Derlega & Chaikin, 1975). In addition to engaging in self-disclosure, individuals in romantic relationships also frequently encourage partner disclosures. These disclosures give individuals an opportunity to respond in various rewarding ways toward the discloser. For example, they may respond empathically to disclosed disappointments or tragedies, respond with enthusiasm to revealed successes, or learn how to adapt more effectively to partners as personal likes and dislikes are revealed.

While self-disclosure is inextricably tied to relationship development, significant personal disclosures involve many potential risks to the disclosing individual, their partner, and their relationship (Miller & Steinberg, 1975; Derlega & Chaikin, 1975). Uncritical and empathic responses to personal disclosures from partners, along with messages encouraging more intimate disclosures, may cause individuals to reveal highly sensitive or even negative information about themselves. These revelations may be met with empathy, understanding, reciprocation, and/or absolution by the partner during this relational period. However, as individuals move beyond the idealization of their partner, they may become more critical of their partner's disclosed past. Such criticisms might be particularly likely to surface during periods of conflict which have departed from the issues and become personal. Dramatic decreases in trust, attraction, future self-disclosure potential, and relational strength would result.

Self-disclosures during the formation of romantic relationships may also involve some degree of exaggeration or deception. Since partners know little about one another's background in most beginning romantic relationships, individuals may choose to reveal primarily the positive aspects of personal information, disclose information in a manner which puts a more positive light on potentially risky or negative information, and even "disclose" information which is untrue. These disclosures may escalate the relationship by making the individual appear more attractive to his or her partner.

These positive relational outcomes could easily be reversed later in the relationship if a more complete and accurate account of the disclosed past becomes available to the partner. This more accurate information may be revealed in several ways. For example, an individual may disclose the whole truth, having forgotten the previous exaggeration/deception, or third parties may unknowingly reveal information that uncovers the individual's previous disingenuous disclosure. Whatever the source of this more accurate information, the negative consequences for relational outcomes would be twofold. First, partners would now have information indicating that the individual is not exactly the person they had been led to believe. More importantly, partners would now begin to question the truthfulness of the individual in other areas and relational trust would inevitably suffer.

One previously ignored negative consequence of frequent intimate self-disclosure in romantic relationship development could explain a common complaint in long-term romantic relationships: that the partners no longer talk intimately and share personal information with one another. The uncritical acceptance and empathy with which intimate self-disclosures are frequently received in rapidly escalating romantic relationships could produce high levels of mutual self-disclosure about each partner's past. However, individuals likely have a limited reserve of important past information available to disclose. It may be that the bulk of these important self-disclosures are frequently provided during this period of rapid escalation. Intimate self-disclosures could continue after this period as individuals share new life experiences, thoughts, and emotions with their partner. However, the rate of intimate self-disclosure may inevitably decline as the partners deplete their reserves of intimate information about their past.

A decline in the amount of intimate self-disclosure would therefore be a natural consequence of having shared much of one's life story with a romantic partner. This reduction in intimate disclosures might well be misread by partners as a signal of a decrease in trust, desire for intimacy, and attraction. Reduced self-disclosure levels would also mean a reduction in the opportunities for experiencing uncritical and empathic partner acceptance. Such repercussions might dramatically reduce the level of positive outcomes experienced in these relationships, increase relational instability, and increase potential for romance loss.

PORTRAYALS OF SIMILARITY

Both research and conventional wisdom support the view that "birds of a feather flock together," at least on certain characteristics. Individuals tend to form relationships with others who are similar to them with regard to physical attractiveness (Berscheid & Walster, 1974), socio-economic background (Kandel, 1978), intelligence (Richardson, 1939), activity preferences (Werner & Parmelee, 1979), communication skills (Burleson &

Denton, 1992), and various other attributes. Whether such similar characteristics actually cause individuals to desire others for romantic relationships
is unclear, but the tendency to pair romantically with those who exhibit
such similarities is undeniable. In addition, much research supports the
view that individuals are attracted to others who share their attitudes and
values (Byrne, 1971; Cappella & Palmer, 1990; Duck, 1976; Parks &
Adelman, 1983). This traditional view of an attitude similarity-attraction
relationship has recently been challenged on several fronts. Three comprehensive critiques of this literature maintain that most established relationships, including romantic relations, do not demonstrate enough attitude or
value similarity to overcome the claim that this is simply an artifact of
demographic matching tendencies (Bochner, 1984; Sunnafrank, 1991;
Huston, et al., 1981).

Despite the scientific controversy regarding whether various similarities
promote attraction, it is clear that individuals tend to believe that similarity is
generally attractive and that dissimilarity and disagreement could be unat-
tractive or promote relational difficulty (Sunnafrank, 1991). Individuals
apparently believe that others will be more attracted to them when they
appear agreeable or similar. When engaged in allurement, individuals would
likely use this belief to guide their choice of behaviors, self-presentations, discussion topics, and conversational contributions. Two specific types of similarity portrayals with interesting consequences for romantic relationships are
examined below: activity preference similarity and attitude similarity.

Similarity in activity preferences is a strong predictor of romantic relationship development (Werner & Parmelee, 1979). Shared enjoyment of the
same activities would seem a good basis for this type of relationship since
partners spend much of their time and life together. It seems likely that during the formation of romantic relationships partners may act in ways which
would produce a high and unrealistic view of the degree of actual similar
activity preferences existing between them. When attempting to allure a
partner, individuals might try discovering the partner's interests and either
suggest or go along with participating in those things the partner likes to do.
In doing so, individuals may sometimes engage in activities they would normally dislike just because their partner enjoys them. In fact, these individuals may even find the activities temporarily enjoyable because of the delight
received from being with and pleasing the partner. An individual's expressions of enjoyment during the activities might be quite real, and the partner
may mistakenly come to believe that the activities are the source of the
individual's pleasure. This perception would heighten the partner's expectations for a future in which the couple could continue to share their joy in

the activities. Later, when the partner discovers that the individual really does not enjoy the activities, these unrealized expectations would produce disappointment and might even lead the partner to perceive that the individual had lied through an earlier feigned enjoyment. Obviously, the more activities involved and the more important the activities are to the individual who enjoys them, the greater long-term difficulty this allurement strategy could produce.

Research on communication behavior and attitude similarity supports the view that individuals attempt to give the appearance of being attitudinally similar to partners during initial acquaintance (Sunnafrank & Miller, 1981; Sunnafrank, 1983). In such situations, interlocutors tend to focus on subjects on which they agree and to avoid conflict by skirting possibly controversial topics. Even when forced to discuss controversial topics on which partners disagree, the discussion proceeds in such a manner as to produce the belief in interactants that their partners actually agree with them more than they do (Sunnafrank, 1984). When individuals wish to allure partners for the possible purposes of developing a romantic relationship such tendencies to appear attitudinally similar may well increase. Focusing on topics of agreement and avoiding or playing down disagreement should be a common allurement strategy. Much research supports this possibility by confirming that spouses and romantic partners perceive that their partners are more similar in attitudes and values than is actually the case (Sillars & Scott, 1983; Sunnafrank, 1986).

Interlocutors who employ this allurement strategy may succeed in getting their partners to like them, and to think this liking is reciprocal; work on opinion conformity suggests this (Jones & Wortman, 1973). The successful use of such strategies should produce high levels of perceived attitude similarity, as well as increase the likelihood of relational development. In some cases, relationships containing partners with highly discrepant perceived and actual attitude similarity levels will successfully progress toward developing a romantic relationship through these conversational processes. When high perceived attitude similarity is combined with very discrepant perceived and actual similarity levels, the likelihood of future relational strain and problems may increase dramatically. High levels of perceived attitude similarity may eventually lead individuals to make relatively bold and unguarded attitude statements. Blunt revelation of attitudes in the presence of actual dissimilarity may lead to several potentially negative conversational and relational consequences. These embarrassing occurrences might produce anger and destructive conflict in some cases, particularly when the attitude in question is important to, or intensely held by, one or both partners. Even when surprising dissimilarities are discovered less directly, individuals may suspect that their former perception of similarity was generated by partner deception or disingenuousness. These discoveries would likely have negative consequences for several key relational variables including trust, perceptions of partner credibility, self-disclosure level, intimacy of communication content, and attraction.

OTHER ALLURING BEHAVIORS

Many other alluring behaviors might produce similar long-term negative consequences for romantic relationships. Various alluring behaviors and strategies could be gleaned from work on compliance gaining processes and strategies (Boster & Stiff, 1984; Dillard & Burgoon, 1985; Miller & Burgoon, 1978; Miller, Burgoon, & Burgoon, 1984: Miller, Boster, Roloff, & Seibold, 1987; Seibold & Steinfatt, 1979; see Chapter 5), ingratiation tactics (Jones & Wortman, 1973), affinity-seeking strategies (Bell & Daly, 1984), and uncertainty reduction strategies (Berger, 1987: Berger & Bradac, 1982; Berger & Calabrese, 1975; Berger, Gardner, Parks, Schulman, & Miller, 1976). While the current presentation makes no attempt to provide an exhaustive list of allurement techniques, three which appear particularly promising in terms of explaining romance loss are briefly discussed here.

Impression management strategies used in forming romantic relationships may provide an inaccurate image of how the self will act in the relational future which could contribute to relational instability. Individuals attempt to create and maintain particular impressions of themselves to obtain liking and other positive outcomes from others (Goffman, 1959; Jones & Wortman, 1973). In the case of romantic relationships, numerous desirable outcomes associated with relational escalation might derive from the successful management of the image romantic partners have of one another. The image generated to acquire these outcomes may frequently produce an unrealistically positive impression of an individual's accomplishments, abilities, power, and status. These impressions could clearly raise partners' outcome expectations to levels that would go unrealized in the relational future.

Promises about future behaviors and relational states are another likely allurement tactic employed in developing romantic relationships. Hopes and dreams for the future may frequently be shared in a manner which implies a promise that the partners will make the dreams come true. When confronted with the reality of the future, many promises, no matter how well intentioned originally, go unfulfilled. Sometimes promises are unrealized because of the actions of the relational partners, sometimes because of the hand of fate, and sometimes a mixture of both forces are at work. Whatever the reasons, this failure would certainly reduce the outcomes experienced in the relationship from the promised levels.

Deception may be a particularly troublesome tool individuals use when attempting to allure partners into potential romantic relationships (see Chapter 4). In fact, deception may be a general approach that can be employed in implementing many other allurement strategies. As suggested earlier, deception may be used in portraying similarity and self-disclosure strategies. It could also be employed in providing disingenuous self-presentations or in knowingly making relational promises which cannot be fulfilled. Miller and his colleague's pioneering work on detecting deception (Bauchner, Brandt, & Miller, 1977; Brandt, Hocking, & Miller, 1980; Miller, Bauchner, Hocking, Fontes, Kaminski, & Brandt, 1981; Miller & Burgoon, 1982; Miller, deTurck, & Kalbfleisch, 1983; Stiff & Miller, 1986) could usefully be extended to examine the consequences of such deceptive allurement practices for romantic relationships. Much deception in alluring potential romantic partners would focus on raising partners' expectations for the relationship. The higher such deception-generated expectations, the more trouble and instability the romance could eventually face. Moreover, negative consequences for trust and commitment should result as deceptions are discovered.

CONCLUSION

One of the enduring myths of western civilization is that each of us has a life partner somewhere in the world who was made just for us. When we meet that special person music will play, fireworks will explode, and we will live happily ever after. Few of us are likely to claim that this myth is reflected in our beliefs about reality. However, processes involved in developing romantic relationships appear to belie these claims. Romantic relationships rarely develop between individuals who know one another well. The music hasn't played for these relationships in the past and, we might reason, it is unlikely to do so in the future. Instead, we keep looking for love among strangers. It is here that the reality of knowing another cannot immediately intrude upon our search for that one ideal person.

Relative strangers can more readily convince one another that the romantic myth has finally been met in them. Alluring behaviors that provide partners with exaggerated expectations for the relationship appear to play a vital role in this process. Since alluring behaviors are unlikely to be contradicted by the limited knowledge relative strangers possess about one another, unrealistic expectations for the relationship may result. Increased positive outcome expectations for these developing relationships should produce high levels of attraction between partners and motivation to further escalate the relationship. If the outcome experiences, attraction, and motivation are sufficiently positive, the music starts to play.

The potential dark side of this myth-perpetuating process isn't revealed until later in relationships. As romantic relationships continue, accumulated knowledge about partners reveals they are somewhat less than perfect, and alluring behaviors diminish in effectiveness, reward value, and frequency. These changes should result in some degree of relational disappointment. Disappointment, in turn, sets in motion processes that may reduce the intensity of the romance, produce romance loss, or even terminate the relationship. The allurement process described here is certainly not the only cause of romance loss. However, the theory offered does explain the long-recognized phenomenon of extremely high relational motivation in the beginning of romantic relationships followed by a precipitous drop in romantic excitement as relationships mature (Miller & Steinberg, 1975). More importantly, it provides a novel and compelling explanation of how relationships that begin with such great promise frequently produce disappointment and disaster. Myths die hard, particularly when we are such willing participants in creating the delusions they perpetuate. Careful consideration of the role that allurement plays in creating these delusions could improve considerably our understanding of romance and romance loss.

REFERENCES

Altman, I., & Taylor, D. (1973). *Social penetration: The development of inter-personal relationships.* New York: Holt, Rinehart, & Winston.

Bauchner, J.E., Brandt, D.R., & Miller, G.R. (1977). The truth-deception attribution: Effects of varying levels of information availability. In B.R. Ruben (Ed.), *Communication yearbook 1* (pp. 229-243). New Brunswick, NJ: Transaction Books.

Baxter, L.A. (1987). Self-disclosure and relationship disengagement. In V.J. Derlega & J.H. Berg (Eds.), *Self-disclosure: Theory, research, and therapy* (pp. 155-174). New York: Plenum.

Bell, R.A., & Daly, J.A. (1984). The affinity-seeking function of communication. *Communication Monographs, 51,* 91-115.

Berg, J.H., & McQuinn, R.D. (1986). Attraction and exchange in continuing and noncontinuing dating relationships. *Journal of Personality and Social Psychology, 50,* 942-952.

Berger, C.R. (1987). Communicating under uncertainty. In M.E. Roloff & G.R. Miller (Eds.), *Interpersonal processes* (pp. 39-62). Newbury Park, CA: Sage.

Berger, C.R., & Bradac, J.J. (1982). *Language and social knowledge: Uncertainty in interpersonal relations.* London: Edward Arnold.

Berger, C.R., & Calabrese, R. (1975). Some explorations in initial interactions and beyond: Toward a developmental theory of interpersonal communication. *Human Communication Research, 1,* 99-112.

Berger, C.R., Gardner, R.R., Parks, M.R., Schulman, & Miller, G.R. (1976). Interpersonal epistemology and interpersonal communication. In G.R. Miller (Ed.), *Explorations in interpersonal communication* (pp. 149-172). Beverly Hills: Sage.

Berscheid, E. (1983). Emotion. In H.H. Kelley, E. Berscheid, A. Christensen, J.H. Harvey, T.L. Huston, G. Levinger, E. McClintock, L.A. Peplau, & D.R. Peterson (Eds.), *Close Relationships* (pp. 110-168). New York: W.H. Freeman.

Berscheid, E., & Walster, E. (1974). Physical attractiveness. In L. Berkowitz (Ed.), *Advances in experimental social psychology* (pp. 158-216). New York: Academic Press.

Berscheid, E., & Walster, E. (1978). *Interpersonal attraction.* Reading, MA: Addison-Wesley.

Bochner, A.P. (1984). The functions of human communication in interpersonal bonding. In C.C. Arnold & J.W. Bowers (Eds.), *Handbook of rhetorical and communication theory* (pp. 544-621). Boston: Allyn & Bacon.

Boster, F.J., & Stiff, J.B. (1984). Compliance-gaining message selection behavior. *Human Communication Research, 10,* 539-556.

Brandt, D.R., Hocking, J.E., & Miller, G.R. (1980). The truth-deception attribution: Effects of familiarity on the ability of observers to detect deception.
Human Communication Research, 6, 99-110.

Burleson, B.R. & Denton, W.H. (1992). A new look at similarity and attraction
in marriage: Similarities in social-cognitive and communication skills as predictors of attraction and satisfaction. *Communication Monographs, 59*, 268-
287.

Byrne, D. (1971). *The attraction paradigm.* New York: Academic Press.

Cappella, J.N., & Palmer, M.T. (1990). Attitude similarity, relational history,
and attraction: The mediating effects of kinesic and vocal behaviors.
Communication Monographs, 57, 161-183.

Cody, M.J. (1982). A typology of disengagement strategies and an examination
of the role intimacy, reactions to inequity and relational problems play in
strategy selection. *Communication Monographs, 49*, 148-170.

Cupach, W.R., & Metts, S. (1986). Accounts of relational dissolution: A comparison of marital and non-marital relationships. *Communication Monographs,
53*, 311-334.

Derlega, V.J., & Chaikin, A.L. (1975). *Sharing intimacy: What we reveal about
ourselves and why.* Englewood Cliffs, NJ: Prentice-Hall.

Dillard, J.P., & Burgoon, M. (1985). Situational influences on the selection of
compliance-gaining messages: Two tests of the predicted utility of the Cody-
McLaughlin typology. *Communication Monographs, 52*, 289-304.

Duck, S. (1976). Interpersonal communication in developing acquaintance. In
G.R. Miller (Ed.), *Explorations in interpersonal communication* (pp. 127-
148). Beverly Hills, CA: Sage.

Goffman, E. (1959). *The presentation of self in everyday life.* New York:
Doubleday.

Homans, G.C. (1974). *Social behavior: Its elementary forms* (2nd ed.). New
York: Harcourt Brace Jovanovich.

Huston, T.L., Surra, C.A., Fitzgerald, N.M., & Cate, R.M. (1981). In S. Duck &
R. Gilmour (Eds.), *Personal relationships 2: Developing personal relationships* (53-88). London: Academic Press.

Jones, E.E., & Wortman, C. (1973). *Ingratiation: An attributional approach.*
Morristown, NJ: General Learning Press.

Kandel, D.B. (1978). Similarity in real-life adolescent friendship pairs. *Journal of
Personality and Social Psychology, 36*, 306-312.

Kerckhoff, A.C., & Davis, K.E. (1962). Value consensus and need complemen-
tarity in mate selection. *American Sociological Review, 27*, 295-303.

Miller, G.R., Bauchner, J.E., Hocking, J.E., Fontes, N.E., Kaminski, E.R., &
Brandt, D.R. (1981). "...and nothing but the truth": How well can
observers detect deceptive testimony? In B.D. Sales (Ed.), *Perspectives in*

law and psychology: The jury, judicial, and trial processes (pp. 145-179). New York: Plenum.

Miller, G.R., Boster, F., Roloff, M. & Seibold, D. (1987). MBRS rekindled: Some thoughts on compliance gaining in interpersonal settings. In M.E. Roloff & G.R. Miller (Eds.), *Interpersonal processes: New directions in communication research* (pp. 89-116). Newbury Park, CA: Sage.

Miller, G.R., & Burgoon, J.K. (1982). Factors affecting assessments of witness credibility. In N.L. Kerr & R.M. Bray (Eds.), *The psychology of the courtroom* (pp. 169-194). New York: Academic Press.

Miller, G.R., & Burgoon, M. (1978). Persuasion research: Review and commentary. In B. Ruben (Ed.), *Communication yearbook 2* (pp. 29-47). New Brunswick, NJ: Transaction Books.

Miller, G.R., Burgoon, M., & Burgoon, J.K. (1984). The functions of human communication in changing attitudes and gaining compliance. In C.C. Arnold & J.W. Bowers (Eds.), *Handbook of rhetorical and communication theory* (pp. 400-474). Boston: Allyn & Bacon.

Miller, G.R., deTurck, M.A., & Kalbfleisch, P.J. (1983). Self-monitoring, rehearsal, and deceptive communication. *Human Communication Research, 10,* 97-117.

Miller, G.R., & Parks, M.R. (1982). Communication in dissolving relationships. *Personal relationships 4: Dissolving personal relationships* (pp. 127-154). London: Academic Press.

Miller, G.R., & Steinberg, M. (1975). *Between people: A new analysis of interpersonal communication.* Chicago: Science Research Associates.

Miller, G.R., & Sunnafrank, M.J. (1982). All is for one but one is not for all: A conceptual perspective of interpersonal communication. In F.E.X. Dance (Ed.), *Human communication theory* (pp. 220-242). New York: Harper & Row.

O'Keefe, B.J., & Shepherd, G.J. (1987). The pursuit of multiple objectives in face-to-face persuasive interactions: Effects of construct differentiation on message organization. *Communication Monographs, 54,* 396-419.

Parks, M.R., & Adelman, M.B. (1983). Communication networks and the development of romantic relationships: An expansion of uncertainty reduction theory. *Human Communication Research, 10,* 55-79.

Richardson, H.M. (1939). Studies of mental resemblance between husbands and wives and between friends. *Psychological Bulletin, 36,* 104-120.

Roloff, M.E. (1981). *Interpersonal communication: The social exchange approach.* Beverly Hills: Sage.

Seibold, D.R., & Steinfatt, T.M. (1979). The creative alternative: Exploring interpersonal influence processes. *Simulation & Games, 10,* 429-457.

Sillars, A.L., & Scott, M.D. (1983). Interpersonal perception between intimates: An integrative review. *Human Communication Research, 10,* 153-

176.*Statistical Abstract of the United States: 1992.* Washington, D.C.: United States Bureau of the Census.

Sternberg, Robert J. (1986). A triangular theory of love. *Psychological Review, 93*, 119-135.

Stiff, J.B., & Miller, G.R. (1986). "Come to think of it...": Interrogative probes, deceptive communication and deception detection. *Human Communication Research, 12*, 339-357.

Sunnafrank, M. (1983). Attitude Similarity and interpersonal attraction in communication processes: In pursuit of an ephemeral influence. *Communication Monographs, 50*, 273-284.

Sunnafrank, M. (1984). A communication-based perspective on attitude similarity and interpersonal attraction in early acquaintance. *Communication Monographs, 51*, 372-380.

Sunnafrank, M. (1986). Communicative influences on perceived similarity and attraction: An expansion of the interpersonal goals perspective. *Western Journal of Speech Communication, 50*, 158-170.

Sunnafrank, M. (1991). Interpersonal attraction and attitude similarity: A communication-based assessment. In James A. Anderson (Ed.), *Communication yearbook 14* (pp. 451-483). Newbury Park, CA: Sage.

Sunnafrank, M., & Miller, G.R. (1981). The role of initial conversations in determining attraction to similar and dissimilar strangers. *Human Communication Research, 8*, 16-25.

Thibaut, J., & Kelley, H. (1959). *The social psychology of groups.* New York: Wiley.

Waller, W. (1938). *The family: A dynamic interpretation.* New York: Gordon.

Werner, C., & Parmelee, P. (1979). Similarity of activity preferences among friends: Those who play together stay together. *Social Psychology Quarterly, 42*, 62-66.

Webs of Influence in Personal Relationships

Malcolm R. Parks

It is difficult to overestimate the role personal relationships play in our lives. While it is certainly true that periods of solitude or relational deprivation can be fertile grounds for creativity and inspiration (Storr, 1988), it is also true that most people view their personal relationships as the most important sources of meaning and satisfaction in their lives (Chappell & Badger, 1989; Klinger, 1977; Long, Anderson, & Williams, 1990). Moreover, researchers have demonstrated that inadequate or disrupted personal relationships pose health risks of the same magnitude as poor diet, lack of exercise, and heavy cigarette smoking (Atkins, Kaplan, & Toshima, 1991; House, Landis, & Umberson, 1988). Understanding how personal relationships develop and deteriorate is therefore of great practical, as well as theoretic, importance.

We typically view personal relationships from the inside out, from their interiors. Both as scholars and participants, we usually focus on individuals' direct experience of themselves and their partners. This perspective emphasizes the psychological world of the individual and the dyadic world of the communication between the partners. The view from the interior dominates studies of interpersonal communication and personal relationships. Thus most studies are concerned with the way dyadic partners feel about each other, think about each other, and communicate with each other (see Chapters 6 and 7). Every personal relationship, however, also has an exterior. It occupies a social space, is an object of others' perceptions and actions, and constitutes a small part of the weave of a larger social fabric. Because the participants in a relationship have other relationships, any given dyad becomes a particular link in a larger network of relationships. Whatever their disciplinary badges, researchers have largely ignored the exterior perspective. Indeed calls for more attention to the social context surrounding personal relationships echo across the literature on personal relationships (Milardo & Lewis, 1985; Parks & Eggert, 1991).

For the last several years, my research has focused on the interplay between relational interiors and exteriors. This chapter is a research narrative, summarizing my own and others' research which has been directed toward understanding how the developmental path of any given personal relationship becomes intertwined with the participants' surrounding social networks. While there is still much to be discovered, we now have substantial evidence showing that social network influences are actively involved across the entire life cycle of personal relationships. To support this claim, I have organized the chapter around three broad phases in the life of a personal relationship: initiation, development, and deterioration. In the final section I will draw together a set of theoretic forces that account for the interplay of network and dyadic factors in personal relationships.

NETWORKS AND THE INITIATION OF PERSONAL RELATIONSHIPS

Perhaps our most common—and certainly our most enduring view—of how personal relationships begin is a romantic one: eyes meet, hearts beat, and the world falls away as future lovers discover each other for the first time (see Chapter 7). A classic expression of this can be found in Goethe's (1774/1971) tragic romance *The Sorrows of Young Werther*. After being introduced to Lotte, the object of his desire, young Werther writes:

> Then I left her, after asking the favor of seeing her again that same day. She granted my request and I went. Since then, sun, moon, and stars may continue on their course; for me there is neither day nor night, and the entire universe about me has ceased to exist. (p. 32)

While the world may be psychically suspended during an enchanted encounter, experience and reality are in fact two quite different things. We may be so focused on the future partner that the world around us seems to disappear, as it does for young Werther, but that does not mean that it actually ceases to exist or, more importantly, that it ceases to influence the course of the romance. It is not my purpose to debunk the romantic image of the "world of two;" it undoubtedly plays a crucial role in energizing the development of the relationship. But its importance does not lie in its empirical reality. Quite the opposite, it is precisely the denial of reality that gives romantic imagery its profound impact. The empirical reality is that the world—the participants' social and physical context—not only exists for prospective relational partners, but is actively involved in the initiation and early development of their relationship.

Some of the ways that initiation and the early development of relationships are influenced by contextual factors are well established in past research. The role of physical proximity, for example, has such a long research tradition that it is rarely examined in contemporary studies (for a review, see Berscheid & Walster, 1978). Sociologists have long noted the impact of social norms that mark groups as acceptable or unacceptable sources for friends and romantic partners (Kerckhoff, 1974; Milardo & Lewis, 1985). Long before one meets the prospective friend or lover, one will have usually followed social dictates by associating with members of the groups in which the future partner is to be found. The physical and social context may be a reinforcer or a source of arousal in its own right. To note just one example, recall Dutton and Aron's (1974) finding that young men's sexual attraction to a woman was enhanced by meeting her under arousing circumstances. In the case of Dutton and Aron's study, the arousing context was a walk across a 230-foot high suspension bridge, but we can easily imagine other positive or arousing contexts that might promote affiliation and attraction.

Our research program has uncovered still other ways that the initiation and early development of personal relationships are tied to social context. One of these is what I would call a *social proximity effect*. To appreciate this effect it is necessary to think about the social context just prior to the time future friends or romantic partners first meet. They are not linked directly yet, but may be indirectly linked through any number of friends, friends of friends, or other people they know in common. The number of people separating the potential partners constitutes their distance from one another in a social network. If these webs of relationships begin to merge, people are carried into greater social proximity with one another and the probability of potential partners meeting directly increases. In other words, the fewer the links separating people (i.e., the greater their social proximity in a network), the more likely it is that they will actually meet (Parks & Eggert, 1991).

The social proximity effect suggests that prospective relational partners should have had common acquaintances prior to their first meeting. Several of our data sets have yielded evidence of this effect at work. These data sets covered a total of 858 subjects who were reporting on either a same-sex friendship ($n = 478$) or a romantic relationship ($n = 380$). About 40% of the sample was made up of high-school students, while the remaining 60% attended a large state university. All subjects were asked to obtain a list of their friend's or romantic partner's four closest family members and eight closest friends. Once this list was obtained, subjects were asked to report how many of the people on the partner's list they had already met prior to meeting the partner for the first time. This procedure yielded an index of the extent to which prospective relational partners had contact with each other's network prior to the time they actually met.

Our results indicated that 66.3% of the subjects had indeed met at least one member of their partner's network of close friends, family, and other significant contacts before they had met the partner for the first time. Although many subjects (32.7%) did not have prior contact, the largest group (47.3%) had prior contact with between one and three members of their future partner's network. Some (13.2%) had met between four and six members of the partner's network, while a few (5.8%) had met over half of the partner's 12 significant others prior to meeting the partner for the first time. If the broader network beyond these 12 closest contacts were examined, it is likely that even greater levels of prior contact would be observed.

These proximity effects did not differ for males ($n = 355$) and females ($n = 503$). Nor did they differ for high-school students and university students. We did find, however, that people in romantic relationships had prior contact with almost twice as many people in their prospective partner's network as people in same-sex friendships (M's $= 2.68$ vs. 1.40, $p < .0001$). Further testing revealed that this difference was even more pronounced in the college-age group than in the high-school-age group. Put another way, young people, especially college-age people, tend to "reach further" for their friends than for their romantic partners. Compared to the people who are to become friends, the people who become romantic partners are people with whom one already has more indirect contacts. In both cases, however, it is typical for prospective relational partners already to have a number of contacts with people in each others' networks prior to the time they first meet.

Social networks are involved in the initiation of personal relationships in still another, more active, way. Network members may play the role of "third party helper" or matchmaker by engaging in strategies that help new relationships get started. To explore this possibility, we conducted an exploratory study on the role of third party help in the initiation and early development of romantic relationships (Parks & Barnes, 1988). Our first goal was simply to identify the types of help that third parties might provide. Using focus group methods, we isolated 14 help strategies, which we classified into three conceptual categories. One of these involved *direct initiations* of the kind that most people traditionally associate with matchmaking: introducing prospective partners to one another, arranging a blind date, arranging a double date, or arranging for the prospective partners to "meet by accident." Another third party strategy type was what we called *direct assistance.* It included all third party activities that helped participants conduct their relationship. Helpers provide, for example, coaching to one of the partners on what to say or how to approach the other. They act as information relays, ferrying information back and forth between the partners. Sometimes they act as problem solvers by, for example, helping the partners with transportation or arranging for a place for them to be alone. The third strategy type contained helper strategies that functioned as *attraction manipulations.* That is, third parties influenced the prospective partners' attraction to one another by saying good things about one person to the other, by downplaying one person's negative qualities to the other, by telling the partners how much they had in common, and so on. It was apparent, therefore, that third parties had quite an arsenal of strategies available to them should they wish to engage in matchmaking.

But how often do third parties actually get involved in the initiation and early development of romantic relationships? To answer this question, a survey was given to 437 university students who were asked to report about their experiences as both users and recipients of helping strategies during the previous year. What we found was that third party help, far from being the exception, was the rule. Fifty-five percent of our subjects reported that they had used at least some of the strategies described above in an effort to help someone's romantic relationship get started. Indeed, subjects had given help to an average of three couples in the previous 12 months. More to the point, 64% of those who had initiated a romantic relationship in the last year reported having received help from third parties. We also found that common stereotypes about third party help were incorrect. One was the belief that females are more likely than males to play the role of helper. We found no sex differences. Males and females helped equally often and were the recipients of help equally often.

Third party helpers are sometimes portrayed as manipulators acting for their own purposes and without their targets being aware of their actions. The truth is that third party help is rarely unknown or unwanted. We found that at least one member of the recipient couple was aware of the third party helper's activities in approximately 80% of the cases. Moreover, 64%

of the helpers reported that one or both recipients had given hints indicating that their help would be appreciated. And, 69% of the recipients reported that they had given such hints. In 45% of the cases the third party assistance had been directly requested by one or both of the recipients.

Our research program has sought to place the process of relationship initiation back in its proper social context. It is fair to say that most of the research conducted in the last 35 years on personal relationships and on interpersonal processes has either ignored the very beginnings of relationships or has failed to place them in any kind of meaningful social context. In some studies, relationship initiation occurs only in a phantom sense when people react to written descriptions or pictures of others rather than interacting with people themselves (for example, Byrne, 1971; Snyder, Berscheid, & Glick, 1985). In other cases, the relationship is arbitrarily created when the researcher pairs subjects and the resulting interaction occurs in a socially disconnected setting, often with little or no reference to the subjects' larger social world and certainly with no consequences for it (Cappella & Palmer, 1990; Sunnafrank, 1984; VanLear, 1987). As we restore the social context to this process, we remember the myriad roles it plays in the initiation and early development of personal relationships. We rediscover the importance of physical proximity and add to it the notion of social proximity within a social network. While only suggestive to this point, our research implies that people are often "carried" toward first meetings as their separate networks merge. Prospective partners, however, are not just awash in the currents of their surrounding networks. Instead, as our study of third party help revealed, they set sail and navigate the social context in search of resources that will facilitate their relational desires. They actively enlist others to, among other things, arrange meetings, relay information, sing their praises, minimize their faults, and paint pictures of rosy relational futures.

NETWORKS AND THE LATER DEVELOPMENT OF PERSONAL RELATIONSHIPS

MYTHS ABOUT NETWORKS AND RELATIONSHIPS

Two of the most enduring views of how personal relationships are influenced by the surrounding networks of friends and family emphasize themes of opposition and withdrawal. In Shakespeare's *Romeo and Juliet*, for example, the young lovers are brought together not only by their virtues, but also by the unyielding opposition of their families. This theme is a common one and can be found in popular descriptions of relationships from antiquity to the present. Opposition from family and friends is thought to foster attraction either because it represents a frustration of goal-directed behavior, which leads to a more intense desire for the goal, or because it threatens the participants' sense of personal freedom and thereby creates reactance effects (Driscoll, Davis, & Lipetz, 1972). These beliefs help explain why many parents decide that silence is the best policy when it comes to their children's poor choices of friends or dates. They believe that expressing their opposition will only drive their children closer to such undesirables.

Withdrawal is another common theme in the literature on networks and developing relationships. Social theorists of many stripes have argued that friends and lovers retreat into the private world of their developing relationships, withdrawing from their other relationships (Freud, 1930/1957; Goode, 1960; Johnson & Leslie, 1982; Krain, 1977). Withdrawal from other relationships is sometimes seen as a way of reinforcing the identity of the developing relationship. In other cases it is simply a natural consequence of spending greater time with the new relational partner. Either way, the withdrawal image suggests that networks play a diminished role in the development of personal relationships. One of my goals in this section is to evaluate the validity of these images of development through opposition and withdrawal. Then I will turn to an examination of additional linkages between networks and relational development, and particularly to the findings on these linkages coming out of my research and others' research.

While the notion that opposition from network members can intensify the development of personal relationships is appealing, the research supporting it is scant. The most supportive and most frequently cited study was conducted by Driscoll and his colleagues in the early 1970's (Driscoll, et al., 1972). These researchers found that perceived interference from the partner's parents was associated with increased feelings of romantic love in both cross-sectional and longitudinal analyses. They dubbed this pattern of findings the "Romeo and Juliet effect." Unfortunately, later studies have failed to replicate such an effect (Krain, 1977; Leslie, 1983; Lewis, 1973). One of the limitations of the Driscoll study was that it focused only on perceived opposition from the partner's parents and did not address the level of support or opposition flowing from the subject's family, the subject's friends, the partner's friends, or from other sectors of the partners' networks. We examined these additional sectors in our studies of romantic relationships and have consistently found only limited support for the Romeo and Juliet effect, and usually only in the case where parents and family were perceived to be opposed to the budding romance, but friends were perceived to be supportive. Even then, the effect did not show up on all measures of romantic involvement (see Parks, Stan, & Eggert, 1983; Eggert & Parks, 1987). Opposition from network members is negatively, rather than positively, associated with the development of personal relationships in our studies.

Doubt has also been cast on popular images of social withdrawal as a cause or consequence of relationship development. It does appear that as their relationship develops, romantic partners reallocate at least some of their leisure, recreational, and other activities from network members to the romantic partner (Surra, 1985). However, the research is less convincing when it comes to the sort of generalized social withdrawal so often envisioned in popular images of relational development. Most studies indicate that withdrawal does occur, but that it is relatively limited both in its magnitude and in its breadth (Eggert & Parks, 1987; Lewis, 1975; Milardo, 1986; Parks et al., 1983; Surra, 1988). One of the most extensive studies to date was done by Milardo, Johnson, and Huston (1983) who used diary methods to track romantic partners' contacts with network members. Evidence of withdrawal was found in only about a third of the tests they conducted. When withdrawal did occur, it occurred with acquaintances and casual friends rather than with close friends and family. While the frequency of communication with network members dropped somewhat, couples maintained the same size networks as their relationship developed. Our findings indicate that withdrawal from some relationships with network members may be offset by expanded relationships with others. Members who are seen as supportive may receive more attention. The individual's network expands to include new members drawn from the partner's network. Thus, social withdrawal is just one part of a larger process in which the participants in a developing relationship reallocate their activities and realign their social relationships. They do not so much withdraw as create a new, more highly shared network.

Images of couples being united in the face of hostile friends and family or of couples withdrawing into the cocoon of their private relationship do not, then, provide an adequate basis for understanding the ways in which developing relationships become intertwined with the participants' broader social networks. In the last ten years we have, along with other researchers, uncovered additional factors connecting network characteristics with the developmental trajectory of personal relationships. Three classes of network factors are critical: 1) the amount of contact and overlap between the partners' networks, 2) the extent to which the partners are attracted to members of each other's networks, and 3) the extent to which members of the partners' networks support their relationship.

I will highlight the findings emerging from our research program, but will also note several excellent contributions made by other researchers. Before turning to the findings themselves, a brief description of the research program is in order. Over the last several years we have constructed a data bank containing approximately 860 cases. As I noted earlier, subjects were drawn from both high school and university populations. They ranged in age from 14 to 36 years ($M = 18.61$, $SD = 2.17$). Somewhat more females (58%) than males (42%) contributed data. Preliminary analyses of portions of the data have been conducted (Parks et. al., 1983; Eggert & Parks, 1987), but the more complete analysis, which I will overview here, is forthcoming (Parks, forthcoming).

Each case in the data bank contains dyadic and network information. Subjects reported on the dyadic development of one of their personal relationships—either a same-sex friendship (44%) or a romantic relationship (56%). We were interested in three general factors associated with the development of personal relationships: the amount of communication between the partners, the intimacy or closeness of their interaction, and the level of commitment to maintaining the relationship. The network data were generated by asking each subject to list the 12 friends and kin to whom she or he felt the closest, and by instructing the subject to obtain a similar 12-person list from his or her dyadic partner. Subjects then responded to several questions regarding communication with network members, attraction to network members, and the level of support they perceived from network members for their dyadic relationship.

CONTACT AND OVERLAP BETWEEN NETWORKS

Relational partners occupy locations in larger networks that may already be merging prior to the first meeting of the partners. Indeed, as I suggested previously, prospective partners may actually be carried toward one another on these social currents. Contact with members of the partner's network, however, continues to be a potent predictor of relational development well after the initial stage of the relationship. We have consistently found significant correlations in our confirmatory factor analyses between measures of the number of people known in the partner's network and the frequency of communication with them on the one hand, and measures of the communication, intimacy, and commitment in the developing dyad on the other hand. These correlations tend to be stronger for university students reporting on their romantic relationships (r's ranging from .48 to .76) and same-sex friendships (r's ranging from .32 to .69). Correlations between the network contact measures and the developmental dimensions tended to be lower for high-school students reporting on their romantic relationships (r's ranging from .16 to .35) and same-sex friendships (r's ranging from .10 to .37). Only about half of these correlations were significant, while all of the correlations involving the older subjects proved to be significant. I think this difference reflects the fact that high-school students inhabit a more structured, less varied social environment than older people. Even with this difference, it is fair to summarize our findings as showing that measures of contact and communication with members of a friend's network or a romantic partner's network are important correlates of the development of that friendship or romance.

Similar findings can be found in a remarkable study of heterosexual relationships by Kim and Stiff (1991). Among other things, these researchers sought to replicate our findings by collecting data not just from dyadic participants, but also directly from the members of their networks. So instead of relying on the subjects' estimates of contact and communication with network members, Kim and Stiff conducted telephone interviews with network members themselves. They found that relational development was positively correlated with both the number of people in the partner's network who reported knowing the subject ($r = .66$, $p < .001$) and the amount of communication they reported having with the subject ($r = .29$, $p < .05$).

These findings imply that the networks of dyadic partners should become overlapping and shared as their relationship develops. Support for this hypothesis comes from a variety of sources. Salzinger (1982), for example, found that the total networks of same-sex friends became more densely interconnected as their relationship developed. More support comes from a study by Milardo (1982) who instructed romantic partners to keep a diary of all interactions lasting 10 minutes or more over a 10-day period. These allowed him to determine the proportion of contacts that the romantic partners shared. He found not only that partners in more advanced stages of courtship shared more mutual contacts, but also that the proportion of mutual contacts grew over time for couples whose romance developed and shrunk for couples whose romance deteriorated. Kim and Stiff (1991) also found that the degree of network overlap and the density of links between networks were positively related to a global index of relational development.

ATTRACTION TO THE PARTNER'S NETWORK

Apart from how often one communicates with them, attraction to the members of the partner's network can have a powerful effect on the development of personal relationships. The theoretic grounding for this will be explicated later in the chapter, but suffice it to say that having attractive friends makes one more attractive. Our analyses (see Parks & Eggert, 1991) show a consistent association between measures of attraction to the known members of the partner's network and measures of relational development. For example, we found that romantic involvement was positively and significantly correlated with the mean level of attraction to the partner's friends and family whom the subject had met ($r = .39$, $p < .05$). This same measure of attraction was also related to measures of perceived similarity ($r = .40$, $p < .05$), intimacy ($r = .35$, $p < .05$), and commitment ($r = .80$, $p < .05$) in same-sex friendships. As far as we know, ours is the only research program to examine the role played by attraction to network members. Instead, most researchers in this area have emphasized closely related variables such as network support.

SUPPORT FROM NETWORK MEMBERS

Numerous studies have examined the extent to which network members are perceived to support the emerging dyadic relationship. Marital researchers have long documented the positive association between support from network members, particularly parents, and marital adjustment (see Burgess & Cottrell, 1939; Locke, 1951). The same pattern has emerged from studies of premarital romantic relationships. Lewis (1973), for instance, found that couples who reported higher levels of support from family and friends also reported increases in attraction, commitment, and courtship progression over a three-month period. I know of only two studies in which a positive association between network support and relational development was not found. One of these was the Driscoll, Davis, and Lipetz (1972) study discussed earlier. The other was a study of parental approval and disapproval by Leslie, Huston, and Johnson (1986). The non-significant findings in this study, however, might have reflected the fact that the developmental measure—change in courtship label—was rather a global single indicator and lacked variation.

Perceptions of relational support from network members have been positively related to indices of relational involvement without exception in our studies. Measures of support from members of the partner's network of family and friends were significant correlates of intimacy and commitment in both romantic relationships and same-sex friendships and across all age groups (r's = .29 to .68). The same held for measures of support from members of the subject's own network (r's = .26 to .69). Perceived support from the subject's own network and from the partner's network were significantly related to the communication between dyadic partners in the older samples (r's = .35 to .59), but less strongly related to this factor among high-school subjects, perhaps reflecting less variance in the communication patterns of younger subjects.

Network support is a negotiated commodity. It is not simply passively received, but rather actively sought and manipulated. Leslie, Huston, and Johnson (1986), for example, found that 85% of the romantic partners in their sample had actively attempted to influence their parents' view of the romance. These influence attempts employed strategies like emphasizing the partner's good points, providing reassurance to the parents, and discussing the partner's background in positive terms. Romantic partners may manage information to such a degree that some network members do not even know that it exists. For instance, Leslie and her colleagues reported that people often did not inform parents of their romantic relationships until the romance had gone beyond a casual stage.

In sum, the development of personal relationships does not proceed in a social vacuum. People do not withdraw from other relationships to any great extent in order to develop their private relationships, nor do their other relationships merely become foils for creating a romantic myth of "two against the world." Instead, the surrounding network of friends and family is the supportive soil that nurtures the participants' developing relationship. Its nutrients are given, but are also sought out and managed by the participants. Obviously, there are a number of theoretic forces at work in these situations, but before explicating them in the final section, I will first extend the analysis by considering the role of networks when relationships deteriorate.

NETWORKS AND THE DETERIORATION OF PERSONAL RELATIONSHIPS

If relationships are put together and held together by contextual forces, it is reasonable to presume that they also can be broken by those same contextual forces. What little research we have points clearly to the role of network structure and social support in the deterioration of friendships and romantic relationships.

CONTACT AND OVERLAP BETWEEN NETWORKS

Just as development occurs within the context of merging networks, the deterioration of personal relationships is accompanied by a loosening of network structure. The private bonds cementing the interior of the relationship and the public linkages creating and legitimizing its exterior come apart at the same time. We found, for example, that romantic couples who broke up over a three-month period had met fewer members of each other's network and communicated less with members of each other's network than couples who stayed together (Parks & Adelman, 1983). Similar results have been obtained in studies using alternative methods. In his diary study of network contacts Milardo (1982) found that the proportion of shared network contacts dropped among romantic couples whose relationship deteriorated over a three-month period.

In broader terms, the stability of any one relationship will be at least partially a function of the density of the surrounding network. Although most of the data on this point are anecdotal, a study of men's friendship networks directly supports the proposition that relationships in loosely knit networks are less stable than those in tightly knit networks (Salzinger, 1982). Salzinger reported that 90% of the men in loosely knit networks changed friends, while only 58% in tightly knit networks changed friends over the same three-month period. In her study of social ties in a factory, a church group, and a doughnut shop, Hammer (1980) found that the probability of any given relationship lasting over time was positively related to the connectedness of the participants' respective networks. At a still broader level, intercultural comparisons have revealed that divorce rates are generally higher in cultures where the spouses maintain relatively separate networks than in cultures where spouses develop a more jointly shared network (Ackerman, 1963; Zelditch, 1964).

SUPPORT FROM NETWORK MEMBERS

Relationships that are opposed by network members are more likely to terminate than those that are supported. Evidence for this proposition can be found in at least three longitudinal studies of premarital romances. The first was conducted by Lewis (1973) who found that romantic couples who believed that their friends and family were unsupportive were more likely to break up over time than those who perceived higher levels of support. We were able to replicate this finding as part of our research program (Parks & Adelman, 1983). In fact, we found that the level of network support was a stronger predictor of relational stability than a number of dyadic factors such as uncertainty about the partner and perceived similarity with the partner. Other researchers have reported that couples whose romances had deteriorated over a one-year period tended to perceive less support from network members than couples whose romances remained unchanged or developed (Johnson & Milardo, 1984). Studies of divorce also demonstrate the negative impact of opposition from network members. They typically show that, compared to couples who remain together, couples who divorce are more likely to encounter parental opposition both before and after the marriage (Thornes & Collard, 1979).

Opposition and support are actively negotiated in the deterioration process, just as they are in the developmental process. As one participant's commitment to the relationships wanes, it is likely that she or he will reveal complaints and problems from the relational interior to those on its exterior. What McCall (1982) called "relational spoilage" is now public. The question of what to reveal and to whom raises complex dilemmas for relational partners. While the complaining partner may obtain support by revealing relational problems to outsiders, such revelations can also create substantial risks for how others see the complaining partner, the other partner, and their relationship (Goldsmith, 1988; Goldsmith & Parks, 1990). Our research suggests that one of the most common strategies for dealing with these communicative dilemmas is to reveal relational problems only to those network members who are likely to be the especially sympathetic (Goldsmith & Parks, 1990). While this may minimize the short-term risks of revealing relational problems, the long-term effect may be to create further rifts in the couple's network, as the partners look for allies and as network members choose sides.

The weight of the evidence, therefore, indicates that both the development and deterioration of personal relationships are intertwined with the dynamics of the participants' networks in similar ways. Relationships develop as the participants increase their contact with each other's network and develop a shared network, become attracted to members of each other's networks, and receive support from them. Relationships deteriorate as rifts form in the partners' joint network, either as a result of their actions or as a result of forces beyond the their control. Relational deterioration also becomes more likely when network members are perceived to be unsupportive or have been enlisted to support the efforts of one of the participants to leave the relationship.

TOWARD A SOCIAL CONTEXTUAL THEORY OF PERSONAL RELATIONSHIPS

The importance of context has long been recognized in explanations for individual behavior. Almost a half century ago, Kurt Lewin (1951) was reminding his fellow social psychologists that their explanations for individual behavior could not be limited to accounts of personal characteristics, but instead had to incorporate the context surrounding the individual. A half century before that, Charles Horton Cooley (1902/1956) already was championing the view that selves were socially constructed. Through processes like the "looking glass self," Cooley emphasized the interdependence of individuals and their social context. He argued on a grand scale:

> the individual is not separable from the human whole, but a living member of it, deriving his life from the whole through social and hereditary transmission as truly as if men were literally one body. (1956, p. 35)

Research has generally borne out Cooley's interactionist insights. If anything, recent research on self-concepts has shown that Cooley and his followers underestimated the communicative character of the self-appraisal process (Ichiyama, 1993). The shift to an interactive view of self has been part of a larger shift in the social sciences, a shift from explaining individual behavior in terms of relatively fixed internal structures like personality traits (see Chapter 3) to explaining individual behavior in terms of interactive, communicative processes (Carson, 1969).

Relationships, no less than individuals, are intertwined with social contexts. The research findings summarized above demonstrate that the entire life cycle of a personal relationship is contingent upon the dynamics of the personal relationships around it. If we move Cooley's contextual view from the individual to the relational level, we might express the central image of a social contextual theory of relationships this way:

> no relationship is separable from the human whole, but a living element of a larger network of relationships; deriving its life course not only from character of its individual participants, but also from its ties to the relationships that surround it.

What is missing in most of the literature to date, however, is a theoretic framework capable of going much beyond this sort of global imagery. The most commonly employed explanatory concepts often fail to identify the more specific processes in which they are manifested or which produce them (Parks & Eggert, 1991). These include concepts like transitivity drawn from structural sociology (see Davis, 1970; Holland & Leinhardt, 1972, 1977) and structural interdependence drawn from social psychology and family studies (see Kelley 1979; Milardo, 1982, 1986; Surra, 1988; Surra & Milardo, 1991).

The principle of structural transitivity describes the flow of positive sentiment across a chain of social relationships. If John likes Bob and Bob likes Carole, then John should also come to like Carole. That is, the probability of two people developing a close relationship increases when they already share mutual friends (Hammer, 1980; Salzinger, 1982). Our findings are certainty consistent with predictions drawn from a transitivity principle. The difficulty from my point of view is that structural transitivity is too abstract a theoretic concept to capture the richness of the interpersonal processes linking relationships to one another. Unfortunately, structural sociologists who employ this principle typically have their sights aimed at macrosocial structures and consequently treat transitivity as a lower order concept, requiring little separate explanation (Berkowitz, 1982; Blau, 1977).

Images of interdependence also have been used to explain the role of network factors in the development and deterioration of personal relationships. In this perspective, changes in the interior of personal relationships are described in terms of changes in the degree of dyadic interdependence between participants (Kelley, Berscheid, Christensen, Harvey, Huston, Levinger, McClintock, Peplau, & Peterson, 1983). Interdependence at the structural or network level is usually described in terms of traditional network characteristics. Thus, the networks of dyadic participants are said to become more interdependent as they become more overlapping and more densely interconnected (Surra & Milardo, 1991). Changes in the degree of interdependence at one level are then "explained" by reference to the degree of interdependence at the other level. Dyadic involvement and network involvement are part of the same pattern of interdependence that emerges as participants' develop "a jointly held orientation" toward one another and one another's relationships (Milardo, 1983, 1986). While this approach is useful because it emphasizes the symmetry of the dyadic and the network levels, it is less satisfying as theory. It merely applies the same term to two different categories of phenomena. It provides no mechanism to account for how the developmental characteristics inside the dyad become linked to the dynamics of the participants' surrounding social networks. In fairness, it should be noted that interdependence theorists do seem to have recognized this problem and have recently begun to articulate some of the more specific mechanisms by which dyadic and network inter-dependence drive each other (see Surra, 1988; Surra & Milardo, 1991).

I believe that at least six specific theoretic forces energize the interplay of network and dyadic factors in personal relationships. These are: 1) the satis-faction of social expectations, 2) cognitive balance, 3) information exchange, 4) relational reinforcement and support, 5) the creation of oppor-tunities for joint interaction, and 6) barrier forces. Together these processes form the basis of a social contextual theory of relationships (Parks & Eggert, 1991). Before briefly describing each of these components, the issue of causal priority needs to be addressed. The processes described here cannot be neatly assigned to either the individuals in the dyad or the individuals in the surrounding network. They may emanate from the actions of either the dyadic participants or members of the network (Parks & Eggert, 1991).

Most people involved in personal relationships expect to meet their part-ners' friends and family. This expectation reflects a widely shared social norm. Meeting those close to the partner therefore helps manage uncer-tainty, while failing to meeting the partner's close associates should raise doubts about the partner's feelings and one's own desirability (Parks & Adelman, 1983). The importance of satisfying expectations for meeting net-work members highlights the difference between two ways of specifying network membership. Researchers may define networks by asking subjects to list people to whom they feel particularly close, or they may define net-works by asking subjects to list the people with whom they interact most often. The difference between these two methods is worth noting because the networks they generate are often quite different (Milardo, 1989). Some theorists give priority to the interactive network of regular contacts (Milardo, 1986, 1989; Surra, 1988). In terms of satisfying social expecta-tions, however, meeting the people who are psychologically close to the partner may be more important than meeting routine, but subjectively less central, contacts. Our research findings, as well as those from studies like Kim and Stiff (1991), show that meeting the partner's significant others is correlated strongly and positively with dyadic development.

A second explanation for the intertwining of dyads and networks can be found in theories of cognitive balance (Cartwright & Harary, 1956; Newcomb, 1961). Structural sociologists have long recognized the implica-tions for social networks of our desire for cognitive balance (for example, Davis, 1970). Attraction to a dyadic partner should create a cognitive strain toward liking the people the partner likes. By the same token, attraction to members of a partner's network should create a cognitive strain toward liking the partner. On the other hand, dislike for the people the partner likes should create uncertainty, a sense of cognitive imbalance and tension, and may lead to reductions in attraction to the partner. This helps explain why we have generally found positive associations between the level of relational development and attraction for the members of the partner's network.

The developmental path of personal relationships is driven in part by the participants' ability to predict and explain one another's behavior (Berger & Calabrese, 1975; Parks & Adelman, 1983). There are many strategies for acquiring the information needed to guide the relationship. They vary from passive observation to direct interaction (Berger & Bradac, 1982). Contact with network members opens opportunities across the entire range of information acquisition strategies. On the more passive side, observing the relationships of network members helps partners evaluate their own relationship through social comparison (Titus, 1980). Observing one's partner interact with network members may yield distinctive clues to the partner's behavior and character. More direct interaction with network members provides not only information about the past activities of the partner, but also ready-made explanations for the partner's behavior and an opportunity to compare one's own observations and explanations to those of others (Parks & Eggert, 1991). Indeed, communication with network members may help relational partners manage uncertainty in ways that communication between the partners themselves does not. We have found, for example, that the frequency of communication with members of the partner's network is actually a better predictor of uncertainty about a romantic partner than the frequency of communication with the partner himself or herself (Parks & Adelman, 1983).

Support or opposition from network members not only facilitates change in personal relationships, but may also reflect changes already taking place. Support or opposition are direct forms of reinforcement for the relationship (Lewis, 1973). They also have implications for the daily conduct of the relationship, especially when the relational partners become dependent on network members for accomplishing relational tasks, providing material aid, or rendering emotional assistance. Of course, the strong correlations we have observed between development and support also reflect the tendency for participants to withdraw from network members who are unsupportive (Johnson & Milardo, 1984). Perhaps for this reason, network members who were silent or critical become more supportive once the relationship becomes firmly established (Driscoll, et al., 1972; Leslie et al., 1986).

Ironically, these same people may change course if they sense that one of the partners is having doubts about the relationship.

A fifth factor linking dyads and networks covers all those still smaller forces that create joint interactions. Many of these forces have less to do with psychological processes than with the dynamics of communicative structure. We saw this quite clearly in our findings on the initiation of personal relationships. People meet in part because they are carried toward one another by the physical and social architecture they inhabit. The location of prospective partners in the structure of their larger communication network influences their likelihood of meeting. Of course, relational partners and network members often add deliberate, strategic dimensions to their progress through the social structure. Our study of third party help illustrated some of the ways that prospective partners use the network as a resource for creating joint interactions (Parks & Barnes, 1988). Even after their relationship is established, participants may organize group interactions involving themselves with network members as a way to spend more time together. Network members may do the same when they wish to gain information, express support, or when they are concerned that the couple has become withdrawn (Parks & Eggert, 1991).

Finally, the network surrounding a personal relationship may impose what Levinger (1979) referred to as "barrier forces" which make it more difficult to terminate the relationship. Being involved in a shared network reduces access to alternative relational partners (Parks & Adelman, 1983). Members of the partner's network may be attractive in their own right or may provide resources that would be lost if the relationship with the partner were terminated. The social, emotional, and financial costs of withdrawing from a partner may be greatly increased because of the need to withdraw as well from the network of relationships in which the partner is embedded. The threat of reduced contact with children, to give just one example, becomes a barrier force that may hold individuals in marriage long after attraction to the spouse has waned. Thus, as Johnson (1982) has pointed out, commitment to a relationship is a function of both its positive features and of the barriers to dissolving it.

Interpersonal relationships are ultimately defined by the patterns of influence that bind the participants to one another and that develop and change over time (Miller & Steinberg, 1975). We may view relationships from several different vantage points; but from any vantage point, it is now apparent that the initiation, development, and deterioration of personal relationships is closely intertwined with the participants' other relationships. Social contextual theory unites the psychological and communicative interiors of dyadic relationships with their social and structural exteriors. In doing so, it not only offers a more thorough account for the life cycle of a given personal relationship, but it also provides theoretic transport between the macro- and the micro-levels of analysis. Higher order structural concepts like transitivity and interdependence are conceptualized as abstractions of micro-processes like satisfying social expectations, promoting cognitive balance, exchanging information, providing social support, creating joint interactions, and imposing barriers. Social contextual theory therefore provides a theoretic avenue for relating the privately experienced interiors of personal relationships to larger societal structures and forces.

REFERENCES

Ackerman, K. (1963). Affiliations: Structural determinants of differential divorce rates. *American Journal of Sociology, 69*, 13-20.

Atkins, C.J., Kaplan, R.M., & Toshima, M.T. (1991). Close relationships in the epidemiology of cardiovascular disease. In W.H. Jones & D. Perlman (Eds.), *Advances in personal relationships* (Vol. 3, pp. 207-231). London: Jessica Kingsley.

Berger, C.R., & Bradac, J.J. (1982). *Language and social knowledge.* London: Edward Arnold.

Berger, C.R., & Calabrese, R.J. (1975). Some explorations in initial interaction and beyond: Toward a developmental theory of interpersonal communication. *Human Communication Research, 1*, 99-112.

Berscheid, E., & Walster, E. H. (1978). *Interpersonal attraction* (2nd ed.). Reading, MA: Addison-Wesley.

Burgess, E.W., & Cottrell, L.S. (1939). *Predicting success or failure in marriage.* Englewood Cliffs, NJ: Prentice-Hall.

Byrne, D. (1971). *The attraction paradigm.* New York: Academic Press.

Cappella, J.N., & Palmer, M.T. (1990). Attitude similarity, relational history, and attraction: The mediating effects of kinesic and vocal behaviors. *Communication Monographs, 57*, 161-183.

Carson, R.C. (1969). *Interaction concepts of personality.* Chicago: Aldine.

Cartwright, D., & Harary, F. (1956). Structural balance: A generalization of Heider's theory. *Psychological Review, 63*, 277-293.

Chapple, N.L., & Badger, M. (1989). Social isolation and well-being. *Journals of Gerontology, 44(5),* S169-S176.

Cooley, C.H. (1956). *Human nature and the social order.* New York: C. Scribner's Sons, 1902. Reprint, Glencoe, IL: The Free Press.

Davis, J. (1970). Clustering and hierarchy in interpersonal relations. *American Sociological Review, 35,* 843-851.

Driscoll, R., Davis, K.E., & Lipetz, M.E. (1972). Parental interference and romantic love: The Romeo and Juliet effect. *Journal of Personality and Social Psychology, 24,* 1-10.

Dutton, D., & Aron, A. (1974). Some evidence for heightened sexual attraction under conditions of high anxiety. *Journal of Personality and Social Psychology, 30,* 510-517.

Eggert, L.L., & Parks, M.R. (1987). Communication network involvement in adolescents' friendships and romantic relationships. In M.L. McLaughlin (Ed.), *Communication yearbook 10* (pp. 283-322). Newbury Park, CA: Sage.

Freud, S. (1957). *Civilization and its discontents* (J. Riviere, Trans.). New York: Norton. (Original work published 1930)

Goethe, J.W. (1971). *The sorrows of young Werther* (E. Mayer & L. Bogan, Trans.). New York: Random House. (Original work published 1774)

Goldsmith, D. (1988). *To talk or not to talk: The flow of information between romantic dyads and members of their communication networks.* Unpublished master's thesis, University of Washington, Seattle.

Goldsmith, D., & Parks, M.R. (1990). Communication strategies for managing the dilemmas of social support. In S. Duck & R.C. Silver (Eds.), *Personal relationships and social support* (pp. 104-121). Newbury Park, CA: Sage Publications.

Goode, W.J. (1960). A theory of role strain. *American Sociological Review, 25,* 483-496.

Hallinan, M. (1974). *The structure of positive sentiment.* New York: Elsevier.

Hammer, M. (1980). Predictability of social connections over time. *Social Networks, 2,* 165-180.

Holland, P., & Leinhardt, S. (1972). Some evidence on the transitivity of positive interpersonal sentiment. *American Journal of Sociology, 77,* 1205-1209.

Holland, P., & Leinhardt, S. (1977). Transitivity in structural models of small groups. In L. Leinhardt (Ed.), *Social networks: A developing paradigm* (pp. 49-66). New York: Academic Press.

House, J.S., Landis, K.R., & Umberson, D. (1988). Social relationships and health. *Science, 241,* 540-545.

Ichiyama, M.A. (1993). The reflected appraisal process in small-group interaction. *Social Psychology Quarterly, 56,* 87-99.

Johnson, M.P. (1982). Social and cognitive features of the dissolution of commitment to relationships. In S. Duck (Ed.), *Personal relationships 4:
Dissolving personal relationships* (pp. 51-73). London: Academic Press.

Johnson, M.P., & Leslie, L. (1982). Couple involvement and network structure:
A test of the dyadic withdrawal hypothesis. *Social Psychology Quarterly, 45*,
34-43.

Johnson, M.P., & Milardo, R.M. (1984). Network interference in pair relationships: A social psychological recasting of Slater's theory of social regression.
Journal of Marriage and the Family, 46, 893-899.

Kelley, H.H. (1979). *Personal relationships: Their structure and processes.*
New York: Wiley.

Kelley, H.H., Berscheid, E., Christensen, A., Harvey, J.H., Huston, T.L.,
Levinger, G., McClintock, E., Peplau, L.A., & Peterson, D. (1983). *Close
relationships.* New York: W.H. Freeman.

Kerckhoff, A.C. (1974). The social context of interpersonal attraction. In T.L.
Huston (ed.), *Foundations of interpersonal attraction* (pp. 61-78). New
York: Academic Press.

Kim, H.J., & Stiff, J.B. (1991). Social networks and the development of close
relationships. *Human Communication Research, 18*, 70-91.

Klinger, E. (1977). *Meaning and void: Inner experience and the incentives in
people's lives.* Minneapolis, MN: University of Minnesota Press.

Krain, M. (1977). A definition of dyadic boundaries and an empirical study of
boundary establishment in courtship. *International Journal of Sociology of
the Family, 7*, 107-123.

Leslie, L.A. (1983). Parental influences and premarital relationship development
(Doctoral dissertation, Pennsylvania State University, 1982). *Dissertation
Abstracts International, 43*, 277A.

Leslie, L.A., Huston, T.L., & Johnson, M.P. (1986). Parental reactions to dating
relationships: Do they make a difference? *Journal of Marriage and the
Family, 48*, 57-66.

Levinger, G. (1979). A social exchange view of the dissolution of pair relationships. In R.L. Burgess & T.L. Huston (Eds.), *Social exchange in developing
relationships* (pp. 169-193). New York: Academic Press.

Lewin, K. (1951). *Field theory in social science.* New York: Harper & Brothers.

Lewis, R.A. (1973). Social reaction and the formation of dyads: An interactionist
approach to mate selection. *Sociometry, 36*, 409-418.

Lewis, R.A. (1975). Social influences on marital choice. In S. Dragastin & G.H.
Elder (Eds.), *Adolescence in the life cycle* (pp. 211-226). New York: John
Wiley.

Locke, H.J. (1951). *Predicting adjustment in marriage.* New York: Holt.

Long, J.D., Anderson, J., & Williams, R.L. (1990). Life reflections by older kinsmen about critical life issues. *Educational Gerontology, 16,* 61-71.

McCall, G.J. (1982). Becoming unrelated: The management of bond dissolution. In S. Duck (Ed.), *Personal relationships 4: Dissolving personal relationships* (pp. 211-231). London: Academic.

Milardo, R.M. (1982). Friendship networks in developing relationships: Converging and diverging social environments. *Social Psychology Quarterly, 45,* 162-172.

Milardo, R.M. (1983). Social networks and pair relationships: A review of substantive and measurement issues. *Sociology and Social Research, 68,* 1-18.

Milardo, R.M. (1986). Personal choice and social constraint in close relationships: Applications of network analysis. In V.J. Derlega & B.A. Winstead (Eds.), *Friendship and social interaction* (pp. 146-166). New York: Springer-Verlag.

Milardo, R.M. (1989). Theoretical and methodological issues in the identification of the social networks of spouses. *Journal of Marriage and the Family, 51,* 165-174.

Milardo, R.M., Johnson, M.P., & Huston, T.L. (1983). Developing close relationships: Changing patterns of interaction between pair members and social networks. *Journal of Personality and Social Psychology, 44,* 964-976.

Milardo, R.M., & Lewis, R.A. (1985). Social networks, families, and mate selection: A transactional analysis. In L. L'Abate (Ed.), *Handbook of family psychology and therapy* (Vol 1, pp. 258-283). Homewood, IL: Dorsey.

Miller, G.R., & Steinberg, M. (1975). *Between people: A new analysis of interpersonal communication.* Chicago: Science Research Associates.

Newcomb, T.M. (1961). *The acquaintance process.* New York: Holt, Rinehart, & Winston.

Parks, M.R. (forthcoming). *Personal relationships and personal networks.* Hillsdale, NJ: Lawrence Erlbaum.

Parks, M.R., & Adelman, M.B. (1983). Communication networks and the development of romantic relationships: An expansion of uncertainty reduction theory. *Human Communication Research, 10,* 55-79.

Parks, M.R., & Barnes, K.J. (1988, November). *With a little help from my friends: The role of third parties in the initiation of interpersonal relationships.* Paper presented at the annual convention of the Speech Communication Association, New Orleans.

Parks, M.R., & Eggert, L.L. (1991). The role of social context in the dynamics of personal relationships. In W.H. Jones & D. Perlman (Eds.), *Advances in personal relationships,* (Vol. 2, pp. 1-34). London: Jessica Kingsley.

Parks, M.R., Stan, C., & Eggert, L.L. (1983). Romantic involvement and social network involvement. *Social Psychology Quarterly, 46,* 116-130.

Salzinger, L.L. (1982). The ties that bind: The effects of clustering on dyadic relationships. *Social Networks, 4,* 117-145.

Snyder, M., Berscheid, E., & Glick, P. (1985). Focusing on the exterior and the interior: Two investigations of the initiation of personal relationships. *Journal of Personality and Social Psychology, 48,* 1427-1439.

Storr, A. (1988). *Solitude: A return to the self.* New York: Ballantine.

Sunnafrank, M. (1984). A communication-based perspective on attitude similarity and interpersonal attraction in early acquaintance. *Communication Monographs, 51,* 372-380.

Surra, C.A. (1985). Courtship types: Variations in interdependence between partners and social networks. *Journal of Personality and Social Psychology, 49,* 357-375.

Surra, C.A. (1988). The influence of the interactive network on developing relationships. In R.M. Milardo (Ed.), *Families and social networks* (pp. 48-82). Newbury Park, CA: Sage.

Surra, C.A., & Milardo, R.M. (1991). The social psychological context of developing relationships: Interactive and psychological networks. In W.H. Jones & D. Perlman (Eds.), *Advances in personal relationships,* (Vol. 3, pp. 1-36). London: Jessica Kingsley.

Thornes, B., & Collard, J. (1979). *Who divorces?* London: Routledge & Kegan Paul.

Titus, S.L. (1980). A function of friendship: Social comparisons as a frame of reference for marriage. *Human Relations, 33,* 409-431.

VanLear, C.A. (1987). The formation of social relationships: A longitudinal study of social penetration. *Human Communication Research, 13,* 299-322.

Zelditch, M. (1964). Family, marriage and kinship. In R.E.L. Faris (Ed.), *Handbook of modern sociology* (pp. 680-733). Chicago: Rand McNally.

About the Contributors

Charles R. Berger (Ph.D., Michigan State University, 1968) is a professor in the Department of Rhetoric and Communication at the University of California, Davis. He is currently coeditor of *Communication Research*, and serves on the editorial boards of seven journals and annuals. He is former editor of *Human Communication Research*. Dr. Berger has authored more than 60 articles and book chapters, and has published *Language and Social Knowledge: Uncertainty in Interpersonal Relations* (with James J. Bradac), a volume that won the Speech Communication Association's Golden Anniversary Award. He has also coedited *Social Cognition and Communication* (with Michael E. Roloff) and *Handbook of Communication Science* (with Steven H. Chaffee). His current research concerns the strategies that individuals use to alter communication plans when they are not understood by others in social interaction situations.

Franklin J. Boster (Ph.D., Michigan State University, 1978) is a professor in the Department of Communication at Michigan State University. His interests center around group dynamics and attitude change, and he has published articles on these topics in various journals including: *Communication Monographs*, *Communication Research*, *Human Communication Research*, *Journal of Cross-Cultural Psychology*, *Journal of Personality and Social Psychology*, *Brigham Young Law Review*, and *Trial*. The initial research that forms the foundation for Boster's chapter was published in *Communication Monographs* in 1977; it received the Charles H. Woolbert Award from the Speech Communication Association in 1989.

179

Michael Burgoon (Ph.D., Michigan State University, 1970) is professor of communication and professor of family and community medicine at the University of Arizona. Dr. Burgoon is also research professor in The Arizona Cancer Center, Tucson. He was previously a faculty member at California State University—Northridge, West Virginia University, the University of Florida, and Michigan State University. Professor Burgoon is the author of more than 150 articles and chapters, and 12 books including *Human Communication, Mexican Americans and the Mass Media*, and *New Techniques of Persuasion* (with Gerald Miller). His work in the area of social influence has appeared in journals in the fields of psychology, communication, medicine, mass media, education, and business. Much of his research has centered on the development of Language Expectancy Theory, which is the focus of his chapter in this text. Dr. Burgoon is a Fellow of the International Communication Association, an invited member of the Society of Experimental Social Psychologists, and a member of the American Psychological Association. He has been actively involved in consulting relationships with a number of media organizations in North America. He did the original research that resulted in the development and launch of *USA Today,* the first national newspaper in this country.

Malcolm R. Parks (Ph.D., Michigan State University, 1976) is associate professor of speech communication at the University of Washington. He was also a faculty member at Northwestern University, Michigan State University, and the University of Utah. Dr. Parks' primary research focuses on the development of interpersonal relationships and personal networks. He has studied the development of business relationships, romantic relationships, and friendships. Secondary research interests include communicative competence and deceptive communication. His research has been published in numerous volumes including: *The Handbook of Interpersonal Communication, Communication Yearbook, Communicating Social Support, Personal Relationships and Social Support, Personal Relationships 4: Dissolving Personal Relationships*, and *Advances in Personal Relationships*. He has also contributed to scholarly journals in the fields of psychology, sociology, and communication. Among these are *Human Communication Research, Quarterly Journal of Speech, Communication Monographs, Journal of Social and Personal Relationships*, and *Social Psychology Quarterly*. Professor Parks sits on the editorial board of *Human Communication Research* and has been on the editorial boards of the *Journal of Social and Personal Relationships* and *Communication Monographs*. He was associate editor of the *Western*

Journal of Speech Communication, and has served as vice president of the International Communication Association and as a member of its board of directors.

Michael E. Roloff (Ph.D., Michigan State University, 1975) is professor and chair of the Department of Communication Studies at Northwestern University. His research interests include bargaining and negotiation, social exchange within intimate relationships, persuasion, and interpersonal conflict resolution. He wrote *Interpersonal Communication: The Social Exchange Approach*, and coedited *Persuasion: New Directions in Theory and Research* (with G.R. Miller), *Interpersonal Processes: New Directions in Communication Research* (with G.R. Miller), *Social Cognition and Communication* (with C.R. Berger), and *Communication and Negotiation* (with L.L. Putnam).

Thomas M. Steinfatt (Ph.D., Michigan State University, 1971) is professor and director of speech communication at the University of Miami. His research interests include the effects of personality variables on communication, intercultural communication in developing countries, research on linguistic relativity, and research in measurement and statistics. Among his previous publications are "Communication in Game Theoretic Models of Conflict," with Gerald R. Miller, in G.R. Miller and H.W. Simons (eds.) *Perspectives on Communication in Social Conflict*, Englewood Cliffs, NJ: Prentice-Hall, 1974; *Human Communication*, Indianapolis: Bobbs-Merrill, 1977; "Personality and Communication: Classical Approaches," in J.C. McCroskey and J.A. Daly (eds.) *Personality and Interpersonal Communication*, Newbury Park, CA: Sage, 1987; "Linguistic Relativity: Toward a Broader View," in S. Ting-Toomey and F. Korzenny, *Language, Communication, and Culture: Current Directions*, Newbury Park, CA: Sage, 1989; and "Communication Factors in the Transmission of AIDS," in *The International Congress on AIDS: Impacts on Developing Countries,* Chulabhorn Research Institute, Bangkok, Thailand, 1991.

James B. Stiff (Ph.D., Michigan State University, 1985) has been associate professor of communication at Arizona State University since 1990. He was also a faculty member at Oklahoma State University, and served as assistant professor of communication for five years at Michigan State University. Throughout his academic career, Professor Stiff's scholarship has focused on information processing and social influence in interpersonal contexts. Consistent with the view that deceptive communication is a form of social influence, the majority of his research examines communicative dimensions of deceptive transactions. Specifically, his research investigates the ways in which verbal and nonverbal features of deceptive messages interact with characteristics of message receivers to affect the process of deception detection. His research has culminated in the publication of more than 20 research articles and chapters in outlets such as *Human Communication Research*, *Communication Monographs*, *Journal of Personality and Social Psychology*, and *Communication Research*. He also wrote *Persuasive Communication*, published by Guilford Publications, and collaborated with Gerald R. Miller on *Deceptive Communication,* published by Sage Publications.

Michael Sunnafrank (Ph.D., Michigan State University, 1979) is currently professor of communication at the University of Minnesota-Duluth. He has been on the faculties of the University of California, Arizona State University, and Texas A&M University. Dr. Sunnafrank has published work on persuasion, research methods, legal communication, and interpersonal communication. His work has appeared in *Communication Monographs*, *Communication Yearbook*, *Human Communication Research*, *The Quarterly Journal of Speech*, and many other journals. He is currently on the editorial board of *Communication Monographs* and regularly reviews manuscripts for *Journal of Personality and Social Psychology*, *Journal of Social and Personal Relationships*, *Human Communication Research*, and other national and international journals that publish works on interpersonal processes. His major lines of research focus on the role of communication processes in developing interpersonal attraction and relationships during the beginning stages of acquaintance.

Index